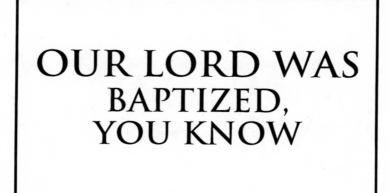

# OUR LORD WAS
## BAPTIZED,
## YOU KNOW

# OUR LORD WAS BAPTIZED, YOU KNOW

## Reflections on a Spiritual Adventure

A Memoir

## MARTA SUTTON WEEKS

iUniverse, Inc.
New York Lincoln Shanghai

# OUR LORD WAS BAPTIZED, YOU KNOW
### Reflections on a Spiritual Adventure

iUniverse books may be ordered through booksellers or by contacting:

iUniverse
2021 Pine Lake Road, Suite 100
Lincoln, NE 68512
www.iuniverse.com
1-800-Authors (1-800-288-4677)

ISBN: 978-0-595-40501-5 (pbk)
ISBN: 978-0-595-84868-3 (ebk)

Printed in the United States of America

# CONTENTS

# PRELUDE

## Marianna (1935)

Marianna, standing awkwardly on the side lines, did not like what she was watching. She didn't really understand, but a sense of the macabre gripped her as she continued to view the unfolding scene.

"Ah … ooooo…. ga. Ah…. ooo…. .ga," Gail was saying.

"In the name of the great spirits and spooks," replied Carey, Marianna's older sister.

Gail and Carey, clutching the corners of a blanket they were holding, stretched their arms skyward as it rose between them into the air.

"Come great spirit."

"Come Great Poltergeist. Ah…. oooo…. ga."

The dusty blanket fell, its center now touching the ground, then rising again in response to the girls' undulating arms.

"Ah…. oooo…. .ga. Ah…. oooo…. .ga."

The only other sounds were the gurgles made by the water flow in the irrigation canal, and the horse flies buzzing near the bank.

"'bout time for the baptism?" queried Carey.

"Yep. Good idea."

The two older girls stopped heaving the blanket, then cast their glances in Marianna's direction.

"Marriana first," said Gail.

"No. I dowanna."

"Come on. It won't hurt."

"I dowanna play," protested Marianna.

"You have to. Everyone's supposed to be baptized."

"You'll go to hell if you're not."

"I don't want to be a Mormon."

"We're not going to baptize you a Mormon," laughed Carey.

"How about an atheist then?" said Gail.

Marianna frowned. "I don't want to be an athooist."

"Atheist," corrected Carey.

Marianna began to back off. "What's an athoo ... atheist?"

"Someone that's nice."

"And doesn't make you eat carrots," added Gail.

"Or rhubarb," said Carey, moving slowly towards Marianna.

A flicker of interest crossed Marianna's face.

"It's really somebody without a God," said Carey."

"It's a person without a rotten God," corrected Gail.

"I think it's someone who doesn't believe in a rotten God," retorted Carey.

Incorrect theological ramifications or definitions did not concern Marianna. But she'd been around Gail and Carey enough to know when they were up to no good.

"I don't like rhubarb," she said, then turned and began running towards the fence.

Dragging the blanket, Gail and Carey moved quickly to cut off Marianna's retreat. A few long strides and they caught up. Twirling the blanket into a make-shift rope, they spun it around her preventing further escape, then reversed direction and began pulling back towards the canal. When Marianna resisted, a hard jerk sent her flying to the ground. She struck her knee on a rock and began to cry.

"C'mon. Get up. It won't take long," said Carey.

"I dowanna be baptized," sobbed Marianna, slumped now in the grass.

"Sure you do."

Carey released hold of the blanket and ran to the canal. By dropping to her stomach and leaning over the bank, she was able to reach the water and scoop it into her hands. She kept them cupped, slithered back, weight on both elbows, then stood and tried to bring back the water; but already it was trickling between her fingers.

Marianna had seen her chance and already, sturdy little legs were propelling her through the deep grass again at the end of the culvert. She reached the barbed wire fence, flattened to her tummy, and was scraping herself under the lowest strand when Gail caught up and firmly gripped her jeans.

"Hey, not so fast. You can't go yet."

"I dowanna be baptized," screamed Marianna. Baptism in her mind had something to do with Mormons and religion, and she knew from her mother and aunts that this was not to her liking. There was something mysterious and evil about religion.

"We're all going to be baptized. Me'n Carey too. You can help," said Gail, grabbing one of Marianna's kicking feet and pulling her back from under the fence. To Marianna's dismay, her oversized hand-me-down shirt caught on a fence barb, followed by a resounding rip which left it open from the collar seam to the middle of her front pocket.

"C'mon four eyes ... it's not going to hurt."

But Marianna's glasses had been knocked off under the fence, no longer earning her that nickname, and her perspective on life just then was blurred, not only from tears, but from the fact that she could not see very well either.

"Pu ... leeese.... don't ... Gail."

"Maybe we should put her in the blanket," Gail said to Carey.

"I don't think they use blankets."

"Atheists ought to be able to use anything."

"I thought they just poured water over your head and said a lot of mumbo jumbo."

"Well, I've heard some churches put you in a tub of water, then push your head under."

By now, all the water had disappeared from Carey's carefully cupped hands.

"We could put her in the canal ..." a slight smile crossed Gail's face ...

"maybe in the blanket."

"We don't want to drown her. She only dog paddles."

"Then let's just do it *on* the blanket."

"Okay."

"I want my glasses," whimpered Marianna.

The older girls began to spread the blanket over the grass, all the while keeping a close eye on Marianna. "You'll get your glasses after you're baptized."

Marianna wiped a dirty sleeve across her nose. It left a muddy streak on the side of her face. Gail pulled her to her feet and herded her into the center of the blanket as Carey went to get more water.

"Pul ... puleeeeese.... don't," sobbed Marianna. "I dowannaa be baptized." She began trying to pull away from Gail.

"Don't make such a fuss, Marianna. This is a religious service." Gail spun her around, standing behind, a firm arm lock under Marianna's chin.

At the mention of "religious," a wave of terror gripped Marianna. "No ... no," she screamed.

Carey returned with the water. "Now?"

"We're supposed to say something."

"Hurry!"

"Come great spirit," chanted Gail. "Ah.... ooooo.... .ga."

"No," screamed Marianna, trying to pull away.

"We baptize you into the great church of atheism," said Carey, throwing her cupped hands open in Marianna's direction. But Marianna had already sunk her teeth into Gail's arm causing her to spin around. In the attempt to extricate herself, Marianna's captor received the full thrust of the water down the middle of her back.

"Good gosh," said Gail, forgetting the baptism momentarily, holding up her arm for inspection. "You didn't have to bite me, Marianna. We're only playing!"

But Marianna was swinging wildly at the air now with the determination of Geronimo.

"Wow, we've made her mad," observed Carey, mentally picturing a windmill she'd once seen in a *Book of Knowledge*. "I don't think she likes to play baptism."

The understatement was not lost on Gail.

Five year old Marianna was standing defiantly now, glaring at them both. Adrenalin pumping, her fears were temporarily forgotten. She was like a small animal that turns valiantly on a larger predator when all chances of escape are gone.

Just then, a voice could be heard calling further down the hill from the direction of the house. "Ca…. .aaaaa…. rey…. .Mari…. aaaaaa … na."

Startled, Gail and Carey looked at one another. "It's your mother," said Gail. "I'd better be going. Auntie Jane might be missing the blanket." She turned towards the damp and now sticker-covered heap lying on the ground. "Tell her we were having a picnic on it in the orchard if she asks."

Gail scooped up the blanket, then turned back to Marianna. "I'm sorry, Marianna," she said, her voice softening. "We didn't mean to upset you. It was just a game." Then she turned to head south along the fence. Further down, where an old log straddled the canal, she crossed to the short-cut that would lead home. At the intersection of the south boundary of the property and the road leading to the canyons, Gail lived with her aunt and uncle.

The disappearance of one problem now left Carey Marianna's ally as they prepared to confront their mother.

"Don't you tell what we were doing," hissed Carey, wiping her hands on the back of her pants, then tossing back hair that seemed to hang perpetually over one eye.

But Carey needn't have worried. Tattling was the last thing on Marianna's mind. Not only was she still shaken by the intended baptism, but now she had to worry about finding her glasses.

Looking over her clothes, hugging the torn shirt to her body, Marianna slid her hands down over her jeans and happily discovered they were not wet. And she was sure from previous conversations overheard between her sister and Gail that water was a necessary part of baptism. This happy turn meant she was still not baptized, a state she was now determined to remain in forever.

"Caaaaaaa.....rey ... Yoo.... hoooooo."

"We're up here on the hill," Carey called back.

"Can you see my glasses, Carey?" I have to have them," Marianna whispered loudly, her voice rising in pitch. "Where are they?"

Carey could see them on the other side of the fence wire where they had fallen next to a post. Under less urgent circumstances she would have at best played cat and mouse with her little sister, or at worst, stomped on the glasses (serve Marianna right for being such a spoil sport), but now was not the time for that. Besides, glasses cost money and "money doesn't grow on trees," she well knew. Worse, Marianna might tell. Talking about religion was almost as bad as taking one's panties down in front of a boy. Or drinking milk with chokecherries. Or saying "ain't."

Marianna was now on hands and knees moving her hands back and forth over the prickly grass. "Carey, I can't find them. Help me, Carey," she pleaded.

"Hey, Dummy.... your glasses are over there. By the fence post."

Marianna whirled about and crawled towards the spot where Carey was pointing and soon grubby little hands were closing thankfully on the black rimmed, dirty lenses.

"Thank you, Carey," she said with relief, wiping them off on her loose shirt tail.

"C'mon. Let's get away from the canal. I hear Mother coming up the trail."

◆     ◆     ◆

**Author's note:**

The preceding scene is fictionalized truth which I thought would be a good way to begin a novel once. But it never materialized.

I was the little girl in this scene and, though only five years old at the time, knew even then I didn't want any part of religion. No one. Absolutely no one would ever baptize me or get me to join a church.

In retrospect, if anyone had told me back in 1935 that not only would I be baptized someday, but that eventually I would end up becoming an Episcopal priest, I certainly never would have believed them. If anything, I would have suggested they might be candidates though for the looney bin.

But time changes things. We all change. Perspectives can change too. What doesn't change is God; the God that loves, looks after, and cares for us. As the Psalmist says: "For you, O Lord, are good and forgiving, and great is your love toward all who call upon you. (Ps. 86:5) and "I will give thanks to you, O Lord, with my whole heart; I will tell of all your marvelous works. (Ps. 9:1)

# PART I

# 1

# THE BIG CHANGE

My very early life revolved primarily around a relationship with my mother and/ or my sister—who always seemed to be present.

It also revolved around my geologist father (a shining knight far away in the jungles of South America)—who was mostly absent.

The one thing that stood out for me in my childhood was the Big Change and what had happened before that. The Big Change was in 1932 when I sailed on my second birthday from Buenos Aires to The United States with my sister and mother, leaving my father behind.

What happened before we moved made such an impression upon me that it remained throughout my childhood. And it's still there, though diminished with time. I've read that people cannot remember before age two or three, but that's nonsense.

What I do remember was being held by someone's arms with a lot of water around us. I was in front of them and they were lifting me up and down, talking and laughing, moving about and splashing me. I thought it was the grandest thing to have happening and was swept up in the exuberance of it all. Then, in the midst of all this excitement, all of a sudden, a beautiful light began to shine around us. There were awesome colors and such a feeling of warmth and ecstasy and love, it left me breathless. I couldn't do anything, could only perceive something very unusual was happening and that I didn't want it to leave. I could only bask in the beauty of this unknown epiphany. Like some kind of angelic mantle coming out of nowhere, it seemed to speak silently, mystically, as it wrapped itself eloquently about us.

I do not know who the person was lifting me up and down in the water. And I could never speak of this experience to anyone. I could never have adequately described it anyway and was afraid too that if I did try to speak about it, that the wonderful experience might never return. So I kept it to myself. Years later, however, I did once ask mother if she ever took me and my sister to any large bodies of water or pools when we were small. "Yes," she said, "near Belgrano where we lived, I used to take you and Shirley swimming." She didn't say if my father ever went with us; and I forgot to ask. But they could have taken us in either January or February of that year when the weather was warm in the southern hemisphere, so it means I would have been 18 or 19 months old when the water episode occurred.

If I'd later been asked to depict my life in terms of color prior to the Big Change, I would have included bright blues and greens and yellows, with some orange and turquoise perhaps, and maybe a little purple with red thrown in too, but all of it slightly subdued in contrast to the wonderful light that had surrounded and embraced me that day.

And if I'd been asked to describe my life for seven years after the Change, I probably would have described it more in terms of gray, with only occasional patches of color to vary the landscape. Still, there would always be that marvelous memory in the background, receding ever so slightly, shining not quite so brightly, as each year passed. In retrospect however, I know now, as I intuitively knew then, that it was my first memorable experience of God's love.

I think my mother and sister were more affected by the Big Change than I was. That's because they had so much more to lose. I hadn't lived long enough to know what not having happy friends or a father close by to help us could be like. Although Daddy was away for long periods in northern Argentina and Bolivia, still he was able to return to Buenos Aires on occasion. I had only my very young unfolding present, then later, the future hope my mother planted with remarks such as: "Won't it be fun to show Daddy this someday?" or "We'll do this when your Daddy comes home."

It must have been difficult for my sister because she was going on seven when we sailed. She had to leave behind her good friends and a vibrant culture, things difficult for her to replace in Utah.

But to put things in perspective as to why at age five I was so leery of religion, it's necessary to fill in a bit on the family history.

My grandmother (Annette, as she was called) was not enamored with Mormons, and for good reason. She had been born in Stockholm, brought up Lutheran, before landing in Utah. Some of her relatives, however, including an aunt and uncle, had converted to Mormonism, emigrating to the United States and settling in the small community of Peoa east of Salt Lake City.

Some time after this, their four children died from a diphtheria epidemic and the parents were so bereft they didn't know what to do. In desperation, they wrote back to Sweden asking if my grandmother's parents would let one of their daughters come to live with them. They needed to have a young person in the house again, anything to get them through their grief. Also, it would be an opportunity for their niece to find a husband. So my grandmother's sister, Karsti (or it may have been Ingree) who was the eldest, was chosen to go. When it came time for her to leave, however, she got cold feet and refused, so my grandmother stepped up and volunteered. She thought it would be a great adventure. So off she went alone across the Atlantic to Ellis Island seasick the entire trip.

But what she'd expected and the reality Annette found in Peoa were miles apart. The agreement with her uncle and her parents had been that he would pay for her passage if she would agree to stay for two years and help with the house-work. This seemed fair. But after some months with the relatives, Annette found them to be increasingly difficult and demanding. After getting over their grief, or perhaps because of it, they increased the chores expected of her to the point where they in effect began to treat her like a household slave rather than a daugh-ter, and her uncle began to beat her. The last straw was when he announced he'd found her a suitable husband. It was settled that she become the third (or maybe fourth) wife of a Mormon bishop some twenty five years older than she.

Grandmother balked, refused to marry a "patriarchal Mormon billy goat" and tried to run away. But they brought her back and took away her shoes so she couldn't try it again. But Annette, a resourceful, nice looking, strong, spunky nineteen or twenty year old was not to be told how to live her life and was deter-mined to fend for herself. She would only agree to finish the two year stint if she could then move to Salt Lake City. This she did, found a place to live with another young woman and was able to take in laundry as a means of support. She earned a dollar a week and was able to save money, she said, though I'm not sure how on those wages. Annette was born in 1869, the year the golden spike was driven at Promontory Point in Utah.

My grandfather James had had a wonderful love affair with a girl he'd expected to marry until her parents also insisted she marry a Mormon bishop who already had several wives. My grandfather was so upset over this experience that it about broke his heart and he determined he'd never take out another Mor-mon girl. Since that's about all there were in Utah at that point in history, James had little social life. When his parents had emigrated from England, they'd also come as converts to Mormonism; however, one of the first things James' father, Joseph, heard on his arrival in the Salt Lake valley was that he should take another wife. This created untold problems with James' mother, Elizabeth Ann, who had known nothing about polygamy before leaving England. So, though Joseph did take a second wife (and possibly several more), these unions did not last. Consequently, Joseph was not looked upon with favor by Brigham Young or any of his cohorts. It didn't help either that contrary to the church's orders, my great grandfather Joseph sold produce from his farm to soldiers stationed at Fort Douglas who had been sent to Utah territory by the federal government. Eventually the Mormon Church's "Avenging Angel" did in (i.e. poisoned) my great grandfather Joseph for his non-conformity and my grandfather James would have nothing further to do with the Mormon Church. (The story goes that the girl James had hoped to marry refused to cooperate and had to be locked up before her wedding to the polygamous bishop. They were later divorced, she re-married eventually but when my grandfather died many years later, she attended his funeral.)

Given their unhappy skirmishes with Mormons, my grandparents—James and Annette—seemed meant for each other. And even though there was a disparity of age between them, James courted Annette. They eventually married and settled south of Salt Lake City on land my grandfather homestead. It was here in the Holladay area they reared seven children, one of whom was my mother.

My parents had grown up and met in Utah. My father's Dad was the sexton of Mt. Olivet Cemetery, so my father came naturally by the nickname of "Spooks" since he had played among the tombstones. He was a graduate engineer and geologist from the University of Utah and had fallen in love with mother before volunteering to fight in World War 1. When he returned, he begged her to marry him.

My mother, on the other hand, wanted to finish her college education and honor the loan her father had made so she could leave Utah to study at the University of California. After receiving her teaching credential along with an MA in English, she stayed there to teach in order to pay off her debt.

In the meantime, my father had gotten a job in Colombia and was still writing letters asking mother to marry him. He lived for the boat mail that would often bring him news from home or from my mother, though he was getting very discouraged that she had too many admirers to pay much attention to him.

But after fulfilling her obligations and finishing up her teaching contract, mother totally astounded him by saying "yes," She arranged to take a boat to Panama; he arranged for an Anglican minister to marry them the day of her arrival in Colón. They then went to Cartagena to live while he could continue his field work not too far away. This was before the depression in 1923.

In the meantime, my grandfather divided up his homesteaded property giving five acres to each one of his children. It was a wonderful present for my parents which offered them the opportunity to begin building a home for their future.

But alas, it also became an albatross of sorts due to my father's inability to find employment in Utah during the depression years. He kept planning to return to the United States, but whenever it came time to renew his contract, he could never find anything remotely the same or better. So from Colombia, he went on to field work in Argentina, then Bolivia, and later, after a year and a half in Mongolia, to Venezuela.

My parents lost one child born before me. Mother had been in Utah supervising the final building of their home when Marla died of pneumonia. With my father so far away, it was impossible for him to be with her. There is so much heartbreak and sadness in the letters they exchanged at that time. So it must have been difficult for mother to leave my father in 1932 and return to Utah again without him. But my father's job kept him out in the field for such long stretches that they finally decided it would be better for mother to return to the States. I think that must account for some of the drab memories still held in my thoughts whenever I look back on those early years. I was both emotionally and physically close to mother so it would have been difficult not to see things through her eyes at times. And though I described my seven early years in Utah as "gray," this is really more the adult in me speaking now comparing other times in my life. As a child, I think mainly due to my mother, life in the thirties was a tremendous adventure. Despite the loneliness she must have experienced, my mother was remarkably upbeat. She often quoted poetry or read to me and my sister, or encouraged us to read and study so we could do well in school. And she also shared with us the things she'd done in her life, which included her experiences in Cartagena and Buenos Aires and growing up in Holladay. It was with happy excitement she often read some of our father's letters to us in addition to those from Dr. Hart who had been her thesis professor in Berkeley. He encouraged her to write. So after tucking us into bed at night, mother often spent her evenings writing letters or composing poems or stories that sometimes brought in extra money.

The following chapter was written by my mother from the viewpoint of when she'd been a nine year old. She submitted it to a "Life in the United States" contest sponsored in 1937 by *Scribner's* magazine. It shows some of what she'd been immersed in as a child which led to her writing this during those long years without my father. It's a vignette about my great grandmother who came to Utah in 1852 over the Old Mormon Trail, and as my mother put it: "Her death ploughed up a whole field of truths." I know it also contributed to my dim view of Mormons. And since that's all I knew about religion—any religion—it took me a long while to dig my way out from under it all. And probably accounts for my writing this book.

# 2

# ELIZABETH ANN
# WALKED ALONE

## June 4, 1906

*Things are happening this year. In April was the San Francisco fire when we sent what clothes we could spare to the needy. In May, Topsy, our buggy horse, died from a jealous neighbor's bullet. And now, grandmother. Her death was not a shock, really, for she has been bed-ridden several years, and was nearly 96 years old. But Topsy was so young. Anyway, the house seems strangely still without her. Without grandmother, I mean. Or rather, without grandmother alive; for she is still with us, really. She lies in the front room with glass fruit jars of cracked ice packed all around her. Mother keeps filling jars with ice and replacing those that have gone to water. The weather is so warm that the ice doesn't last long; and sometimes the bottles crack and leak. Then mother has an awful time and has to be quick as anything or grandmother will get all wet. So mother is afraid to leave her for very long. She has stood there all day, manipulating bottles, and did the same all night. Her face is almost as pale as grandma's and her hair isn't so tidy as usual. She looks so small and thin from overwork. But no wonder! For many weeks mother has carried grandmother about as if she were a baby. "Shift me," she would say, "for I am in pain." Then mother would change her position in bed. Before mother could leave the room, grandmother would say, "Shift me again." So mother turned her over toward the wall. In a moment came a shriek of pain, and the cry, "Shift me again. It eases the pain when you move me about!" So mother would gather her up in her arms and carry her about the room. Poor mother! No wonder she looks all tuckered out.*

*Last night grandmother had no appetite for her chicken broth and seemed so utterly weary. Although the doctor had to come ten miles by horse and buggy, he arrived finally, carrying a black bag. He said the time was short, gave her a sleeping tablet to ease the pain, and departed. I had not been in bed long when mother asked me to get dressed. Grandma was dying.*

*As we entered the chamber, we were aware of a peculiar throaty noise accompanied by labored breathing. "The death rattle," said mother. I stared in silent wonder overcome by awe, fear, and a new emotion I cannot quite describe. Perhaps it was the feeling every person experiences in the presence of death. I couldn't take my eyes away. Being a bundle of skin and bones, her slight figure left the bedspread almost flat. It trembled violently as she rattled for breath, and then was still until time for another inhalation. Her head was pressed backward into the pillow so as to obscure her hair, almost. Her face, full of little wrinkles and tinged with yellow, resembled a freshly peeled walnut on a piece of cotton. The nose was long and sharp, and the chin came out to meet it. From where I stood at the foot of the bed, the eyes were out of sight, lying in the black shadows of deep sockets. Upon the coverlet lay two bony sticks terminating in claws. One could hardly call them hands since the fingers were too long and thin, the hands themselves too narrow and hard. They resembled, rather, the cold talons of an eagle or the claws of an animal. I shall never forget how white the knuckles looked when the hands closed convulsively. I wanted to look elsewhere but my gaze seemed glued on those strange hands. They held me spell-bound until I became aware that the rattling noises were fainter, farther apart. I looked up just as they ceased and am sure the long pointed nose became suddenly sharper, the chin more firm and sharp too. It was all over. Said mother in apostrophe, "Now you do not have to walk alone any longer." And I looked timidly about to see if any spirits had come for grandma.*

*So mother washed the dead, and laid her out, and put coins on the eyelids to keep them shut. In the morning father sent telegrams to people in Idaho and lost an argument with local relatives to have grandmother embalmed. "That would cost money," they argued; and stood pat. Such silly nonsense! So father bought ice to preserve the body and although mother was horrified, she said nothing.*

## June 6

*The house is cluttered with our Mormon relatives come to see grandmother who is now dressed and in her coffin, her hard little hands folded across her breast. Although the hands are shockingly grotesque and the face unlovely with age, yet there is something beautiful about her as she lies there resting. Perhaps the peace which is death, is also beauty. Cousin Elsie walked up and kissed her on the forehead; so did her sisters. It must have been like kissing a cold, brown stone. Aunt Celie towered above the casket comely and straight. I had to look way up to see her face for she is tall enough to be queenly. Her voice seems to come from way down deep in her stomach as if a little old rusty machine down there were grinding out the words with difficulty. They come out one by one, hard and clear-cut, but get together into meaning, somehow, like a string of sausages. Cords in her neck tightened as the little machine began to work.*

*"I brought flowers for the funeral tomorrow, Nan," she said, looking across the room at mother. "A strawberry crate full of pansies. You can make them up into a wreath. Here they are on the sofa."*

*Mother looked a little startled and her mouth tightened but she uttered no word. I could almost here her thinking. It went like this: "I don't have enough to do with ice and bottles and funeral arrangements and out-of-town relatives and the usual routine, so you bring me extra work. On top of everything, I am to weave your pansies into a wreath." And I wondered why mother did not pick up that crate of pansies and throw them right across the coffin into Aunt Celie's face. Grandmother would have loved that and chortled, if the dead could chortle. But she lay so still. The dead are too darn still. The machine was grinding out advice.*

*"Of course, it won't be necessary to buy flowers. The pansies will be enough."*

*Mother's voice in reply was as hollow as a dry churn. "I mean to buy a floral spray," she said "And if your husband and John can't spend that much on their own mother's funeral, it is a pity. She's my husband's mother, too. I assure you we'll pay for a floral offering, even if you won't."*

*Aunt Celie pulled up her straight back into a straighter line. "Too bad," she said, ignoring the subject and looking down at the white burial dress. "Too bad that grandma isn't dressed in Mormon garments. The green apron with the fig leaves would look a lot better. She used to be a good Mormon, you know."*

*"Used to be, yes," said mother, who had selected the burial clothes. "But she left the church many years ago as you very well know."*

*"Yes," ground the machine. "But it was too bad."*

*"Too bad, nothing!" said mother, ceasing to look tired. "Wasn't she bitterer than gall against the church when grandpa was commanded to take another wife? And when he added two more, wasn't she like one possessed? Hasn't she told us that a hundred times? And didn't she resolve to leave the church as soon as it was safe? 'How would you feel,' she used to say, 'if your husband left you for a young bride's bed and ruined everything beautiful you had built together over a long period of years?'"*

*Mother's face was flushed now; her eyes snapped fire, and there was apprehension in everybody's eyes. Were these two sisters-in-law going to quarrel over grandmother's dead body? Ada and Elsie moved nervously about without going anywhere; Uncle John sighed deeply and knitted his fingers; Aunt Edna pulled at her dress as if it were wet against her body. Father groped in his beard and blinked owlishly as is always the case when mother gets her wind up or when he wants to enjoy a situation that isn't quite proper to enjoy. Everybody glanced sidewise at everybody else. Someone in the group breathed a breath unnaturally deep as if to inhale the black blanket of flies gathered on the screen door. I caught myself breathing fast and was aware of the pecu-liar odor of the dead and of a faint pansy fragrance. Mother went on.*

*"You know very well that grandfather could scarcely afford to keep one wife prop-erly, let alone three more. And you know, too, that his principles were against polyg-amy. But the church commanded it and the church was all-powerful. Unless he obeyed, the Avenging Angel followed with swift punishment. He knew only too well what that meant since some of his friends, refusing to obey, had been murdered in their beds. Being a practical man and a lover of life, he decided to keep his position in the church even if it meant changing his whole manner of living. But as time passed, the Lord's promised glory did not reveal itself to him, as such, in quarrelsome wives, numerous children, and insufficient funds. Instead, he yearned for the peace of monog-amous years. Though the church had changed his mode of living, they could not change his thinking. So he apostatized; and the Avenging Angel got him post haste. Everyone of you must know all about it; how he had to be buried within a day of his death because his body was swelling so fast they were afraid they couldn't put the coffin lid on. A clear case of poisoning, it was; and everybody close-lipped with fear. That was almost 50 years ago, Celie. Fifty long years that grandmother has walked alone; and almost as many since she heard her own name, Elizabeth Ann, on kind lips. Can't you see, Celie? Won't you try to understand? Knowing her life as you do, how can you stand there and say that grandmother should wear Mormon burial garments? Please, Celie, just this once, try to look at those long empty years from grandmother's point of view?"*

*Aunt Celie might have spoken but mother continued with this longest speech of her life.*

*"Try to see her stripped of the security to which she was accustomed, her home life suddenly meaningless, her children betrayed, her life full of daughters not her own. How could she reconcile this mess with real religion? She couldn't, of course. And nei-ther could you nor I; nor anyone else. O but her life was lonely for fifty long years, I tell you. Bleak as winter, Celie. Bleak! Bleak!!"*

*Suddenly I understood something in a puzzling past. Often have I seen grand-mother huddled under her old gray shawl in her accustomed rocker. She might sit qui-etly for a long time. Suddenly she would leap out of her chair like one possessed, talk and sputter about the room in bewildering manner, and end the paroxysm by spitting vehemently into the coal scuttle. Observing neighbors who called her "cracked" were wrong She was smarting from wounds that would not heal. She was remembering events in a tragic past; things repulsive to the delicately feminine heart. Spitting them out of her system was perhaps a natural physical reaction. Who knows?[1]*

◆     ◆     ◆

My mother and her brothers and sisters never spoke much about the fact that my maternal great grandfather had been a polygamist. I must have been thirty years old before I knew for sure. I think there was such a great sense of shame on their part that this was in the family history, I'm sure they felt the less spoken about it the better. And I was almost sixty before reading many of my mother's notes and poems confirming it.

My early years in Utah very much related to the Mormons too, though more perhaps by their absence than their presence. Mormon children didn't naturally go out of their way to play with gentiles, so my only playmate in childhood was my sister and occasionally our older friend named Mary (a.k.a. Gail in the Prelude) who lived a short distance from our home. In my framework of religion, there were only Mormons, Non-Mormons, Anti-Mormons or Jack Mormons. (The latter were those Mormons who did not practice their faith.) At that point, I'd never heard of any other kind of faith, so if one were to speak about religion, I viewed myself as Non-Mormon. I didn't mind being categorized as such, even though it meant in the greater community, I was a non-person, but to me and my sister, this was a badge of distinction. In first grade, not being among the chosen, I still recall a Jewish boy named Clarence and I who were the only two gentiles in our class. A block from our school was a Mormon ward where most of our class went for after school activities. Of course, we were never part of those.

Aside from having only my older sister and Mary to play with on occasion, what little I knew about Mormons in my early life was that they often upset my mother, grandmother and aunts, especially when on the subject of polygamy; consequently, a cloud formed in my mind relating to anything that smacked of religion, and it followed me for a long time.

The first church I ever entered was the Unitarian Church in Salt Lake City. That was when my mother's younger sister was married. There were lots of flowers and everyone was dressed up which made a big impression on me because we seldom went to anything. Putting on my best dress I knew was very special. Mother liked the Unitarians and even took my sister and me back once to visit their Sunday school. I was six by then and recall the teacher in the class I was placed in discussing the theory of evolution that day. Mother wanted to take us back, but the drive into town was just too far to go on a regular basis, so that didn't happen.

As a youngster, I often used to think of myself as living in a private garden under the shadow of Mt. Olympus rising up behind us. I knew far away over the mountains towards the southeast, my Daddy worked in mountains and jungles. And I knew he was big and strong and loved us and would some day come home for good. And sometimes when I'd climb the hill behind our house, when looking westward, I could visualize California beyond the Great Salt Lake and imagine Mother's thesis professor sitting somewhere far away at his desk. And there would be an invisible cord stretching from Berkeley all the way to Utah, then on to South America.

# 3

# THE LONG SEVEN YEAR STRETCH

I can recall seeing my father twice between ages 2–7. He came home once on foreign leave for three months around 1936. Later, when he returned from doing geology in Mongolia and finding oil in China, he was with us before his transfer to Venezuela.

When I was three, mother invited some people in for my birthday. Having seen only my sister, mother and a few individual relatives over my first year in Utah, to whom I'm told I often said "Go away," I was not at all prepared for all those strangers. I think it was supposed to have been a surprise. And indeed it was. Mother had a large china cabinet in the corner of the dining room under which I took refuge where I spent nearly the entire evening. No one could coax me out until almost time for the cake to be cut. It would be ten years before mother ventured to give me another birthday party!

Other strange incidents still stand out in my memory.

One was my cousin Hal and how inventive he always seemed to be. He once constructed a remarkable underground which was a large hole in the ground covered with boards, then camouflaged with dirt on top. I guess he viewed this as his private club house of sorts. Dispersed along the walls, he'd inserted recessed vertical halved tin cans from which lighted candles could reflect light. I crawled down into the entrance once through a short tunnel and was quite amazed to see how large it was. The second time I was invited in, I saw a mouse running out the exit, however, and decided never to return.

Hal was much older, so Shirley and I saw little of him, but one day he invited us over to play. He said he had a surprise for us and took us into my aunt's basement. There he pointed out a large upside down wash tub and asked my sister if she'd sit on it. But Shirley suspected something and declined. Then it was my turn. I tried to accommodate my cousin and was about to sit down when my sister pulled me back. "Look!" she said. I looked to see where Shirley was pointing to see an electric wire attached to the tub's handle. Hal was trying to get us to sit on his "electric chair" which he'd hot wired! I have no idea what that might have done to us. But when I later heard Hal had gotten hold of his father's loaded pistol and shot it off in his parent's closet, thus putting holes in all their clothing, I never really thought of him as a suitable playmate.

The other unnerving thing that happened to me was when my piano teacher had an epileptic fit right in the middle of my piano lesson. I was so traumatized by the experience I had difficulty trying to read the bass clef after that. That's the assignment I'd been told to work on for the day. When I got home, I told mother I didn't want any more lessons. She must have had a bad day too because she never asked me why, although she suggested I could learn from Shirley if I wanted to continue later.

Little children like to be included with their playmates and I was no exception. The problem, however, was that I was much younger than my sister and our friend, Mary, so could not always keep up with them. Five years in childhood makes a huge age difference. When I was 6, they were 11 or 12. For this reason, I was often either "ditched," or else made the object of games they concocted in which I was often made the target or guinea pig. This ensured they would have fun at my expense or else get rid of me altogether. But mostly, I really didn't mind. I just know rather than being left out, I loved to be with the "big girls," even if their rules and games were questionable. But when left alone, I learned how to make the best of it. I always felt blessed in a way because of that wonderful light I'd once seen, and I could always play make-believe that Daddy was coming home and then figure out what I would say to him someday when he did.

Shirley and Mary both knew how to read, something I could not do until I went to school. My sister had learned to read when she was 4 or 5, but I had not had that experience, even though I was taught my blocks and could fit a lot of them together to make words. I was apprehensive about going to first grade because I was afraid I'd be the only kid in the class who couldn't read. What a wonderful surprise it was to discover that no one else could either.

I think because my sister had read so many western cowboy stories by Zane Grey and others, she'd been influenced into thinking it was important to be a "tough hombre," certainly one who didn't cry. "People who cry are sissies," she insisted. So she was stoic whenever punished. Her only way to "get even" when she thought our mother had unfairly punished her, would be to say *brat, shit, poop, bugger, damn, hell, ain't* under her breath, words she knew mother disapproved of. Neither of us had heard of the F word back then, or I'm sure it too would have been included. Shirley complained she always had to "break the trail" for me, because she got punished much more than I did. Then again, there were times when I thought she really deserved it.

One of these occasions was when she and Mary played a game with me, the idea being that the winner would get to be "queen." I'm sure they arranged the game so I would win which meant I'd get to be "crowned." Only their idea of a crown turned out to be a big round prickly arrangement of purple and green burdock thistles which got so entangled in my hair that they were impossible to remove. After a painful period of trying to comb them out, mother finally had to cut off most of my hair. I rated that game the second worst ever after their attempt to baptize me near the canal.

But the good times outweighed all the negatives, and I still remember the excitement of going to Lagoon (an amusement park with a marvelous swimming pool) as well as Warm Springs where there was also a large pool. I loved water and couldn't wait to learn how to swim. My grandmother's pond had cold springs that fed into it which made it pretty chilly; nevertheless, we tried even though the moss tickled our feet and the two big carp she had would swim by and eye us.

Mother also took us hiking up Tolgate's Canyon, or towards the road that paralleled the mountain east of our home where Indian Rock jutted out. That's where my mother killed a rattlesnake once. And I fell in love with a tap dancing class down town too but which we did not continue. I suspect Mother might not have had enough money for it, or it may have been the long drive which took away from things that had to be done at home. We always kept plenty busy helping to weed or irrigate or pick raspberries and strawberries. In the fall, we'd pick up walnuts off the ground too which, when dried, could be cracked during the winter to be used in fudge or cookies. And helping to pick cherries, apples, pears or apricots I always thought was fun.

Since we weren't church goers, often on Sundays, we'd also play poker at Mary's. Her relatives ran a "take out food" and restaurant and were usually very busy on weekends due to the weekend traffic heading for the canyons. There was a round table in the back of their house where we'd sit in our blue jeans and green shade hats pretending to be tough desperados. We'd pile up the chips and play for stacks of caramels which Mary somehow was always able to acquire.

One highlight of our childhood was when Professor Hart and his wife invited my mother to visit them for a week in California. This did not include me or Shirley, of course, so mother well prepared us for her absence. She trusted us, said she knew we'd be good, would go to school on time, study hard and take care of the place. My aunt lived across the street and my grandmother lived about fifteen acres away down the field and Mother reminded us we could always call on them if we needed anything. Shirley was thirteen at the time and I was nearly eight. We both felt like really Big Girls to be trusted with so much responsibility. And we did live up to our mother's expectations; at least most of them! In this day and age, I see on TV that parents who leave their young children alone even for a weekend sometimes end up in jail. But times have changed since the '30's.

We were in hog heaven being given so much leeway in how to spend the money she left us for "extras" and the option of getting up or going to bed when we pleased, just as long as we went to school. Because we so loved waffles, after mother left, we first made us a large batch to last the entire week. Then we went to a weekend movie (double feature) with some of the money and then squandered the rest on root beer, bubble gum, candy and milk shakes for the rest of the week. We didn't make our beds even once until it was time to change the sheets and do the laundry, but we didn't miss one day of school. It was in early May that she went, so the weather was good and we cut the grass once and got the garbage out on schedule. The one game we played that we loved consisted in turning all the lights off in the house after it got dark, then one would be "it" while the other would hide. The idea was that the person who was "it" had to wander around in the dark waiting for the person who was hidden to jump out and scare them. I don't think I'd really enjoy that game now! The Saturday before mother returned, we cleaned the house from top to bottom, polished the silver and scrubbed the kitchen.

I am indebted to my sister for never having taken up smoking. Once when rummaging about in the trunks in our basement, Shirley and I found a box of Cuban cigars which our father had packed away. I was about four years old as I recall. Shirley thought it would be great fun to smoke them. I was a little leery of this, but she found some matches and encouraged me, even demonstrating how I should take a deep breath and then blow out the smoke. After a few puffs, as well as swallowing some smoke, I knew then and there I would never be a smoker.

When our father got his foreign leave and was able to return to the States for three months, Mother took us to Chicago to meet him part way. Shirley and I had never stayed in a city, nor in a hotel, so it was a real adventure. After getting reacquainted, Daddy suggested he treat me and Shirley to some movies which we thought was a great idea. We saw two double features on two consecutive days which was about the only way our parents could get rid of us now that I think of it, just so they could have some privacy.

What really fascinated me about Chicago though were the spittoons by the elevators in the hotel. I wondered for days what they were for. Mostly though I remember Errol Flynn in *Robin Hood*, as well as *The Adventures of Tom Sawyer*, a restaurant with great pancakes and a toy our father purchased for us that we could spiral high into the air and watch float down. This was hard to do in a city and we didn't know where any parks might be, so we figured out how to get on the top of the hotel's roof and played with it there. After umpteen launches, it floated down and landed past us on an adjoining roof next to the hotel we were in; so it took us a while to figure out how to retrieve it. Reaching the other building necessitated having to climb the upper fire escapes, however, and when someone saw us, they were horrified and told us we couldn't play our game anymore. After climbing trees all our lives, we never gave a thought to its being dangerous.

From Chicago, we went to Detroit where our parents had ordered a new Plymouth automobile. We got to watch our car being put together on an assembly line all the way from start to finish. I can still recall a mechanical brush painting the red line around the outside of our car just below the windows. After that, lunch was served in the cafeteria and then our father drove us all out of the factory in our new car heading for Utah.

# 4

# MARACAIBO

When I was nine, my father was transferred to Venezuela when housing opened up for him in Maracaibo. This was after he'd spent a year first searching for oil in China and Outer Mongolia. My mother and I went to join him in Venezuela leaving my sister with an aunt. Shirley was already in high school and had to stay behind since the oil camp school did not extend beyond 8<sup>th</sup> grade.

From being somewhat of an exile in Utah to an accepted freckle-faced, red-headed *Maracucha* in an oil camp in South America was as different and exciting as I could have ever hoped to imagine. There were no discussions about polygamy; no one got upset over Darwin; people spoke different languages and no one ever asked me if I belonged to the TRUE church. In fact, no one ever asked me if I even went to church! All the kids played together like a large family. My school was a polyglot of Dutch, American, Venezuelan and British kids primarily, who lived either in the Mene Grande, the Lago Petroleum or the Royal Dutch Shell oil camps.

Spanish was taught. There were outdoor movies under the stars which gave me an opportunity to start a popcorn business. It flourished despite the fact that a German sub sank the tanker that carried my first order of canned popcorn.

We sometimes fished or swam in Lake Maracaibo and many of the women played bridge or gave teas. One started a Girl Scout troop. We kids played kick-the-can or Tarzan or pomp-pomp-pull-away. I chased iguanas and one summer got to go to La Mesa de Esnujaque for camp in the Andes where I chased and sometimes caught butterflies too along the Butterfly Trail. My father drove us through the mountains also, often explaining the various geological formations. I still remember the iznotu of the oligocene and the bettijoque of the miocene. When we'd get off the beaten track in the Andes, looking for gas or for some geologic outcrop, people would come out and look at us. Surprised children would run to their parents and point at me or my father and I'd hear them say *milagrera*.

Some in those areas had never seen red-headed people, and seeing two at once really caused a commotion.

My mother happily worked for the American consulate too and later wrote a book on Venezuela. She was also a contributor to various publications including the *Caracas Journal* when my father was transferred to Caracas.

There was endless swimming. And every year there were Christmas pageants and Easter sports. It seemed grown-ups were always giving outdoor parties too adjacent to a tile dance floor near the club house and swimming pool, where a large mango tree afforded enough foliage for us kids to hide in so we could spy on everyone. There were many barbeques given too for the service men who came through whenever a submarine or navy ship docked nearby. This gave all us kids a chance to collect autographs and hear stories first hand about what was happening in the war. I often told myself if there were such a place as heaven, I knew I'd already arrived. Certainly it was a world I'd never remotely experienced in Utah.

But one summer, some of the parents got together and decided their children could benefit by going to summer school and improving their Spanish. A local Catholic school run by nuns was trying to raise money and agreed to take us all. It was a grade school and the desks in the room they put us in were so small that we could barely get our knees in under the desks. None of us wanted to be there and felt we were being robbed of our vacation time. About our third day there, one student named Philip became especially boisterous. When the sisters tried to discipline him, he managed to get hold of a fire hose hanging in the outer patio and turned it on them. Of course, we were all kicked out, to the chagrin of Philip's parents, but to the delight of the rest of us.

After a short time, my parents sent me to Sunday school. The church existed only because one of the oil workers, an Englishman named Charles Teckmeyer, had become concerned that the children were not getting basic religious training. ("Don't want to see them all end up little heathens.") So he returned to England to study, became ordained, then returned and set up an English speaking church for expatriates. It was open to all the families from the various oil camps regardless of denomination or nationality and included Catholics and Protestants alike. The things that stand out to me now, looking back on it all, were the organdy dress I had to wear which always scratched my prickly heat, the tight shoes I had outgrown, the *lochas* we put into the collection plate to equal our age whenever it was our birthday, and my father, reading his *Time* magazine, sitting patiently in the back waiting to take me home.

I was given a Bible; my mother even gave me a Bible in Spanish which I never read. But I did learn all the books of the Bible which I could rattle off as fast as I could speak. And we all learned the Beatitudes, the Lord's Prayer and various Bible verses from time to time. But some of it confused me. My scientifically oriented father made it very clear to me once that the Virgin Mary could not possibly have been a virgin, so, though mother always said "take the good and forget the rest," I looked at the Bible with a skeptical eye. The Bible was a book I packed around with me whenever I moved (which was often) with the idea that someday I would take time off to understand what religion was all about. My Bible was a lucky charm. It sat on the book shelf and got dusted.

There was one boy nicknamed Ceako about my age whose mother I was told was a Christian Scientist. They lived several rows away from our house in the oil camp. There was something special about Ceako that made me think of light long before some one told me his mother taught him prayers and read the Bible to him. Ceako didn't swear or pick on the younger kids and he was always polite and considerate of others. He was never a goody-goody, but he and his mother always stood out to me as special people. One evening a group of us were playing hide-and-go-seek in the Lago camp. It was my turn to hide and I found myself a spot between two hibiscus shrubs which I thought would conceal me. Ceako was nearby behind a palm tree. As we hid, I suddenly had the most unusual experience of what I can only say was God's presence. And I knew it emanated from Ceako. It was like a lighted rope connecting us. It was an amazing experience that left me overwhelmed. I relegated it to my God file because I couldn't begin to explain it to myself, let alone to anyone else. But I knew it was somehow related to that time when I'd been in the water in Buenos Aires.

We all attended the Bella Vista School which was supported by the various oil companies for the benefit of their employee's children. Most of the teachers, with the exception of our Spanish teacher, were hired from the United States. One day a group of us decided to make a special valentine for our teacher. The practice was to have a box in the classroom for the valentines so they could be handed out during our party. After constructing a very attractive one, we all tried to think of something to say on it, but nothing seemed quite right. Then one of the kids came up with a verse that wasn't a bit complimentary and it was all down hill after that. After much trial and error and laughter, and because she was a very tall woman, the verse finally decided upon was:

> "Rose are red, violets are blue
> Giraffes like you should live in the zoo."

I'll never understand why I went along with this. But there seemed to be a sense of "okay-ness" since the entire group thought it was funny, so I did nothing to veto it. (After all, I'd done much worse when I'd been around Mary once when she relieved her uncle of one of his prize bottles of good scotch, then enlisted me to help her lace the chicken mash with it in order to get all his chickens drunk.) Of course, none of us signed the valentine, but she was such a fair, out-going, good teacher, I can't believe now on looking back we were sure she'd see it as the joke we all intended it to be and laugh with us.

The day of the party, we couldn't wait for her to open her valentines. She distributed all of ours first, then sat down and began to read through hers, thanking each one that was signed. When we saw her pick up the one we had made, we couldn't wait for her to read it. Only after looking it over, she didn't laugh. She just stared at it, then laid it aside on her desk, looked down at her lap for a bit, then looked up. Her lower lip was trembling and we could tell she might cry. Then ever so quickly, she got up and excused herself. Only those of us involved knew what had happened. The rest of the class kept on partying.

I can't speak for the others, but I know I died a thousand deaths that day. I knew I'd knowingly contributed to hurting a lovely person. I took it so personally, I could hardly breathe. I knew I could have said it wasn't nice to do this to our favorite teacher. I could have opted out, but I didn't. I hadn't done a thing. I'd just gone along with it all. Self-loathing didn't begin to describe what I felt. I just knew I'd never had such a sickening feeling inside of me. No one had to remind me I'd been involved in something wrong. That's when I learned first hand that Christianity basically involved relationships. And some of those Bible verses I'd memorized began to come alive. (Try 1 Corinthians 13: 4–7).[2] In no uncertain terms, even though my name was not on that card, I knew I had to personally apologize to my teacher; and for my peace of mind, the sooner the better.

It was a Friday, and there was no opportunity to speak with her before going home, so I spent two days over the weekend, agonizing over the valentine, hoping I would run in to her.

I finally spotted her unexpectedly under the big mango tree. She was in a good mood, awaiting her escort who had gone to get them both a *cerveza*.

"No one seems to be on duty," she told me.

"I guess not." I responded, then blurted out how sorry I was, how I hadn't meant to hurt her feelings. "We all like you, Miss Sloat." Then, despite my sister's rule that "only sissies cry," I began to cry. "We all thought you'd think it was funny. But I know now it wasn't."

"Marta, I'm sure it was funny to all of you. I guess Friday wasn't one of my better days. It's all right. You're forgiven. Thank you for owning up to being part of it."

Just then her escort returned with their beer, and as I turned to leave, she said to him: "Marta and I have been having a discussion about giraffes. They're lucky. They get to see all kinds of things others close to the ground never see at all." She winked at me and hoisted her glass. The following year, I heard she and Mr. Refshauge were married. And five years later in New York City, God gave me a chance to make it up to her.

One other time when I really goofed was when my parents had an opportunity to go to the mountains for a brief vacation. Since school was in session, I couldn't go with them, but they felt I was in good hands with our maid—Chila. Since we also lived in a fenced oil camp where all our friends and many other employees lived, there was no problem about getting help if one needed it.

My sister was in the States at the time but later sent me an essay which she wrote for one of her English assignments after coming to spend the summer with us in Maracaibo. The following is her take on what happened.

# 5

# MARTA DEFIES GRAVITY

*It happened the early spring of 1941, just a couple of months before I came down on summer vacation to Maracaibo, after a long year at boarding school. I had already heard some of the more gruesome details from Mother's letters, but steeped in maternal horror as they were, I suspected her of giving me only one side of the story, and my suspicions were readily confirmed by Marta's non-apologetic post-scripts and squawks of righteous indignation as to the odiousness of her offense. So when I stepped off the Pan-Am clipper that hot Saturday evening in June, I was greeted not only by my family, but by an enormous white cast, prominently displayed at a rakish angle where Marta knew I could not miss it. It covered her right leg from the knee down, and when she walked, it was only with a pronounced limp, which, from the rear, gave her a certain swash-buckling air that must have made her the envy of all the kids in camp. And so, bit by bit, from different people ranging from the gardeners to the camp boss and Chila, who remembered more and more each time I asked her, I pieced together the brief episode of Marta's great folly.*

*In Maracaibo that year, the rains came soon and lasted long, and each wet, sweet-smelling day brought with it heat, the steaming, stifling heat that comes up from the ground in waves, and beats down from above your head, and presses in from all sides till your clothes stick to your body, and you sit like a lump all day and sweat and swear and gasp for relief. It was partly the heat, and partly the fact that Daddy's local leave had come around, that drove him and Mother to the Andes for a two-week vacation that February. And though Marta howled with indignation and wept crocodile tears, Mother remained firm: she had to stay home with Chila and go to school, and that was that.*

*Now the children in camp had found various and diversified ways of amusing themselves, and at this time of year, when the palms were green and supple and the great under-fronds hung low from their own weight, the favorite sport was palm-*

*swinging. This dubious art consisted of first finding a palm tree with a suitable low-hanging frond, the longer the better, and then running madly to it, catching hold, and swing back and forth until it died down. In due time the abused frond gave up the ghost, and the children went off in search of another. All went well that spring until the camp was exhausted of palm trees with low fronds, and then some adventuresome lad pointed out that those huge fronds away up there out of reach looked much more exciting, and definitely more Tarzan-like. At which suggestion there was an immediate murmur of approval, and the group set out bodily for a thorough canvass of the camp's potentialities. And there, half-way down "jefe" row, in front of an empty house, stood an old tough coconut palm, with long rippling fronds ending about ten feet off the ground. The kids stood, hands on hips, and ran a critical eye up and down the tree, to the roof of the house, back to the tree; then with one accord they walked silently around to the back, climbed up a mango tree, jumped onto the roof, and one by one, with screeches of joy, dived head-foremost into space, grabbed a big frond on the way down, and swung unharmed to the ground. It was at the unhappy moment that Marta was on her third or fourth trip, that Mother glanced casually out the dining room window in the midst of packing for the trip. It is hardly necessary to describe the scene that followed, but the up-shot of it was that Marta was threatened with no movies for a month if she ever tried it again. And it was in this frame of mind, with Marta, slightly subdued but still belligerent, and Chila watching the proceedings with great joy from the butler's pantry, that Mother and Daddy left for their trip to the mountains.*

*Several days passed and all went well. Marta's unaccustomed freedom was without a doubt a source of irritation to her little friends who still had to go to bed early, and lead a more or less well-regulated existence. But Marta and Chila were in seventh heaven. Chila flicked a dust cloth vaguely in the direction of the largest pieces of furniture once a day, and spent the rest of her time trotting from back-door to back-door with all the latest gossip. She borrowed Mother's curlers regularly and pranced in front of the long mirror in the master bedroom, admiring her chubby self for hours at a time. She entertained her maid-friends in the living room while Marta was at school, and they all sat and wriggled their dirty bare feet on the oriental rug, and talked of lofty things, and smoked Daddy's cigarettes.*

*And Marta spent her time at the club playing ping-pong and pool with the men, and talking Julio, the bartender, into giving her two scoops of ice-cream for the price of one. At night, after the movie, she and Chila went and sat on the back-steps of the club and ate ice-cream and threw rocks at the frogs that appear so suddenly and in such numbers each night during the rainy season. And in the afternoons, when Francisco, the gardener on our row, sidled around to the back door to speak of love and what-not to Chila, Marta leaned out of her bedroom window, and haggled over the price of a baseball mitt Francisco wanted to buy from her, and frustrated the poor man no end.*

*And so life went for a few hilarious days. Much to Marta's sorrow, her friends kept swinging on the palm fronds that had been forbidden her. The scene of operations had been moved by this time to another old withered palm in front of the guest house, a higher palm, and a higher house. She looked on sadly for the good part of an hour while that particular frond became weaker, and, as needs be, wilder, and much more exciting. For a good part of the same hour she endured the taunts and disparaging remarks about her courage, of her friends who had envied her freedom the last week. At last, to prove she wasn't a sissy, and could swing as far as anyone, and to satisfy a secret longing to swing on that particular palm, she forgot Mother's threats, climbed up on the roof, took a deep breath, and with a lusty whoop, dived out and down. The ill-treated palm frond parted company with its better half, and together, it and Marta crashed to the ground. Marta limped home and went to bed, and Chila went to the club, and bought two dishes of ice-cream, and thus fortified, Marta decided all would be well, and swore Chila to secrecy. But in the morning, on discovering her leg to be swollen to twice its size, numb, and black in color, Chila dashed next door in a panic, and with a rush of Spanish which left the "señora" dazed, dragged her to the house and into the bedroom, where Marta sat sheepishly, clutching a copy of Superman, her wounded limb propped up on a pillow.*

*So Marta went to the hospital. And when Mother and Daddy finally drove into camp a week later they were met at the gate by a delegation consisting of Chila, wringing her hands, half the married women in camp and all the bachelors Marta played pool with at the club, all talking at once, trying to explain that she was in the hospital but was all right and happy. And when they finally got there, she was sitting up in bed, her red hair in pigtails, talking with her latest friends, the Venezuelan nurses.*

*The next day a whole retinue of gardeners armed with machetes, attacked the innocent, long-suffering palm trees, and gave them a trimming which put further swinging out of the question for months to come.*

◆     ◆     ◆

*And that night, after I got home from the airport, Marta and I went over to the club, and while I ate an ice-cream and looked at the calendars on the back wall, Marta rested her cast on the bar rail, and tried to talk Julio out of another package of gum.*

◆    ◆    ◆

Despite not being allowed to swing anymore on palm branches, that three and one-half years spent with my parents in the Lago Oil camp were the happiest years of my childhood. Shirley didn't mention I went swimming during a Girl Scout outing to Lake Maracaibo while I still had the cast on (which was not a good idea!) because the salt water dissolved the cast. My doctor was not happy with me because it meant he had to put on another one. Then, several days later, he caught me riding my bicycle and about had apoplexy. After that, I led a very quiet life until the cast was removed.

# 6

# ST. MARY'S

I eventually outgrew the school in Maracaibo and had to continue my education in the United States.

My father had arranged for Shirley to have an office job during the summer before her return to college in the fall; so in late August, she and I flew to Miami on a Pan American Airways clipper, landing in Coconut Grove. We stayed overnight in the city where we'd never seen so many sailors in one place, then took a train to Chicago where we could catch another train for Salt Lake City. Since the war was still underway, trains and hotels were terribly over crowded. When we arrived at the Palmer House in Chicago where we had reservations, we were told the only space left was a bridal suite.

"We only have enough money to pay for a room with two twin beds. Or one, if that's all you have," we assured the clerk. "We have a reservation." The manager hummed and hawed, checked with his superiors, then finally put us in the bridal suite.

"Boy, this is something, isn't it?" said my sister, viewing the big room and bed. "Wait till we tell mother we've slept in a bridal suite." She also couldn't wait to tell her friends.

That night we ate dinner in the hotel dining room. It was the first time too either of us had ever seen lamb chops with little white skirts on them.

My Aunt Alice met us in Salt Lake City. Shirley went back to school and I spent a year going to a local junior high while living with my Aunt Alice and Uncle Harold who were Hal's parents. Hal didn't seem quite as intimidating to me as he had when I'd been smaller, though I still held the memory of that electrified wash tub in mind. By now, however, he was interested in more important things such as being a ham radio operator, college and girls.

My sister had already graduated from St. Mary-of-the-Wasatch, a girl's school on the east bench of Salt Lake City. So that's where I was also sent the following year. Shirley had already regaled me with tales of crucifixes and depressing paint-ings, but "you'll like Sister Patty Anne. She's a lot of fun."

St. Mary's was run by the Sisters-of the-Holy-Cross and my parents knew them to be good teachers. But I was enrolled with the proviso I was not to be taught any religion. Mother did not want the sisters turning me into a Roman Catholic. I'm amazed the nuns accepted me under these conditions, but they needed students and agreed to abide by my mother's injunction. It was agreed I would take a class in "character education" in which other students, whose par-ents shared my mother's outlook, were also enrolled. My mother's views of the Catholic Church had all been drawn from years of living in South America where she equated the Roman Catholic faith with superstition and a corrupt hierarchy. Some of my father's experiences did nothing to diminish my mother's take on things either. He had been a keen observer of the church when working in Bolivia and Argentina. The rural priests often took young Indian girls into their homes to help clean and cook for them. When the girls became pregnant, they would be returned to their villages in exchange for other young girls, something I'm sure mother equated with the polygamy she so detested from her upbringing in Utah. And throughout South America, in contrast to the population in many places, the church was very wealthy with vast land holdings in many countries. However, the hierarchy at the time identified only with the power structure and did little if anything to help improve the lives of the poor and uneducated. Mother could think of nothing worse than having a daughter become a Roman Catholic. To her, it was almost as bad as Mormonism.

Of course, there was an Episcopal boarding school in downtown Salt Lake where I might have gone, but mother saw how awful the smoke and smog could be, especially during mid-winter temperature inversions in the valley, and didn't want me living in all that city soot. To her, health had priority over religion. Any-way, she'd heard the Episcopalians were wealthy and didn't want me thrown in with students I couldn't begin to keep up with, certainly not on my minimal allowance. With two daughters away at school, there was little for extras.

I don't think she had any concept of what total immersion in a Catholic boarding school with thirty nuns could do to me. On more than one occasion, I had to remain at school when it was financially impossible for me to return home for short school vacations. So St. Mary's became my second home for three years where I truly loved the sisters, but questioned everything they taught, especially if it smacked of religion.

My first week or two at school, I tried hard to fit in. I also tried not to look at all the religious paintings in the halls, many depicting the life of Christ. I'd never thought of Jesus like this. One painting showed him in terrible pain with a crown of thorns on his head. It reminded me a little of when I'd been crowned "queen" experience. And there was one picture of a saint that looked half-starved. The only painting I liked at all was the one of Christ in the garden of Gesthemane, I guess because of the light streaming in, reminding me ever so faintly of my early memory of Buenos Aires. There were a few statues too of the Virgin Mary, crucifixes in every classroom, bells announcing mealtime, prayer time, class time or bedtime. And always, there were black serge-garbed sisters with their flowing veils, clicking beads and cheerful dispositions, ever punctuated by the white material framing their faces.

The sisters insisted all boarding students go to church on Sunday, if not at school, then to a church of our own choosing in the valley. Of course, I didn't have a church and my meager allowance could not be stretched to pay taxi fare to the city and back anyway. Mother begrudgingly relented and the sisters won that round. So, in order to please both the sisters and my mother, my body was always in their chapel on Sunday, but my mind was usually elsewhere. Looking about me my first week there, I was struck with the realization I'd come from being "non-Mormon" now to being "non-Catholic."

This was painfully evident the first time I went to Sunday church with my new-found friends. Most were Catholic and I wasn't sure what to do.

"Just follow us," said one of them. "Do what we do."

So I bobby-pinned the veil I'd been issued and got in line and followed into the chapel. I skipped the holy water and crossing myself, then looked up to see Christ hanging on the crucifix above the altar. By then I should have been used to it, but this still unnerved me. As for my guide, it seemed to me she was always getting up or down during the service, standing first, then kneeling on a little kneeler that folded out from the bench in front of us. I didn't have to worry about following what the priest was saying because I didn't know a word of Latin. I didn't know a thing about Communion either, or why they rang little bells during the service, but when the girls all got up and filed in line to the altar rail, I followed them too. They all knelt again and so did I, waiting to see what would happen next. That's when I felt a heavy hand on my shoulder and a very tall sister practically lifting me off my knees.

"Miss Sutton," she said. "You are not allowed at the Communion rail," then motioned me back to my seat.

Here I was, my first Sunday service, and I'd done it wrong in front of all those people. I felt so humiliated.

My new friends came from all over the west, many from ranching families in Nevada. There were also a few day students from Salt Lake City. The rest of us were "boarders" and I guess I was the farthest from home. But I made friends quickly. Sr. Patricianne, whom my sister had mentioned, had a niece there named Mary Margaret. She was a freckled redhead with a mischievous smile and I was drawn to her immediately. She turned out to be my best friend all through high school.

I really appreciated the nuns with their stress on scholarship and learning. Since my sister had gone on to the University of Utah, they assumed I too would go to college. "Do you know what school you'll be attending after high school?" they asked. "Do you know what you plan to study?" I wasn't sure, though I'd thought about English or geology, but only because that's all I'd been exposed to. But I knew I wanted to attend Stanford. "Then you should take all solid subjects," they advised me. So that's what I did.

Mother had always said a girl has to prepare for two things. She must be able to support herself first, then if she marries, she has to be able to be a good wife and mother as well. My mother had done both and I knew the same was expected of me.

Well into my second year at St. Mary's, it was announced there was to be a silent three day retreat. I wanted to attend, but the nuns told me parental consent was required. I dutifully wrote home for permission and my father, knowing how loquacious I was, wrote a note back to them: "If Marta thinks she can keep quiet for three days, she's welcome to attend."

Father Sampietro, the retreat master, was tall, dark and handsome. I suspect the entire class had a crush on him before the three days were up. I know I did. I also know that retreat changed my life. Midway through the three days, I sensed God's presence in a new way I'd only until then read about. For the first time in my life, I also began to think seriously about spirituality and faith.

Fr. Sampietro told us he would be in a private office if any of us wished to speak with him, so I signed up.

I couldn't believe I told him I'd been thinking about becoming a Catholic.

"And what do your parents think about that?"

"I haven't told them."

"Would they approve?"

"No. I know my mother wouldn't."

"Then you should not become one. Not now. How old are you?"

"I'll be sixteen in May."

"How long have you been here?"

"About two years."

"I suggest you wait until you are twenty-one. Think about it. Pray about it. But don't upset your parents. A lot can happen between now and when you are old enough to make that kind of decision."

His response amazed me. I was used to proselytizing Mormons. And here this priest was putting me off. Father Sampietro really understood teen age girls—at least this one—and what being far from home and wanting to fit in and be included meant. But there was something else about him—a holiness—that really hit me. When I left his office, all I could think was that I wanted to be a Catholic priest someday. Never mind that I wasn't even baptized, nor was I Catholic, nor was I male.

During the end of that year, I began to visit the back of the chapel with a favorite book to read during Holy Hour, just so I could experience the awesome stillness before Benediction and the feelings of peace that pervaded the atmosphere. Something unseen that I could not grasp seemed to filter through the genuflections, the Latin, the bells and incense. It left me very much at peace and it was something I knew I did not want to lose. Without realizing it, being around those who prayed was becoming an important part of my life.

Something also that left a lasting impression on me and which I've never been able to explain, has to do with what happened my senior year before turning seventeen. It was about a month before graduation and I contracted a kidney infection and was sent to the infirmary. Sr. Emelita was in charge and properly called the doctor who prescribed a sulfa medication for me. I must have had a fever because I was put to bed and can recall Sister's taking my temperature quite often. After a few days, everything cleared up, but I still had to remain in bed until a urine sample was checked and the doctor released me. I was getting bored beyond belief lying in the infirmary wishing I could get out and back to school. My final day there, I recall Sister came in to visit, as she often had, and told me she was on her way to Benediction and that I would be sent supper shortly after. So off she went to Benediction leaving me to lie there looking at the ceiling. About ten or fifteen minutes after she left, I suddenly found myself (my spirit or conscious self anyway) floating in the far corner of the room. There was this beautiful light all around me and the same incredible feeling of love I'd experienced enveloping me as a young child. I couldn't believe it was happening. "Have I died?" I wondered. I looked down at my body lying in the bed and couldn't believe I wasn't in it. "If this is death," I thought, "it's wonderful." I know I did not want to return to my body, but wanted to remain with that fantastic sense of love and light. The experience probably lasted two or three minutes, maybe longer, and then suddenly I found myself back in bed. I didn't dare mention it for fear someone would think I was crazy. Or *really* sick. But since it happened while Benediction was going on, I decided perhaps the sisters had prayed for me. And that in some mystical way, my spirit had been in touch with theirs and been lifted upwards. It would take a long time before I had the courage to share that experience with anyone.

The Diocesan Catholic bishop was among those who presided at graduation. I didn't see why we were expected to kiss his ring when he handed our diploma to us, so I reached out and shook his hand instead. I'd earned my diploma fair and square and felt shaking hands was more to the point.

By the time I graduated as a non-Mormon and a non-Catholic, I had both Catholic and Mormon friends. Since both sides seemed to claim to have the one and only "True Faith" and to be the one and only "True Church," the implication to me then was that half of my friends (according to this paradigm) would never see the "True Light" and were going to end up in Hell, or at least they'd never make it to heaven. And as for me? Well, I figured someday I'd try to make some sense of it all and decided after high school I should continue to stay in my "church of the non-churched." I still had lots of time to decide. And though I doubted I'd ever stand up and be baptized by anyone, I still thought a lot about that beautiful light and the peace that other's prayers had often brought me. I knew it all somehow related to God and that someday I was going to have to come to grips with it.

# 7

# COLLEGE

My mother came to see me graduate and spent part of the summer in Utah before her return to Venezuela. Unknown to me, she'd been influenced by a visiting sister of the American consul in Maracaibo where my mother had worked. This woman who was the French teacher at a mid-western college was trying to recruit for her school. She convinced my mother that a small college would be much better for me after three years in a small boarding school.

Mother agreed

"But Mother, I've been accepted at Stanford already."

"Beloit is smaller than Stanford. I think it would be best if you went to Beloit. With your grades, you won't have any trouble getting in."

"Mother, I want to go to Stanford!"

But there were times when there was no point in arguing with my mother. And this was one of them. I was disappointed, but in my generation, one did not argue with those who footed the bills. So I went to Beloit College in Wisconsin. It seemed so far from Utah and Venezuela, and the winters weren't much to write home about either. But it was a solid school. I was given a wonderful roommate; the professors were great; and I made lasting friends.

Beloit was not specifically a religious school, but they had chapel once a week which was required. Mainly, it involved having a good speaker come and talk to us about a particular field. I vaguely recall there was an invocation or prayer of some kind given, but after Catholic boarding school, it never struck me as being what one would call a religious service. It was more an educational assembly if any thing. Carey Croneis was president of the college then and had been to the Galapagos Islands. I still recall the marvelous slide show and talk he gave about his trip which later compelled me to visit there also.

Basically, Beloit was non-denominational. Still, I was often reminded how the nuns warned that "a secular college will destroy your faith." I wondered if Beloit fit their secular definition. I also wondered if they'd ever been allowed to read about what went on in the middle ages and why the Reformation came about. My mediaeval history class had a slant to it that I'd never heard discussed at St. Mary's.

After two years, when two of my best friends decided to transfer elsewhere, my dream of going to Stanford came back. I wrote to my parents and told them I still wanted to go there.

My father answered: "If you really want to transfer, we don't object. It's closer to Utah anyway." I knew he thought my mother pushed my sister and me pretty hard at times when he added: "Take some time to learn how to play golf, or bridge, Marta. College doesn't have to be all study." I think my father feared I was becoming a book worm to the detriment of my social life.

By now, my father had been transferred from doing field work out of Maracaibo to an office in Caracas. It was arranged I take the Grace Line from New York to Venezuela with other students sailing to South America for the summer. As it turned out, I was scheduled to go to an apartment of a company couple who now worked in the New York office who had offered to help out with the students, the idea being that we would have places to stay until the boat sailed. Before my arrival, however, I was told the people who lived there had been called out-of-town unexpectedly on an emergency. So they made arrangements for me to be let into their apartment and have me picked up and taken to the boat by someone else. When I got there, I was surprised to discover it was the Refshauage's apartment. I could also see they must have been in a big hurry because they hadn't had time to straighten up much. So I saw this as a gift from God, an opportunity to do something constructive for my previous teacher for my earlier thoughtless behavior in Maracaibo. I never worked so hard in my life to make a place look really shipshape!

All summer I was bothered with the idea that I had to declare a major. My father had suggested I take some geology courses "but only so you'll understand what I do," he'd told me. I'd already taken three and loved them.

"Maybe I should major in geology."

"I'm sure you could be a good geologist, but women would never fit into field work. That's pretty much a man's world."

"What's the point of studying then? Why aren't women treated like men? They're just as smart, Daddy."

"Marta. Many of them are smarter. But that's the way it is."

Then I thought I'd major in English. That's what my mother had done and she'd loved teaching. But what would I do with it? I wasn't sure I could be a teacher.

Behind all my concern was the voice of my mother heard for so many years that "A girl has to have two goals in life: Some type of profession for self-support if she doesn't marry, and the ability to be a good wife and mother if she does."

Some of my concerns were answered when I was able to get several jobs that summer. One was with the Centro-Venezolano Americano teaching English part-time at night to immigrants coming in from Europe. The other was working as a typist-librarian during the day for an oil company. I found I loved being around people and especially those who spoke different languages and came from other countries. That reminded me of the job my mother had held too in Maracaibo when she'd been with the American Consulate. From there, it was a short hop to thinking I might be able to succeed in the U.S. Foreign Service.

In retrospect, it was not a good decision on my part to leave Beloit. I just knew I had the feeling that my life was going in the wrong direction and it was essential for me to go back and try to pick up earlier threads. Some of it I know had to do with religion and the confusion that living in such disparate circumstances had instilled in me over the years. It also had to do with missing my parents and the role I wondered women should really have in society. The nuns were doing good things. But I didn't want to be a nun. I wanted to date more too but was terribly shy of men. I knew so little about them. I felt I was missing out on the important things in life. And even though my mother's letters were always cheerful and encouraging, I could still read between the lines. My father was not very well. She thought he smoked too much. "It could be his heart." But he'd been to a good clinic provided by his company and they hadn't found anything wrong. Then someone wrote me about Ceako's mother. I didn't have his address but thought about him for a long time. She'd apparently had a ruptured appendix and refused to see a doctor. Her faith had not been strong enough and she'd died. "What a waste of a good life," was all I could think. And I could not help wonder how that would affect Ceako's faith as well.

I transferred to Stanford and ended up in a two room dorm suite with two roommates who either talked or played the radio incessantly. One was a math major and liked to work her problems to music. The other was a theatre major and was always practicing her various roles aloud. I was forced to spend most of my first quarter in the library just so I could study. No matter how many times I nicely asked them to quiet down, my roommates never really heard me.

One day, before a test, I finally snapped. I picked up a metal waste basket and threw it at the wall, then walked to the student housing office and asked for a transfer as soon as possible. It was my good fortune that a room was available in the Casa Española, a lovely housing unit that served as the center of Spanish

Stanford. We were expected to speak Spanish much of the time and also help entertain visiting dignitaries from Spanish-speaking countries. I loved it and stayed there until graduation.

Just to finish filling out a form, I had put down English as my major the beginning of my junior year, but finally decided it wasn't what I really wanted. Winter quarter was a miserable, rainy time. My mother's letters had lost some of their cheerfulness also and my father's health was not improving. After getting a depressing grade on a paper written about Chaucer and the mediaeval sciences, I switched my major to political science thinking I might go on to graduate school in international relations.

Looking at a campus bulletin board one day, I noticed a sign asking for riders for skiing, riders who would share gas expenses with the car owner for a weekend at Yosemite. I signed up and it turned into a fun weekend. There were two other boys and girls as I recall now and the driver, who was an older, fairly mature man, said he hoped he'd see me again.

Spring quarter the weather finally cleared up and I was happily on track again. I wasn't wild about some of my political science classes, but that didn't matter. I was feeling more adjusted to the big campus, was making friends, and I'd had more dates in one quarter than I'd had in four semesters at Beloit.

Then the ski weekend driver called and asked me to dinner. I accepted and we had a nice evening. I thought he was way too old to get involved with (he was 31 and I was 19), but he was interesting to talk to and I'd never been on a date with a man who ordered wine with dinner, so when he called a second time, I accepted. About half way through a stimulating and somewhat heated conversation relating to Nietzshe, he said "That's what my wife used to say."

"Your wife?" I took a deep breath.

He nodded and went on with the discussion.

"You didn't tell me you'd been married."

"It never came up."

"Did she die?"

"No, she's still alive. But we don't live together. We're getting a divorce."

I couldn't believe what I was hearing. "You've asked me for two dates and you're still married?"

"Sure. Why not? I haven't seen her much lately."

I felt as if I'd been punched in the stomach. This was wrong, certainly for me anyway. I wanted to end the evening as soon as possible.

The conversation switched to why he thought I should continue to see him. It was clear, he was used to having his own way.

"Have you tried counseling?" I asked.

"We've drifted apart. Counseling won't help."

"But have you tried? How can you know it won't help? You must have liked her enough to marry her."

"We had an arrangement when I was in the service. When I came back, things were different."

"An arrangement?"

"Sure.... we had our own lives when we were separated."

"You mean ..." I didn't know for sure what he was saying, but he'd already said more than I wanted to hear.

"It's not cheating when you both agree."

"I think it's time for me to get home."

He finally took me home, but said he'd be back in touch.

I tried to be polite and thanked him for the evening. But the words coming out of my mouth felt like ashes.

Two days later, he called and asked me out again. I firmly declined. He then showed up at the Casa unexpectedly asking if I were in. For nearly a month, he would not leave me alone. I didn't know how to get rid of him. And I didn't know where to go for help. He would be waiting on the porch when I came back from class, or hanging around the library on occasions when I was there. I think now what he was doing would be considered "stalking". And I'm pretty sure it's illegal. I only knew then that I was way out of my league. He was upsetting me; and I didn't know how to deal with it. It was in the course of this depressing experience that I received a phone call from my cousin in Utah.

"This is Hal," he said. "Your mother asked me to call you. She's not up to talking to anyone right now."

"What's going on?"

"She put your father in the hospital as soon as they reached Salt Lake yesterday. He's not doing so well. She wants you to come home if you want to see him alive again. The doctor says he's not going to live much longer. Do you have enough money to buy an airplane ticket?

I couldn't believe what Hal was telling me, but finally managed to say "yes ... I think so.... .I'll come home as soon as I can."

# 8

# DEATH, ENGAGEMENT
# AND BAPTISM

Mother was still in shock when I reached Utah the next day. We were all in shock. Dad had decided on an earlier retirement and had been looking forward to coming home. He and mother had gone to Barbados for a short vacation first; but my father hadn't felt too well, so mother had taken him to an island doctor.

"He was just kind of a horse doctor in this little town. I couldn't find anyone else. When he looked at your father, he said I should get him home as soon as possible. But it was the Easter holidays. The island was jammed. It took us three days to change our flight out."

"What's wrong with him?"

"The doctor in Barbados did several tests, then told me it was as he suspected. Your Dad has some kind of nephritis. It's his kidneys. He said it was something he's had a long time. I took him straight to the hospital."

My experience in high school when I'd had a kidney infection crashed in on me. I finally said. "Does Daddy know he's dying?"

"No, and we're not going to tell him. There's always hope. Things might improve. I never dreamed he was so sick."

For two days, I sat with my mother and watched my father die, all the while wanting to put my arms around him so I could say goodbye and thank him properly for being such a neat father, even though I hadn't spent much of my life with him. I wanted so badly to say something meaningful and to share that wonderful experience I'd had when I'd been recovering from a kidney infection. But I just sat there like stone, afraid to feel or say anything, lest I fall apart. I had to honor my mother's wishes. She might have been right and I didn't want to jeopardize any chances of his getting better.

He died that April when the lilacs were in bloom and was buried in the family plot, in the cemetery where he'd grown up. He never even made it home one last time to the house he'd worked so hard to pay off so he and mother would have a comfortable place in their retirement.

I didn't go back to California to finish spring quarter. With my father's death, I felt my entire future disappear. There were so many things we'd all planned that we'd now never get to do together. Mother needed me to help her get settled anyway. So I enrolled at the University of Utah for summer quarter in order to pick up some credits, then made plans to return to Stanford in the fall.

It was later in the summer when a young man, whose father and mine had both worked together for the Standard Oil Company of Argentina, obtained a job in Salt Lake City. As a courtesy call, he phoned my mother and said his parents knew her and had suggested he look her up. He turned out to be an unexpected angel.

"I thought I might get a free lunch," Austin jokingly told me later.

Indeed, Mother did invite him to join us for lunch.

He was very pleasant, a geologist, and we all hit it off nicely. He asked me out quite a few times before I went back to Stanford and I thought he was very interesting. I'd never met anyone quite like him.

My big concern on returning to school though was to figure out what to do about my major. Going into the foreign service was something I'd contemplated when my parents were both alive and living in South America. With my father gone now, that idea no longer held much appeal. My mother was totally alone in the house; my sister was off and married, expecting a first child, and I was more than depressed.

Austin began writing to me after I returned to Stanford, so I reciprocated. I'd been brought up writing letters, so that was the easy part. We exchanged quite a few before I went home for Christmas break. What I desperately needed at that time was a support system, and I didn't have one. So Austin filled the gap, and not only for me but for my mother as well, and gradually, the black hole I'd fallen in to when my father died began to fill in.

I was thinking a lot more about God by now too and had taken a class in Chinese philosophy at Utah, as well as Indian philosophy at Stanford, in order to extend my faith in, and a better understanding of, religion and the Almighty.

One happy discovery when I became a political science major was that it only required thirty units in the subject to graduate. That left me with lots of extra credits from which I could pick and choose classes. Thinking I might never again have the opportunity to be in college, I signed up for everything I could think of that interested me in some way. High on my list were astronomy, Greek tragedy,

Russian literature and music. The man who had stalked me finally dropped out of my life too and occasionally I'd go out with someone really nice.

But at Christmas break, I saw a lot more of Austin. He and my mother had become good friends too when he'd had an unexpected appendicitis attack which landed him in the hospital. Mother offered to take care of him after surgery. He was not only a nice person, but filled a need for her just then due to the huge gap my father's death had left in her life. He was also connected to our past in such a very real way because our parents had all known one another for years. There was even a picture of Austin in my sister's baby album taken of them both in a play-pen long before I'd arrived on the scene.

Shortly before New Year's Eve, Austin asked me to marry him. In a way, I'd almost been expecting him to ask. On the other hand, even though I liked the idea he was a geologist and very comfortable to be with, I just wasn't sure I was ready yet to make a commitment to marriage. Other than his letters, I hardly even knew him. Besides, I'd always planned to work at least a year before ever being married. That was the understood rule in our family. But Austin wanted to settle down. He was four and one half years older than I.

"Mother, Austin wants to get married as soon as I graduate. I haven't even supported myself yet."

"He'll be a good provider," she countered. Suddenly all the rules I'd taken as gospel when growing up were being tossed out Mother's window. There was no question that she approved of Austin. She'd been playing cupid from day one. "I think your father is helping us from the other side," she said one day. This rather surprised me. Mother had never been one to talk about the "other side."

So after several more evenings together, and two more proposals from Austin, I said "yes." But I insisted on discussing several things before that. I'd had a lot more time to think about God and church and religion and decided I wanted to be a Christian. That meant I wanted him to agree to rearing any children we might have in the Christian faith. Secondly, I asked him if he would consider giving up smoking. My father had smoked heavily all his life and I knew this had not helped his health. I wanted a long married life. Austin agreed he would try to stop smoking and "yes, if we have children, they can be raised Christian." At the party we attended New Year's Eve, he borrowed my lipstick and wrote "A + M" on a big white handkerchief, then hung it on the Christmas tree. I went back to college feeling really good about my decision, despite the fact that I still hadn't come to terms with my own self-support.

The last quarter passed quickly. I flew back to Utah at spring break when Mother gave a luncheon for me officially announcing our engagement. Then in

June, Mother, my sister and her husband, Tom, came to my graduation. This also gave mother an opportunity to introduce us all to her old thesis professor—Dr. Hart. Shirley said later he reminded her of Tweedle Dee; or maybe it was Tweedle Dum. What I most remember was the lovely book of poetry he gave to me.

Up until this point, I had not met either of Austin's parents. All they knew about me was what Austin told them. But they seemed delighted we were going to be married and I received various letters welcoming me into their side of the family. Several weeks before the wedding (which was scheduled for mid-August), Austin's mother came to Utah to get acquainted. His mother was a proper Anglican, born and reared in England. Somehow, she discovered I had never been baptized. "My son marrying a heathen?" she exclaimed. "Goodness!" I gathered that would never do. She called the Dean of St. Mark's Cathedral where we were to be married and told him I should be baptized. Never mind that I might have had other plans, though I could not have articulated them at that point. I'd come a long ways in deciding I'd want to rear any children Christian, but nothing had been said about what church. In many ways too, I was still trying to sort out Catholicism. And never mind (though I did not know it at the time) that only one of a couple needs to be baptized to be married in the Episcopal church. I also had no way of knowing how little interest Austin had in his mother's faith. His experiences in England in a British boarding school had seen to that. He later often complained how they'd knocked all the fun and joy out of him and it was much later into our marriage that I discovered how much he disliked anything to do with church. Of course, he had agreed we bring up any children in the Christian faith. But I was still trying to define the best way to go about this. When I found out my father had once been an altar boy at St. Mark's years earlier, it was a comfort to know I was going to be married in the church where he had once worshipped and not just the church where I'd attended his funeral. At the time, I never connected the Anglican Sunday School in Maracaibo with St. Mark's Cathedral in Utah.

If left up to me, I'm not sure if I would have ever gotten baptized on my own, but I knew I did not want to start off married life on the wrong foot with my future mother-in-law either, so found the required two witnesses and made an appointment to be at the cathedral the following week. Austin was out in the field, the Dean had to be away, so the newly appointed Episcopal Bishop, Richard Watson, agreed to baptize me.

I was rather unsettled when I walked in to St. Mark's. I had tried to forget my only experience with "baptism" some years earlier, but that plus the usual premarital jitters made me think about postponing my wedding, at least until I'd worked for a year. But the invitations had gone out, the wedding dress was purchased and I could not burden my mother with all this. I knew she had decided long before I that Austin would be a fine addition to the family. But I was filled with questions and kept thinking we should wait another year while I had a job. After my mother's striking out on her own years earlier and leaving home to attend school, then teaching before joining my father in Panama, I was left confused that she wanted me married so soon. But she saw things so differently after my Dad's death. And I know, though she never said so, that she was afraid I might meet and marry a Mormon. My sister had already married a Jack Mormon (whom we all loved) but I think mother had decided one Mormon, even a Jack Mormon, was enough.

Austin's father agreed to be a witness as well as Betty Walton, a friend whose husband also happened to be a geologist.

The bishop sailed in, decked with appropriate vestments for the occasion and holding some prayer books. I introduced him to the witnesses.

"So Miss Sutton, you're here to be baptized." It was more a statement than a question.

I had such mixed feelings, I didn't know what to say. On the one hand it was a little like waiting for the guillotine to descend, and I could hardly say I was there because of my future mother-in-law, or that no one had even asked me if I wanted to be baptized. It had all been assumed. But finally, I said "I understand it's required since I'm to be married here next week."

The bishop was a big man, with a kind face and purposeful twinkle in his eyes. He looked at me intently. "Christian initiation is mentioned in the Bible. Our Lord was baptized, you know."

I guess I hadn't really known. At least I couldn't recall if it had ever been brought to my attention. Certainly John the Baptist had never been very high on my radar screen. But I didn't say anything. I just looked around. This place looked pretty Catholic to me. "Do I have to wear a veil?" I finally asked. We'd always had to wear veils at St. Mary's when in chapel.

"That's up to you. You may if you wish."

His answer totally surprised me. After St. Mary's and the unbending rules of the sisters, I hadn't anticipated any flexibility. So I opted not to wear one.

The bishop opened the prayer books to the appropriate pages; then handed one to each of us.

"Holy Baptism is full initiation by water and the Holy Spirit into Christ's Body the Church. The bond which God established in Baptism is indissoluble," said the Bishop.

He then began the service: "Blessed be God: Father, Son, and Holy Spirit."

And we answered: "And blessed be his kingdom, now and forever, Amen."

When he got to the question "Do you desire to be baptized?" I was surprised that I had no difficulty saying "Yes."

I was amazed at how nice the bishop was and how quickly the little service went. Bishop Watson gave a little homily afterwards, but I didn't hear much of it. Happily, I reminded myself this was a far cry from the day I had nearly been baptized into atheism.

There was still turmoil inside of me. But I could not have begun to tell the bishop about it, or why I felt the way I did. I just knew my prayer life mattered, only I wasn't sure how to retrieve it at times. But I knew it was trying to surface through layers and layers of emotional confusion that I was still attempting to sort out. And that this was a good place to start.

# 9

# MARRIAGE AND MOVING

We were married mid-August. Candles placed earlier in the church were bending over from the heat. I don't recall if there was air conditioning. I had wanted my sister to be the matron of honor, but she was very pregnant by now, so a friend from Stanford took over for her, two others were bridesmaids and two of my little cousins were flower girls. My Uncle Arch, my father's brother (whom I'd only seen two or three times in my life), gave me away; and Austin came in from doing fieldwork two days before the wedding. Mother planned the reception to be held at our home in Holladay and we drove to Carmel for our honeymoon.

I had carefully planned the wedding date so it would not coincide with my monthly "period," but it didn't happen that way. My period came two weeks early, the day before we were married. Since we couldn't do very much about it, I brightly suggested that perhaps God had intervened.

"Let's dedicate these first nights to God and ask Him to bless our marriage," I said. I knew marriage could be wonderful; I also knew it could be difficult. And I wanted ours to last. I saw nothing wrong with bringing God into the picture.

Austin was already nervous (he'd been trying to give up smoking) and he probably thought now he'd married a religious nut. "Didn't we just do all that in front of all those people at St. Mark's?" he said, possibly thinking of the phrase he'd recently repeated at our wedding about taking me "for better" or "for worse."

"Well, yes. But it was so public."

"Then if that's what you want, darling."

Our slightly delayed honeymoon began a beautiful time of intimacy and love that we shared for nearly fifty-four years. But I had to admit later, if only to myself, that my subconscious brought about that sexual postponement. It was because I so wanted God to be part of both our lives, echoes no doubt from St.

Mary's where the nuns had always said it was important to put God first in every-thing. It was also because I was apprehensive. I knew so very little about men; and, if I were going to be honest, not all that much about God and religion either.

We found an apartment in Salt Lake City near the state capitol and stayed for a year before being transferred to Colorado. After a year in Durango, Austin was called back to Utah where our first two children were born. It was also at that time Austin's mother became ill and died, but at least not before getting to see her two grandsons.

Austin had to be out in the field a lot, but I'd expected that. I just couldn't help wonder, while changing diapers or cleaning floors, what all those years of study had done for me. The one thing I was unable to put to rest, however, was the fact I had never shown I could totally support myself. Now, looking at two lively little boys, I could not help think *What could I do if something happened to Austin? How could I support all three of us?* I thought about it for quite a while, then finally decided for my own peace of mind to return to school part-time. I made arrangements for a babysitter and began making plans to enroll at the University of Utah for the following semester. They accepted me into the Master's program for English and the day following my notification of acceptance, Austin came home and informed me that we'd been "transferred to Los Angeles."

We lived in California for five years. Since neither of us wanted to live in the city, we invested in a home near Palos Verdes Estates which entailed a fifty-four mile daily commute for Austin. I felt stranded in a community where I didn't know a soul. There was a song popular at the time about "little houses made of ticky-tacky, little houses in a row. There are blue ones and green ones and purple and yellow ones, and they're all made out of ticky-tacky and they all look just the same." I was always reminded of that song whenever I'd drive into our subdivision. After several years there, the company Austin worked for was dismantled and everyone lost their jobs. It was at a time when the oil industry was going through one of its cyclical depressions. Since he was one of the last geologists to be dismissed, most other available jobs in the area similar to his had been taken. So by the time he went looking for employment, he was told by one employment agency that he was probably the "most unmarketable man in Los Angeles."

We had three very difficult years. And to top it all off, despite precautions, I discovered I was pregnant again.

Meanwhile, Austin was sending out resumes and letters to every company he could think of asking if they might wish to employ a geologist. But there were no immediate responses. He found he could get all kinds of part-time jobs, none of which were lasting. Mostly, he was told he was over qualified, so many were reluctant to hire him, knowing full well he'd leave when something better showed up.

He had a friend in commercial real estate who encouraged him to join his firm. It didn't pay any salary, but Austin studied for and obtained a real estate license, then was given one day a week when he would get any incoming calls on his "floor day." With no back up clients, however, and little long term knowledge of the real estate in the area, he had a difficult time. He soon discovered that after knocking himself out for people to help find what appealed to them, some would then wait until the listing time ran out, then go in and buy directly from the owner, thus cutting Austin out of his commission. It was a discouraging experience and one which totally soured him on Mr. Average American Public. My fear of never having established myself in a profession of some type now really hit home. My worst nightmare had come true. I'd had summer jobs that required typing, and I might pass for being bi-lingual, but now I was pregnant and firmly believed in staying home while I had young children. Austin read there was a shortage of science teachers in the area, so began commuting to Long Beach State College to get the required teaching credential. He had master's degrees in both geology and bacteriology with a good background in biology, physics and chemistry. So I joined him thinking if he became a teacher, perhaps I could too eventually. That way, we'd have summers off when the children would not be in school. But the baby sitter we employed quit mid-semester and I could not find another one, so I had to drop out. With the exception of several useful classes relating to audio visuals and grading, Austin thought the classes were "pure drivel."

Due to his real estate experience, however, he had found a small, new apartment house going on the market which he thought would be a good investment. It was called the ISLE and he felt he could use the money from some stock he had to make a down payment. We both felt it better to invest, rather than spend the money for living expenses, but it meant we'd have to move since we could not afford a manager. This meant school changes for the boys, not to mention dealing with the public when trying to rent the units. Austin was always good at theoretical ideas on paper. I was the one who had to ask the hard questions: i.e. "Who's going to fix the dish washers?" or "replace the outside lights?" or "evict people when they don't pay their rent?"

The tenants left a lot to be desired. One couple was always fighting. The wife (a former beauty contest winner) finally locked her husband out of the apartment one day and he broke down the door trying to get back in.

Another couple had two small children and seldom bothered to change their diapers. The carpets all had to be replaced when they moved. The security and cleaning deposits didn't begin to pay for the rugs.

Another lady Austin called the "weird one" complained that "the dark kept showing through the draperies." (Figure that one.) She kept asking him to her apartment to show him. The third time Austin finally figured out she was trying to seduce him.

Just when things couldn't get much worse, Austin was offered a job in the Antarctic collecting samples on a naval research vessel. ("Plucking plankton," as he put it.) Since our funds were dwindling rapidly, he jumped at the opportunity and began making preparations to meet the ship whenever the orders came through.

One day before he left, I ran out to buy some groceries and on the way home drove by a Lutheran church. I'd often driven by, but hadn't paid much attention to it. But this day, something told me to stop. So I parked in front of the church and went in. I didn't see anyone around, but as I sat in a back pew, I was overcome with a wonderful sense of peace. It was so overpowering that the tears began streaming down my cheeks. That's when it dawned on me that I didn't have to go it alone. All that peace and holiness was coming from other people's prayers. I realized how much I was missing by not belonging to a church. That's when I became more fully aware too how difficult those early years much have been for my mother. At least she'd had some of her family near by. I knew after Austin left, however, I wouldn't have anyone except the children (who were a handful) plus the apartment house (which was becoming a pretty big chore as well). So I filled out a little card in one of the pews and went home with a renewed sense of hope, and a few days later, the pastor called. I still recall his name was Marvin Riggs

Fortunately, before Austin had to leave, we were blessed with a lovely baby girl. And a few weeks later, while cleaning the apartment stairs, I thought to myself: *Now I have three children, an absent husband and a crazy apartment house. But at least now I have a profession of sorts. I'm a manager!* And by the time Austin returned a few months later, I'd learned a lot about being a landlady.

"If you can't get another job," I told him, "we can still become teachers and sell the units separately. Prices are way up here now in Redondo Beach." I'd never heard of condominiums; I don't know if anyone had, but the ISLE had the possibility of success. This was in the mid-sixties. I was all for settling down at least long enough to make the place work. And I wanted to get Austin's money back out too. By then, I knew how to replace solenoid switches and evict tenants. Buying a share in our apartment house would be very enticing to the kind of tenants who rented them. Many could not afford a down payment on a house, but to be able to buy into the ISLE would be helpful to some. It would also reduce our share on the real estate taxes. Austin was not keen on holding on to the place, especially now that some of the resumes he'd sent out earlier were beginning to bring hopeful responses. He thought the ISLE had become a big mistake. And who would want it?

Eventually, he was offered and accepted a job in Washington, so the ISLE went on the market and almost immediately, we got an offer. We couldn't figure out why anyone would want the place given its current balance sheet. But this buyer wanted a tax loss and it just suited his tax situation perfectly. What an unexpected angel he turned out to be! We even got all our investment back.

So we moved to Washington D.C. and settled in Camp Springs, Maryland. After finding a house near schools for the children, one of the first things I did was to look for a Lutheran church, I'd been so delighted with the one in Redondo Beach. But there was none close by. But there was an Episcopal church where a Boy Scout troop met regularly. By then, the boys were cub scouts and I was a den mother, and recalling Bishop Watson who had baptized me, I decided it was time to learn more about Episcopalians.

The rector at Nativity was a young man who had been a Methodist minister but who was in the process of attending the Episcopal seminary located across the Potomac in Virginia. He was being "re-treaded" you might say so he could fit into the Episcopal Church. He was down to earth and I found I related easily to him. He was also practical, I thought, because he liked to stop the service after preaching the sermon, give everyone a chance to get a cup of coffee if they wished, then have coffee hour mid-service where anyone and everyone could ask questions or discuss the sermon if they wished before continuing with the Holy Eucharist. Rigid Episcopalians (there are a few) did not approve of this. But I thought it was great. He brought his class work into his sermons, giving us all an opportunity to become acquainted with theologians of all stripes. I found the discussions challenging and fascinating. The service was so Catholic in so many ways, yet everything else about it was so Un-catholic. Never at St. Mary's had there been these types of discussions. Everyone had followed the party line there. You didn't question the pope, or the bishop, or the sisters. But anything was okay with Bob. And if you asked something he couldn't answer for sure, he'd offer to look it up and get back to you; or he'd suggest one of many books which the church library held. It was a thinking, as well as a worshipping church, one to which I was drawn immediately.

Bob and his wife, Beth, had three young children and made their house open to inquirer's groups. Whenever I could find a sitter, if Austin were not in town, I spent a lot of time in their living room.

Bob also believed in educating the congregation to the needs of the community. Once, he took a group of us to St. Elizabeth's Hospital in down town Washington. It's where the mentally ill were warehoused. I'd never in my life seen anything like this. In fact, he opened my eyes to lots of things I'd never even thought about, for which I am still grateful.

Over a period of several years, I found I really liked the Episcopal Church and decided to be confirmed in it; however, I felt compelled to return to Utah for this. After finishing the confirmation class, Bob wrote a note to Bishop Watson.

*I believe Marta is ready to be confirmed and has told me she would like you to do this for her.*

Bishop Watson still remembered me. "So you want to be confirmed now do you?"

I didn't mince words. "I'm here to un-do my baptism," I said.

"Hmmm? Come again?" he asked.

"I'm here to un-do my baptism," I repeated.

He looked a little puzzled, then finally said: "Then if that's what you want, that's what we'll do."

Though we became very good friends over the years, I never tried to explain it all to the Bishop. I probably couldn't have anyway. But by undoing things, I meant I wanted to belong to a church at last. He'd baptized me when I'd mentally been a member of a "Non-Church," and that wouldn't work for me anymore.

So I became a confirmed Episcopalian. And it all seemed right then for me. It also helped me deal a little better with my father's death, to incorporate both my parents' thinking into my own views of church and religion, and to still keep me in touch, not only with that wonderful light of my childhood, but with all those praying sisters I'd known who, unwittingly, had become such an invisible, yet important part of my life.

# PART II

# 10
# ANOTHER MARRIAGE

Some time after Austin's mother died, his father, Lewis, decided to go into consulting work when he retired. Having worked his entire life in geology, it was all Lewis knew and all he still wanted to do; so he set up an office in Connecticut and also went on a lecture tour for one year. During that time, he passed through Salt Lake City more than once in order to see the family. It also gave him an opportunity to call on my mother.

Before Austin and I had left for California, we were surprised when my mother said: "Your father's asked me to marry him, Austin. What do you think of that?"

Austin didn't say much at first. Then, finally, shaking his head, he answered: "I'm not sure that would be such a good idea, Anne."

"Why not?" asked Mother. It was her turn to be surprised.

"You just don't know what Dad's really like. I think you'll find him difficult to live with."

"Oh? How do you mean?" Mother asked.

Austin was reluctant to get into details. He told her, however, from what little he'd heard about my father that he had been much easier to live with. "You might be happier to stay single. Or find someone else," he finally said.

My mother laughed off most of Austin's remarks, reminding him that his mother, Una, had also told her more than once over the years that Lewis could be "difficult" at times. She had so looked forward to retiring in Utah with my father; but after his unexpected death, could not even begin to contemplate spending the rest of her life alone in what she still viewed as a "bastion of Mormons." Getting remarried would be an adventure which she frankly looked forward to.

After our move to California, she eventually called and said they'd decided to marry. This meant Austin and I would soon be step-brother and step-sister to one another. When trying to explain that one to people, Austin often joked with a straight face that "incest begins at home."

By this time, Lewis was beginning to get various consulting jobs. He'd already been "down under" to Australia several times.

A few months into their marriage, we began getting unsettling letters from Mother. At first, just little comments here and there like "You were right, Austin, Your father *is* different in some ways." Or "I can't believe how frugal he is. Has he always pinched pennies until they screamed?" Or. Or. Or. I didn't know what I could do to help. Austin said there was nothing we could do.

"Dad is Dad," he said. "He acts one way in public and another way at home. He'll never change. And he usually gets his way. You know I warned your mother."

I recalled indeed he had. I'd never in my life heard mother complain, but I also knew she was not a quitter. In some ways, (along with many others) I'd thought theirs was a marriage made in heaven, but at first, for a while anyway, from mother's viewpoint certainly, it was the marriage from hell.

Our parent's first year together was not easy, certainly not from my mother's account. In all fairness, they were both trying hard to adjust to the loss of a mate, only Lewis' idea of marriage and my mother's did not coincide at all. She was used to making her own decisions, especially in running a home; he was used to a great deal of control. He had always kept Austin's mother on a very tight, strict budget and expected to do the same with my mother. But Mother was very adept at handling money, something she did well and which my father had always encouraged. She also had access to the insurance money and pension left her plus a little money she'd earned on her own, so was not about to be told what to do with it. She couldn't begin to understand my father-in-law's attitude.

At first, he followed her around the grocery store with a shopping cart and replaced foods she had chosen with some that were cheaper (and inferior) "in order to save money," he told her. My mother had never been one to waste anything, and having raised a great many fruits and vegetables in her life, knew good produce when she saw it. I found some of her stories hard to believe. Austin could only say "I told her so."

"Why don't you go to the store by yourself?" I asked once.

"He hides the keys to the car," she told us. "But I'm getting things sorted out." Knowing my mother, I was sure she would. Knowing his father, Austin was highly skeptical. From my viewpoint, I began to see my father-in-law as a real study in contrasts. One moment, he could be incredibly generous; ten minutes later, he could be the personification of Scrooge.

Shortly after they were married, he told her he wanted her to have Austin's mother's mink fur coat. Mother didn't particularly want it nor did she need it, but since she didn't have a fur, Lewis insisted she have this one. She finally accepted and graciously thanked him for it. A few weeks later, he presented her with a bill saying he'd given her a real bargain since he hadn't charged her as much as it was really worth. After being accustomed to my father's unconditional generosity, Mother was dumbfounded.

When he eventually told her he expected her to pay half of the income tax bill (since they would soon be filing jointly), I suspect that's when my mother laid down the law. He clearly had so much more income than she that it would have left her penniless. She made it very clear his behavior was unacceptable. In time, they worked things out nicely, but I know it was only because of my mother's independent, no-nonsense spirit. It was also because she had some money of her own, something Austin often told me had been his mother's greatest disadvantage.

Mother and Lewis eventually moved to the top of Bluewater Hill in Westport, Connecticut in a lovely home overlooking Long Island Sound near Compo Beach. Here they gardened together, entertained, swam in the Sound, walked daily and were involved with many of their neighbors and business friends. They built a really nice life together and it was sad Lewis died in 1977. My mother lived another twenty years after that and was just a few weeks short of her one hundredth birthday before passing on. She had wonderful care-takers and friends who looked after her and was always happy she'd married and moved East. In retrospect, she had two good marriages but with two totally different men.

Although my mother would never have said so, I think she was the original feminist. But they just weren't called that back in her day. After she and my father were married and were living in Cartagena, mother had to be alone quite a bit when my Dad was working in the field. Walking down the street one day, a man, exposing himself, followed her. Mother ignored him the first time this happened, but then it happened again and she was very put out by his behavior and went to a policeman standing on a corner. She pointed out the offender and told the policeman he should do something about this. My mother, a very attractive blonde, was used to having people stare at her, but this was not appropriate and she didn't like it. "That man's been following me," she told the policeman.

The policeman just looked my mother up and down, then gave her a leering grin and said "Can you blame him?"

Realizing she would not get any help from the police, mother went out that very day and bought herself a gun with plenty of ammunition. The following morning, she found a spot, not far from town, where she could practice shooting at cans and bottles. The word got out fast. "*La señora tiene pistola.*" She said she was never bothered again.

My mother was never one to stand on ceremony either. Once in Bermuda for business meetings, we were dropped off at a Bermuda Yacht club for dinner. There were several cars full with both men and women. As we all got out, the women in the group began to walk one way and the men went the other direction towards the front entrance. Mother and I stood there not quite understanding where the women were going until one of them waved us over and said, "we have a separate entrance."

"What do you mean?" asked my mother.

"This club has two entrances," replied one of the women.

"One for men," said another woman. "And one for us. We women use the back entrance."

Mother was shocked. "I've never heard of anything so ridiculous," she said. "You mean your husbands treat you like second class citizens?"

The women laughed a little uncomfortably and said "well … uh … that's the way it's done …"

"Not to me," said my mother. "Come on, Marta. Our money's just as good as theirs. And since some of them are earning it, we should be able to walk through the front door too." And so we did.

But back to the 1960's, Lewis' consulting in Australia really changed our lives. After his retirement as chief geologist from Standard Oil, he had been approached by BHP, a large steel and mining company. Its name, Broken Hill Proprietary Co. Ltd. came from the fact that the prospectors who started it had mined silver, lead and zinc ore at a place called Broken Hill. Over time, it had grown to become Australia's largest industrial enterprise.

The entry of BHP into active petroleum exploration resulted initially due to the Rough Range oil strike years earlier (1953) where a small amount of oil had been found at Exmouth Gulf in western Australia. This propelled other companies and syndicates to seek petroleum titles over various sedimentary basins which included the coal fields in New South Wales, some of which were held by BHP. As a protective measure, BHP also took out petroleum leases in the Sydney basin area because they feared their coal fields might be disrupted if another company found oil in the area. They weren't particularly thinking of oil at the time, but felt there might be some chance of finding natural gas which could be used in their steelworks. Still, they also wanted to know if there might be any chance for oil.

So eventually Mr. J.D. Norgard, the general manager for operations and distribution, made a trip to the U.S. early in 1960 with the task of finding the "best consultant petroleum geologist available." Lewis was chosen and agreed to go to Australia to inspect the area.

He later told them the presence of commercial supplies of crude oil in the Sydney Basin were unlikely and that natural petroleum as accumulations would be found in small volumes but largely of submarginal commercial value.

Before returning to the States, however, he asked them if they were really interested in finding oil. When they said "yes", he told them he could point out where oil would be found that would be accessible to 90% of Australia's market. They agreed he should speak with someone higher up, and he eventually met with Sir Ian McLennan. Lewis was offered and accepted a 2.5% royalty deal, and when asked "Where's the oil?", he went to the window and pointed "Out there … in the Bass Strait, and particularly off the Gippsland Coast."

Until then, there had been 140 wells drilled along the coast, but deep sea drilling had never been considered. Even though Bass Strait had some of the roughest waters in the world, BHP felt Lewis knew what he was talking about and took the risk. They did an initial aerial survey, later an offshore seismic survey that indicated several possible oil traps in the Gippsland Basin. In 1960, an aerial magnetometer survey was flown over 1500 miles and later a more detailed survey that covered an area of 17,371 miles. This depicted very pleasing results showing a clear outline of the Bass Basin.

In 1964, they convinced Esso Standard Oil of Australia Ltd. to join them in a 50–50 partnership and a drilling rig brought from the Gulf of Mexico spudded the first well. This was in 42 meters of water at a depth of 1318 meters when they hit gas February 18, 1965, known later as the Barracouta gas field. In June of that same year, another gas discovery was brought in at Barracouta 2. Then in March of 1966, oil was discovered at Marlin l. The Kingfish oil discovery followed and since that time a host of others in quick succession including Halibut, Dolphin, Perch, Flounder, Tuna, Snapper, Mackerel and Bream.

Before any of this occurred, however, Mr. Weeks had put some of any future royalties into the names of the family members which included Austin and me and our children as well as my sister, brother-in-law, and their children. Mother said she had enough from my father's pension, didn't need any more money and encouraged Lewis to give to my sister's family instead. When oil was discovered, it catapulted every one of us into millionaire status. This money did not all come to us overnight, but as the drilling continued and more oil fields came on stream, our good fortunes began to rise. We began receiving our first royalty income payments in 1969.

Because of his bonanza, various people persuaded Lewis to start a company. It was assumed all the members of the family would be willing to put a percentage of their royalties back into it so that it could have continued funding for exploration activities. My sister and brother-in-law, speaking for their children, and Austin and I, speaking for ours, did not want to do this. Austin tried to dissuade his father from this plan because he knew Lewis was much better at research than business. "Why not just keep your office where you can continue your consulting? You don't need business problems at this stage in your life."

We had all discussed the pros and cons, deciding we'd all be much better off if left to our own devices, taking care of our own monies in our own ways. So a meeting was held at the Princeton Club in New York wherein all adult personalities involved were asked to be present. Those in favor of going ahead with the company totally ignored everything we said. They just kept on talking about their plans as if we did not exist. It was clear to us they were all anxious to become tycoons—captains of industry—as one later put it, but at our expense. The royalties, which at the time of gifting had not had any value, were now, since the oil discovery, worth a considerable amount, and Lewis wanted to have a say now in how they would be spent. We could have refused, but Austin's father wanted the company and had pretty well committed us to the venture long before the Princeton meeting. Since it was all because of him we had any royalty at all, we could hardly refuse. So an exchange of producing royalties for stock and options was made and Weeks Natural Resources which had been set up eventually became Weeks Petroleum. For my part, I was already so delighted with my good fortune, knew I could happily manage with my remaining royalty. What upset me and Austin, however, was the way no one wanted to hear us out, or take any of us seriously. Nevertheless. I tried to see it as a great new adventure in my life while Austin predicted "life will never be the same."

# 11

# ENERGY PREDICTIONS

In addition to his remarkable generosity to our entire family, one thing I most remember my father-in-law for was his insistence on the need to save energy. We all agreed with him, but I don't think he thought we took him seriously enough. So to emphasize his point, when Austin and I were once visiting him and mother, he turned off the engine of the car "to save gas," he said, whenever we'd get to a stop light. This finally propelled Austin to say: "For God's sake, Dad, you're going to ruin your starter motor. It'll cost a lot more to get that fixed than the amount of gas you're saving!" But Austin had missed the point as far as Lewis was concerned because he wanted to save energy, not starter motors. That was the same visit when, after we'd all been drinking iced tea, he also insisted we wash off our ice cubes and put them back into the ice maker "in order to save energy."

Ever since Austin's and my marriage in the early 1950's, Lewis had often written us that someday there would be a decline in world oil production and that it was essential for all of us to reduce our dependence on petroleum. It was because of him that I joined the International Solar Energy Society. Even though at that time, there was little concern by most that we were running out of fossil fuels, the seed was planted, and though it didn't begin to sprout until we had saved enough money to build our own dream home, we did get involved with an architect to design an active/passive solar home for us. By then, into the seventies, I was driving a small electric car which somewhat horrified Austin. Not because it was electric, but that I might end up as a grease spot on the highway. Then when I replaced it with a wonderful Volkswagen Rabbit that had good mileage, he looked at that with disdain also for the same reason. Our architect agreed to go to various meetings with me to find out what was available in solar energy, but after much investigation, it was terribly disappointing to learn that much of what we wanted was not yet state-of-the-art. Then our second son, Christopher, was killed in a helicopter accident, so the entire idea got put on hold for a year. By then too, our lives were getting so complicated that we couldn't keep up with everything.

Nevertheless, we did get a few energy-saving ideas put into our new home which included solar hot water for home and pool, recessed window overhangs, a heavy R factor on the roof, plus a design that created a venturi effect that would suck hot air out of the patio and upstairs windows when they were open, as well as a house built to withstand 150 mph winds. Since we were later in the north wall of the eye of Hurricane Andrew, it was this latter addition that saved us from being totally blown away.

Back in the fifties, not many people really thought we would ever run low on fossil fuels. But Austin's Dad was insistent with charts and lectures showing the rate of population increase, usage, plus rate of discovery (at that point in time) which clearly showed that something in the future would have to give; so we set up a memorial endowment in Christopher's name, the proceeds of which were to be given every other year for the best ideas contributed to the "practical application of solar energy." The amount generated in the alternate years went back into the fund to help it grow. Our government often "talks the talk" but doesn't always "walk the walk," so many of the prizes have been awarded to people from other countries. In the fall of 2005, for example, the prize went to a Chinese professor who had, among other things, helped install 20,000 hot water solar collectors on roofs in China.

In his speech in 1976 when he and my mother were at the groundbreaking for a new tower building for the Oklahoma headquarters of the American Association of Petroleum Geologist's Foundation, Lewis reminded everyone that it took God 600 million years to lay down the world's petroleum supply, but that man will have used up most of it in 200 years. Given new methods of extraction, the reworking of older oil fields and better technology, we'll certainly be able to add a few more years now to that figure.

My father-in-law's memoir, written 35 years ago, pointed out that if we continued to rely solely on fossil fuels that our energy problem would be insoluble. The reason for this lies in the fact that petroleum was laid down during a relatively short period of geological time, only in sedimentary rocks, and the sedimentary rocks with commercial quantities of petroleum are a very small part of the total. He estimated when all the significant oil fields on land are found, they will only occupy a mere 60,000 square miles of the 17 million square miles of land underlaid by sedimentary rock (this out of 57 million square miles of land surface). In addition, there are another 20 million or so square miles of continental shelves and slopes to explore. But here there will be the usual shrinkage. The occasional large off-shore finds can help only for a time to meet part of the yearly increase in the demand for oil. He thought we should encourage research and development of an adventuresome and out-reaching nature, or "we will not solve our problems." Lewis felt world oil production would peak late in the 20th or early in the 21st century. After the peak passed, oil production would gradually fall off for a hundred years to a mere trickle. "The final reserves will be hoarded for lubrication, to reduce the loss of other sources of energy caused by friction. When that is gone, if we have not learned how to synthesize petroleum from hydrocarbons in the environment, we will be reduced to using bear grease to keep our oxcart wheels from squeaking."[3]

According to an article in *Barron's* by Sandra Ward (quoting Charles Maxwell, October 16, 2006), statistics show that in 1964, we used about 12 billion barrels of the 48 billion barrels of oil found. In 1988, we began finding less than we were using. In 2005, 5–6 billion barrels of new oil were found and we used 30 billion! If this last statistic doesn't say something, I don't know what will wake us up to do something drastic about our modes of transportation. China's current double-digit economic growth has created a burgeoning market for cars. They are now the world's second largest vehicle market after the United States.

Of course, there are major areas of exploration and development going on throughout the world (both in tar sands, oil and gas). Some of these include such places as Northwest Canada, the Rocky Mountains, East Texas, the shallow and deep water areas offshore our Gulf Coast, Sable Island, the Labrador Shelf, Mexico, the Orinoco in Venezuela, Trinidad, Brazil, Angola, Nigeria, Algeria, Egypt, the Chad, Sudan, Iran, Qatar, Saudi Arabia, Iraq, India, Myanmar, Indonesia, Malaysia, Australia's Northwest Shelf, Vietnam, Bohai, Sakhalin, the Azeri Megastructure, the West Siberian Basin, Tengiz, Kashagan and Norway. But geo-political problems as well as the harsh climates in many of these areas will impede fast development.

Also, statistics through 2015 show Canada, Russia, the Caspian area, North Africa, West Africa, the Middle East and Latin America expecting increased production of petroleum while Western Europe and the United States can expect decreasing production.

At a meeting of the American Association of Petroleum Geologists I attended in San Antonio, Texas in October, 2006, Robert Esser, a consultant for Cambridge Energy Research Associates, told us that many of the dire predictions about the near term peaking of oil that we've been hearing recently are because the doomsday types "have not included the oil from recent significant discoveries, oil that is yet to be discovered, and unconventional oil. Unconventional oil includes Canadian oil sands, Venezuelan Orinoco, and gas-related liquidscondensates and natural gas liquids (NGL's) and gas to liquids (GTL's). These liquids also meet the demand for 'oil'. Also, peak theory advocates do not recognize reserve growth in discovered fields which exclude more production, than production from new discoveries."

Nevertheless, We're long overdue in developing good transportation programs in our country, not to mention improved car mileage. Each of us needs to cut down on the amount of gasoline used while simultaneously finding ways to convert to other modes of transportation. There are solar cars being developed, but the need for recharging them from solar stations needs to be encouraged. Some cars have switched to hydrogen, but one has to know where to go for hydrogen. The hybrids are encouraging, but they don't get high enough mileage. We need a rational government that will encourage industry to meet the problems head on. It's an embarrassment to admit we have upwards of 5–6% of the world's population now using some 35% of the world's resources.

# 12

# MONEY

Austin and I didn't have much time to worry about an impending energy crisis. We had three active children and it was all we could do to keep up with our own lives. From Maryland, we'd been moved to Miami and Austin's father wanted him involved with the company. Eventually, Austin gave up his position with the government and joined the board of Weeks Petroleum. Almost from day one, the money, the traveling, the company and entertaining affected all of us. I didn't want the children to be disrupted, but there was no way to avoid it. I had to leave them once with a baby sitter I wasn't wild about. (Years later the children told me she had smoked a pipe among other things.) And I recall telling an investment banker one day: "The most important dates in our lives used to be our children's birthdays, Christmas, and school vacations. Now, the dates we pay attention to are when quarterly taxes are due, meeting for IRS audits, or seeing our tax accountant."

Keeping track of the monies coming in and trying to understand all the government regulations pertaining to our investments didn't leave us time for anything else. We began seeing less and less of our friends, more and more of accountants and attorneys.

Of course, compared with the mega fortunes of billionaires, we weren't even blips on the money screen, but compared with the small income we'd been accustomed to living on our first eighteen years of marriage, it was like having the skies open and being pelted with cash.

At the end of the first or second year, when we had wired in funds for all five of our quarterly tax payments due in January, the manager of the bank, along with his vice-president, showed up on our doorstep one day with a bottle of scotch, profusely thanking us for boosting their year-end deposits to an all time high. (This was before the Reagan years when the government could take 70% of an individual's income.) Our deposits apparently helped his career, because shortly after, the manager was transferred to a larger bank!

Since we had not grasped the enormity of some of the problems we would be facing, I took it upon myself at first to handle all the investments. Austin did not have the time and I felt I should know all I could in order to help the children understand all this someday. At that point, I could not imagine *paying* someone to take care of money. We intentionally did not let the children know about their wealth because we wanted them to slide into it gradually and learn to handle it wisely. Kermit was already fourteen by then, Chris twelve, and Leslie was going on five. Left to our own devices, I think we would have succeeded far better than we did, but my sister's children were older and knew more; consequently their younger cousins were told things we would have preferred they not be told so soon. Nevertheless, our children's small allowances did not change. To add to his spending money, our older son worked at a Publix market during his high school days. And when Chris got older, before his accident, he had a job in a local restaurant kitchen. I still recall the night he came home proudly announcing he had been promoted from scraping plates to cutting butter!

In retrospect, some of this sounds humorous. But at the time, it really wasn't. I recall what mixed emotions we had when the children's first checks arrived. We were so terribly grateful for this good fortune; at the same time, it seemed incongruous that one of the first checks received almost amounted to what Austin and I had been able to save and set aside up to that date. We had denied ourselves so many things over the years trying to save for our children's college education someday.

Still, from the very beginning, I'd never thought of the money as truly mine. It was God's. For some reason, however, some of it had ended up in my bank account. I had not earned it, although I spent a lot of time trying to conserve and care for it. But I felt from day one that the money was a gift which I had an obligation to care for and share with others. My church, of course, was one of the first recipients. When I raised my pledge and began to put larger checks into the collection plate, the treasurer then at St. Andrew's (Jack Lincoln) later told me a counter saw the check one Sunday and remarked: "Boy, this person must have done a lot of sinning to donate this much in one week!" (I think that says a lot about the counter!) He couldn't know I was giving out of joy, from just the sheer pleasure of having this wonderful windfall. But for the grace of God, I knew rather than being among the well-to-do, I could just as easily have been among the very poor.

Though we knew the Bass Strait production could not last forever, we had no idea then what actual reserves would be. And due to the vagaries of the oil business, OPEC, offshore drilling problems, strikes, unpredictable weather in the

Straits, foreign exchange, governmental regulations and taxes, my immediate goal
with the arriving funds was to put away as much as possible, with the hope that
someday we would have enough income from our investments to have something
to fall back upon in tough times; or better still, to have enough to retire earlier
than planned.

A consultant for the Episcopal National Church's Stewardship Commission
has said: "We need to see the abundant and generous kingdom which Jesus envisioned, instead of the scarcity projected by our current economic culture."[4] She
thinks the cultural climate of scarcity is also tied to the experience of many members in the Episcopal Church who relate to the Great Depression of the 1930's
and that these early challenges became part of a collective memory of never having enough. Her remark caught my attention because I am a product of that era,
and I well know what happened to my parents. Their savings were wiped out in
the market crash of 1929. We were never without essentials, but because of that,
I have never taken money for granted. Of course, we have to keep our eyes on the
generous kingdom, but I also happen to be one who believes it's wise to put away
for a rainy day. I don't believe in spending everything I have, nor do I believe
debt should be a status symbol. And I question the honesty of people who always
want to use other people's money to finance their ventures without putting up
hard earned monies of their own.

I have also never felt monies should be invested in the same place. So this
meant all kinds of savings accounts, bonds, stocks and real estate. If it was sensible, name it; I invested in it. Given the circumstances at the time, I believe the
goal in itself was laudable; but the paper work this generated was horrendous. I
had to plan my schedule so that I would have time to spend at the Dixie National
Bank the day the coupons came due for clipping. Once, I had to meet a New
York banker there. He took one look at the bank, then said: "This is really a small
branch, isn't it." When I told him to my knowledge this was the main bank, he
almost choked. The Dixie Bank was meeting our needs. I saw no reason to
change.

Five years into this madness, when things began to get a bit out of control, in
response to a remark I must have made, one of the investment people involved
with some of my father-in-law's interests asked if he might visit the next time he
was in Miami and answer any questions we might have. I said "Of course." I was
tired of doing all the investing and bookwork. I was also coming to realize by
then that everyone else in the family was having a pretty good time with their
money, and I wasn't. And I didn't always get the feeling they were very appreciative.

The gentleman came down and I told him what I was doing. He just sat there with his mouth open. Finally, he got around to asking me about cash. "Do you have any bank accounts?"

"Yes," I nodded.

"How much in each?" he asked, expecting no doubt there would be an account for each one of us.

"I guess we could add them up," I told him as I proceeded to drag out forty account books. (I hadn't wanted to put more money into the accounts than they could be insured for, so had just kept opening new ones as cash became available.)

The banker didn't quite know what to say, but I suspected by then he was equating us with the Beverly Hillbillies.

It was agreed I would send the municipal bonds north. I was sick of clipping coupons and could not wait to get rid of them. Before returning to the airport, he told me to "make a transfer through your broker," then suggested as an afterthought, "you should first get an armed security guard."

I didn't like that idea at all, but didn't tell him. I just knew the more innocuous I looked, the better; so the following day, went to the safety deposit box, stuffed the bonds into a large brown paper shopping bag and took them to my broker. He ushered me into his office.

"John," I said, when I was inside. "Mr. X_____ tells me you can transfer some muni's into my new account."

"Certainly. When do you want it done?"

"Right now," I told him, and put the shopping bag on his desk.

He opened the sack and looked inside, then turned rather pale. "These are bearer bonds," he said. "These are negotiable. Do you realize that anyone could have cashed these?"

"Yes," I said, as I watched his eyes open wider.

"How many are there?" he asked, looking into the recesses of the bag.

"A bunch," I replied.

# 13

# BISHOP DUNCAN

It was such a gradual awakening that I can't recall a specific date, or place or moment when I knew I was going to be a priest, but I can pinpoint one instance that hit me so unexpectedly, I was at a loss momentarily to explain it.

After moving to Miami and getting involved with St. Andrew's, I became involved at the Diocesan level. This was at a time when the national as well as the local church was agonizing over whether to ordain women to the priesthood. I thought it was a no brainer and couldn't understand why anyone could object. But Bishop Duncan who was in charge of the diocese at that time was firmly opposed to women's ordination. Everyone knew he would never ordain a female. For reasons I couldn't totally understand at the time, I decided I should get involved. There was no practical or impractical reason why women could not be priests and I felt it was my duty to campaign for them. There were women with advanced degrees teaching in our seminaries who were every bit as smart and capable as men. "What if one of them wants to be ordained?" I asked. I'd never viewed myself as a feminist, yet here I was jumping in with both feet to support women.

I made it a point to confront Bishop Duncan over this and he graciously put me on a committee which was going to present the various aspects to our local diocesan convention. That was a real eye opener to me and I couldn't believe the close-mindedness of some of the members on that committee. We all met together as a group, until after the second meeting it was quite evident we could never work together. I took the assignment seriously and wrote what I thought was a good position paper addressing the theological issues involved. When we got back together to review what each side had written, I recall one paper giving as its only argument why women should not be ordained was because St. Paul had said "women should be quiet in church."[5] (This from a supposedly educated man.) He had no concept of the cultural background wherein this statement had been made and had no desire to be further educated on the matter. I tried to be

"Christian" about it, but finally concluded that people like him were so wedded to tradition that he'd never change his mind. And he was incapable of reason. I hoped the Bishop would be more flexible.

At some point, either at the convention or possibly it was at a pre-convention meeting, I got up and gave my position paper with the reasons favoring women's ordination. After I had finished, before sitting down, I added "As a matter of fact, I feel called to be a priest, and I think it's absurd that we have church members saying we should not be ordained." I couldn't believe I'd publicly stated that. Yet I had. And I knew in my heart it was true. It went all the way back to my meeting with Father Sampietro thirty years earlier. I also felt God was tired of my procrastinating and knew he was telling me it was time I stood up and be counted.

I had written Bishop Duncan in December of 1976 to ask for admission to the program called Theological Education by Extension. Though I said nothing at the time, my personal intent was to continue on into the ordained ministry. At that time, women in our diocese were only being ordained deacons. I was admitted as a postulant for Holy Orders September 24, 1977; and by this time, the national church had voted to ordain women as priests. Some bishops, however, including Bishop Duncan, still refused to go along.

Bishop Duncan had set up a program to bring seminary education to students, and Jim Rasnick, then the assistant to the Bishop for Ministry and Mission was put in charge. The TEE Program (similar in some ways to what is now called Education for Ministry or EFM) consisted of a weekly seminar to assist students to achieve ordination to the diaconate. There was a need also for more ordained blacks and the bishop hoped this would draw some in. There were four others in my group—Lynn Ramshaw, Caroll Mallin, Louis Duty and Cyril White. (Lynn and Caroll and I were white women; Louis and Cyril were black men.) After a period of time into the program, we were scheduled to appear before the Commission on Ministry.

When it was my turn to be interviewed, and after answering a few questions, I told them I was applying to be a *transitional* (as opposed to a *vocational*) deacon, since it was my intention eventually to become a priest. They mostly smiled at one another, ignored what I said, and gave me the equivalent of a little patronizing pat on the head. Since women were not being ordained, I was told to continue in the diaconate program then underway. Only one member of the group took me seriously. After the interview, he took me aside and told me I could get a head start if I found myself a teacher and began studying Greek. "You'll need it someday," he told me.

Since most of the members on the Commission didn't take me seriously, I didn't take them seriously either. For the most part, I tried to put them out of my mind and trust that God would help me cross the priestly ordination bridge when I got to it.

Bishop Duncan and I could not have been farther apart when it came to our opinions about the ordination of women. Despite this, I really liked him. We discussed various other subjects too, played golf together several times and I wrote ember day letters to him regularly as required by the canons. Ember days are traditionally observed during Lent plus one day at Pentecost, Holy Cross Day in September and St. Lucy Day in December. I always looked forward to what the Bishop had to say in response. He had a full plate with his diocesan duties and some of my correspondence with him relates to the grief the Church of the Holy Spirit gave him when they broke with the Diocese. This was not only over the ordination of women, but abortion, divorce, homosexuality and the changes being made to the *Book of Common Prayer.* I rather enjoyed reading the statement that the founder of that parish made to the newspapers at the time: "The rector hollers about abortions and lesbians and women's ordination, but he doesn't say anything about priests who are queer. It's always against women. If you took women out of the church, there wouldn't be any church."[6]

In one of his notes to me, Bishop Duncan said: "I've had my meeting with the rector, his vestry and congregation. It's pretty well a disaster area as far as supporting the diocese.... .I agree with them in their doubts about women's ordination, but their methodology of continuing to fight and refusing to live with the situation gets my goat. Thank you for your prayers. Keep them going. I'm going to need them."

Before the church's vote (185–14) to sever ties, Bishop Duncan had been barred from leading the service and speaking at the meeting, and he'd had to sit in a back pew of the church while the service was held.

In December of 1976, I asked Bishop Duncan to lunch. I decided I needed to know him much better, so I could pray for him honestly. After all, I concluded, Christianity concerned relationships—one's relationship to God and, by extension, those we know and meet on a daily basis; so prayer, most especially those with whom we disagree, I felt was in order. The Bishop couldn't come at first, but later, in January of 1977 we got together. Half way through lunch at a place called *Arthur's,* Bishop Duncan said: "Don't you have something to ask me, Marta?" I know he expected me to bring up the subject of ordination.

"No, not really," I replied. "I just want to get to know you." He seemed relieved.

When it was time to leave, I picked up the tab (after all, I'd invited him), and he said: "Oh no ... let me pay that."

"Bishop," I told him. "You're my guest! I wouldn't think of letting you do that."

"I was raised to be an old Southern gentleman, Marta."

I could see he was very uncomfortable. But I couldn't help that. I paid the bill. As I did so, I could see him looking around, hoping no one would see this. But that told me something about Bishop Duncan. Certainly he was struggling with the changes going on in our society. He was very human and I was glad I'd asked him to lunch.

In the meantime, I continued writing ember day letters to him and enjoyed the correspondence and relationship that developed. Despite our differences, I always viewed the Bishop as a good shepherd. The following excerpt is from a letter written May 9, 1978:

> Dear Bishop Duncan,
>
> Pentecost is nearly upon us which means I'm supposed to check in again with the High Command. I often ask myself if I should continue in this program. My feelings last week (and this will probably please you) were to drop out completely. What I am reading and studying in the TEE program is so far removed from what I am doing with the rest of my life that it all seems like a waste of time. I saw Bishop Watson last week in San Diego, told him this all seemed like a "dull, boring round-about way to affirm life." I expected him to encourage me to drop out (like you, I don't think he's wild about women in the priesthood); instead, he said "Marta, you haven't earned the right to drop out yet." When I told him I really couldn't see where I would fit into the Diocese as I currently saw it, he suggested I might explore in some way the possibility of helping to define the ministry of women in the church. As I see it, there's an open field ahead, glistening white, like a vast expanse of newly fallen snow. I guess I'm hesitant to make tracks, for fear I might spoil the beauty of it. I think that's a hopeful image of the future, though how it relates to me and the church—if at all—I just don't know. If I don't dwell on the kind of tracks I make, perhaps they'll develop into an acceptable pattern to our Lord. I read John Coburn's book—<u>Hope of Glory</u>—which you recommended. Also James Fenhagen's <u>Mutual Ministry.</u> I think I shall read Fenhagen's book again. The statements that impress me are:

"The greatest gift a pastor has to give to another is not the right answer, but the authenticity of his or her own search," and "the deeper answer to anxiety does not lie in increased certainty, but in the courage to live creatively in the midst of ambiguity and paradox. This is what faith is all about."[7] I guess this spoke to me because I'm not finding very many answers right now.

The Bishop answered on May 15, 1978:

*Dear Marta,*

*Thank you for your good letter. Don't think about my being the High Command. I'm just down here struggling away the best I can.*

*I'm sorry you're still involved in the obligations resulting from the death of Austin's father. I know what difficulties it presents to you when you're trying to get things all straightened out. Please give Austin my regards.*

*Don't worry about meeting with the Examining Chaplains at Biscayne College. It's going to be fun to see what goes on.*

*I can understand your sense of frustration and the dichotomy which exists between what you have to know in terms of Biblical criticism, Biblical background, and Pauline theology, and the whole process of living. So I would have to agree that you don't want to drop out yet.*

*I'm like you. I see some great potential possibilities of women in the Church and in the ministry, but I'm not necessarily thinking it ought to be in the priesthood, as I've said before. It seems to me we need to make some new tracks in the snow as to what we mean by ministry and how we do ministry. Just teaching someone to celebrate the sacraments, say communion, is not what we mean by ministry, and the priesthood is not where it really is.*

*I look forward to seeing you at the meeting with the Examining Chaplains. I hope we'll get a chance to sit down and just talk.*

*With best wishes. Yours,*

*James L. Duncan*
*Bishop*

As for the meetings, I don't think I ever had an opportunity to talk to the Bishop. I can't recall that he even attended. Certainly it was not a fun day. I know I came away feeling psychologically battered and abused. The tensions were unbearable. Either Caroll or Lynn, I can't recall which now, threw up in the ladies room. The meetings could not have been worse in terms of the acceptance of us as women, as *persons* even. I couldn't believe we were supposed to have been in a "Christian" setting. The priest in charge was not Bishop Duncan, but another priest in the Diocese. Perhaps the relationship with his wife (I found out later he was in the midst of a divorce) colored his remarks to us. In retrospect, I'm surprised I put up with all that happened that day. Or that I even continued with my course of study. But by then, the TEE course and all that went with it had become not just my vocation, but a *principle*—a quest for all women's vocations,

and a sense of calling that dated back to high school days—which I was not prepared to give up. That priest and his obnoxious behavior and attitude only served
to help me dig my heels in deeper. Had I been aware then that I would have to
come up against him again in the future, under equally, if not more stressful conditions, perhaps I would have just said "forget it" and walked out. But I couldn't
foresee the future. Anyway, my guardian angel came to the rescue and helped me
devise a victorious way to deal with him.

At Snowbird, Utah, where I love to ski, there is a ski run called STH that cuts
off the trail below the Gad 2 lift. The name of the run translates into "Steeper
Than Hell," and indeed it is, just that. I have only been into the area twice, both
times by mistake, both times by myself. The first was in a white-out when I lost
all sense of direction. It took me some time before I was able to work my way
back to the upper trail. I don't recall now why I ended up there the second time,
but swore it would be the last. There's a very steep cliff-like section where the hill
is so vertical that one almost has to go into free-fall to reach the trail beneath. I
can't believe it's a marked ski run. Perhaps I made a wrong turn somewhere and
never found the real trail. Not only is it steep, but extremely narrow as well. If
there's the least bit of ice or hard pack, it's difficult to turn without winding up in
the trees. Fortunately for me, the snow was unusually deep, which helped slow
me down considerably the second time I got in there. I shudder to think what
could have resulted if I'd hurt myself—broken a leg or something—and been
unable to get out, because I doubt anyone would have found me. There were,
understandably, very few ski tracks.

It was due to my experience on STH, however, that my prayer fantasy developed for this priest. How could I pray without getting so mad all the time—at
the church, at the narrow minded patriarchal-oriented commission, and specifically, at this priest and his ilk?

My guardian angel gleefully came to the rescue, and this fantasy surfaced in
my prayer life. Whenever I'd feel myself getting angry over some of the statements he'd made ("It'll be over my dead body that any woman is ever ordained in
this Diocese"), I'd picture him lying along the trail of STH, unable to dig out of
the deep powder snow. He would be cold, and miserable, and calling for help. It
would be snowing. I'd have my face mask and goggles on so he wouldn't recognize me, and I'd just happen along and ask if I could help. And he'd be so glad I
was there and so thankful. And I'd get him dug out and help him get his skis back
on and then I'd lead him out the easiest way I could find and admonish him for
going into an area clearly beyond his skiing ability. Then I would help him get all
the way back down the mountain and deliver him safely to the skier's bridge that

goes across to the upper deck of the plaza. That's where I would say goodbye and wish him well. He would be effusive and so appreciative and ask "But can't I buy you a drink or something?" But by then, all I could sense was my guardian angel, perched on top of his ski cap, laughing uproariously. I would struggle over whether to let him know who I was, or whether to go my way. Then the fantasy would begin to fade out and I'd feel so much better inside. Vindicated in a way, but very much at peace. After a while, I developed such positive feelings about him, I was able to see the good points that I knew he had, and there was no further need for fantasy.

A later letter to Bishop Duncan was dated September 12, 1978. He had just returned from Europe, where Austin and I had also been.

> Dear Bishop Duncan, Welcome home. I thought about you and Elaine when we were in Switzerland and wondered how Lambeth was going.
> *Austin, Leslie and I got back the end of August. Europe is far away in my thoughts right now, but I still remember a blur of*
> *Quaint chimneys and shingled roofs,*
> *And sail boats on Lake Lucerne,*
> *Aerial trams hanging over glaciers,*
> *Corded wood by mountain homes ... waterfalls ... wildflowers,*
> *Happy cows and tinkling bells,*
> *And eider down.*
> *Croissants and cheese with breakfast,*
> *Shopping for Swiss army knives,*
> *Sidewalk cafes with French menus,*
> *Carved clocks,*
> *Covered wooden bridges ... petunias and geraniums in potted boxes,*
> *And stately swans.*
> *A city wall with towers, parapets,*
> *Fresh raspberries, "rostis," succulent lake fish*
> *And mountains.*
> *Shilthorn, Pilatus, Titlis, the Rigi,*
> *Dinners with friends, hot bread, good wine.*
> *When the exorbitant prices and Humphrey Bogart in German on television seemed normal, we knew it was time to come home.*

I went on to tell him about my classes and activities and reading.

Bishop Duncan's answer included: *"We truly enjoyed everything about it* (his trip to Europe), *particularly being in the Hotel in Baden-Baden. Boy, I could get used to that kind of luxury"* to *"I still come back to the conclusion that the Church is going to be saved, not by the priesthood, but by the lay ministry. To hear and to see what's being done throughout the world by the un-ordained is one of the greatest thrills of the Lambeth Conference. We'll have to get together and talk about it one of these days soon."*

Clearly, Bishop Duncan was never going to embrace women's ordination. And by then, my life was so confusing and complicated in other spheres that I doubted I would ever be able to find the time to continue in the program. But for reasons I couldn't always even explain to myself, it was important to me. Somehow, I managed to remain. In December of 1978, I again went before the Commission on Ministry and it was then I definitely stated I was there to apply for the priesthood. To my knowledge, I was the first woman in the Diocese of Southeast Florida to do that.

# 14

# CHRISTOPHER

Fred Masterman was a wonderful and caring mentor and I loved the two years I was part of the TEE (Theological Education by Extension) program. I gave up every other Friday night for months driving down town to the cathedral where classes were held. But the city was changing. The caretaker would have to open up, then lock us in because of all the transients and the increasing crime in the area. There were often drunks or homeless people sleeping in the cathedral yard when it was time for us to go home.

We were finally scheduled to take our first canonical exam—Bible content—in mid-February, 1979. Anticipating this ahead of time, I had been studying hard and was well prepared. But in the midst of getting my winter clothes in order for a planned ski trip after, someone notified me that our son—Christopher—his passenger, and the helicopter he'd been flying back from a hunting camp over the weekend, had disappeared in the Everglades.

My life shattered into a million pieces that week. Austin was in Bermuda attending business meetings. I was so numb with anxiety that all I could do was go through the motions of living. Kermit, our other son, enlisted many of his friends with planes to help us search and he and I flew back and forth over that desolate "sea of grass" looking for any clues that might lead us to Christopher. Mostly, I can only recall now seeing alligators, or deer gathered in groups on patches of higher ground, surrounded by water; or the occasional airboat with flurries of disrupted birds in its wake. Because Kermit was in the air so much, I'd always had a healthy concern for his safety and was constantly admonishing: "Do be careful." Since Chris flew also but was not involved with aerobatics, it never occurred to me we might lose him in an air accident. I was usually more concerned with the fact that he owned and drove a motorcycle! After two days of fruitless searching, a pilot flying north, not far from Andytown, finally spotted the helicopter wreckage.

After the recovery of the bodies, Austin's return, and the sad drive to Broward County to identify Christopher's belongings, we then had to get through the funeral. I can't remember much about it. I just know I was floating in what I can only describe as a surrealistic nightmare. When anyone spoke to me, I could be terribly focused and present to the moment, but when the conversation was over, I'd retreat into my world of grief. And Austin and I grieved so differently, we couldn't be of much support to one another. I think also we were trying hard to keep a stiff upper lip for our other two children. But as Kate Wiebe says in her book—*Border Crossing:* "A stiff upper lip in time of sorrow may be good stoicism, but it's not good Christianity."[8]

The funeral was at St. Andrew's Episcopal Church, the *old* St. Andrew's before the new church was built. There were faces in the congregation I could not recognize. I didn't want to be there, but knew I had to be. All I could think of was how I'd wanted to get Chris' friends together and make a wooden box for him so he could be cremated. I wanted to do something that related to him and his friends and his life, because they had always been making and doing things together, or tinkering in our garage, fixing their bikes, or watching Kermit build his airplane. They'd always kept things stirred up in ways only teenagers can do. And somehow, I thought making him a coffin, rather than doing nothing, would have been a constructive, creative outlet for all of us, some sane way to deal with the shock. It would have been a time to be together and talk, and remember. It would have been an opportunity to touch his spirit one last time. I could almost hear him saying: "Go for it, Mom." But everything was so out of kilter. No one heard me, or took me seriously, or even tried to listen. So it never happened. Standing in that church, I just tried hard to hang on to the last time I'd seen him.

He'd just moved into his own place and come by the house to see us the day before Austin left for Bermuda. Radiantly happy, he was excited about going to the Everglades. Friends who had a fishing camp had invited him to join them. Since he'd recently qualified for a license to fly helicopters, he decided to rent one and fly out.

We weren't always demonstrative with our children, and I don't know why it came up that day, but Austin and I both made a point to tell Christopher we loved him and that we didn't expect him to try to compete with his brother. Kermit had always excelled in just about anything he attempted, bringing home one trophy after another, which had always made it difficult for Chris, who wasn't always able to keep up. So Chris left the house that Friday afternoon laughing, excited and happily looking forward to the weekend. And that's the last time we saw him.

My mother's sister and husband drove all the way from Gainesville for the funeral. There were lots of people and wonderful food sent from the parish, but I recall so little of that week. My spirit went into nuclear winter and stayed that way for a long time.

I didn't rejoin the TEE group although I did try to go back once about a month after the funeral, but it wasn't the same. It was like having salt rubbed into an open wound. Reading the Bible kept throwing me back to the week studying for exams, the week we'd lost Christopher.

"Marta, if God meant for you to become a priest, He'll lead you back when the time is right," said Father Masterman. I knew he was correct. So my vocation got put on hold; for nine years.

Those years were crammed with activity. I intuitively knew it was the only way I would ever be able to cope. When you keep busy, you don't have time to think, or feel or blame. You also don't have time to wonder what might have been had things gone differently. And one day, you wake up, and the pain doesn't seem quiet as bad.

At the time of Chris' death, Martha Peterson had been trying to get me to join the board of trustees at Beloit College. She'd been Dean of students at the University of Wisconsin, the Dean at Columbia, then President of Barnard College, eventually becoming President of Beloit. Our association not only related to Beloit, where I'd spent four semesters as an undergraduate student, but also to the international oil business. She was the first woman to be named a director of Exxon Corporation which, at that time, was the world's largest oil company. As president of Barnard she also became one of the first women to chair the executive committee of the American Council on Education.

Both Austin's and my father had worked for Esso, before it evolved into Exxon (and later ExxonMobil) and our own involvement with Esso-BHP through Weeks Petroleum continuously brought us into contact with people in the petroleum world. Knowing I would not be going back to my class with Father Masterman, I accepted and remained on that board for three years.

Martha Peterson was a delight to know. Beloit College was going through a real financial crisis when she'd been asked to become their President and it was through her leadership that the college got back on its feet. Whenever I went to Wisconsin for meetings, she always made a room available for me where she lived. Her guests for the most part were fascinating and I loved being at those trustee gatherings. She was full of delightful stories about the many celebrities and academicians she knew. The last time I stayed with her, Garrick Uttley—the news commentator—occupied the room across the hall from me.

I guess because I'd been involved with Beloit, President Foote asked me if I'd become a trustee of the University of Miami. Austin and I first met him at a luncheon arranged by the Director of Development. "Tad," as he was called, was new on the job at that time and trying to get acquainted with people in the community, doing all those nice things that create good will for an institution. We thought he was charming. At first, I declined his invitation to join the board, but finally agreed when he called back later a second time. I was still trying to pick up the pieces of my life and this seemed like a good place to continue. Too, there were other things closer to home which included numerous church and community activities and we were also being more and more drawn into the international oil business.

# 15

# WEEKS PETROLEUM

Since Weeks Petroleum ended up being an international oil company based in Bermuda, many of the directors were foreign. There was an English lord on the board, a marquis from Spain, a Norwegian businessman and an ex-ambassador from Australia. As the headquarters were in Bermuda, there were also directors from there as well as the United States. The company was involved in taking out leases all over the world which meant continuous travel to board meetings which were usually held close to the place where some of the operations were taking place. These included the South China Sea, Australia, Turkey, the North Sea, West Africa, the Santa Barbara Channel and the Caribbean. We had meetings in Curacao, Bermuda, London, Norway, Spain, South Korea, Key Biscayne, Hong Kong, Sydney, New Zealand, Istanbul, Switzerland, Aruba and Hawaii. I could have gone to Ras al Khaima, but the Arabs wouldn't allow women to travel to the rigs; so I sat that one out. I saw no reason to fly all that distance just to sit in a hotel!

I was exposed to quite a bit of business during those early years with the company. That was the period when the television series—*Dynasty*—was running. Austin and I would watch it and laugh ourselves silly at the antics of either Blake Carrington or his ex-wife, Alexis (who was always overdressed). There were few similarities between their lives and ours, though at times we could see glimpses of the power and political struggles in the corporate world which we could translate to our own as well. Austin was stressed out much of the time, consuming enormous amounts of Di-Gel or Rolaids whenever he had to attend director's meetings. As Austin had feared, at times, his father's personality (and those of some of the other board members) generated friction, leaving Austin to feel as though he were "piggy in the middle" as he termed it, always trying to soothe people's ruffled feathers. Added stress towards the late 1970's also resulted when his father developed cancer and insisted we tell no one.

Entertaining, or being entertained, was also very much a part of our lives. It went with the territory. If we weren't going to dinners or cocktails with Weeks Petroleum involvement, we were attending community affairs or else making our home available for charity functions. At first, I thought it was wonderful to be able to afford to do all these things we'd never had the money to do, but gradually, it became too much, and we couldn't seem to extricate ourselves from the social merry-go-round we'd ended up in. I thought on occasion too that the stress was leading to Austin's occasional overindulgence; however, he always seemed to be in control, so I let it pass. But as our lives became more complicated, I was constantly torn between obligations to my children, my husband, or our parents, much of which seemed to revolve more and more around the company.

Once when emphasizing Lewis' many good points, my mother told me she thought he "might be a genius;" but after a little hesitation, added "and I've decided that geniuses can be difficult to live with at times." I didn't really understand until I went to seminary later and studied family systems how much of a control issue was involved here. I became concerned for Austin's health too as the company kept generating problems, and as the oil business became more complicated, Austin and I kept remembering the meeting at the Princeton Club, when no one had listened to us. The biggest dream of our lives then had been to rent, or possibly buy, a camper, drive into Canada with our children, and take them on a family vacation. Of course, that never happened.

By then, the company had gone through several managing directors, a great deal of money and spent a good deal on leases and exploration activity, but with little additional oil's being found. Even though we had received stock and options, had it not been for the built-in royalty flow supporting all these ventures, the company would never have survived. One managing director also saw the royalty as his personal slush fund and spent needlessly on extras that had infuriated my father-in-law. At this time also, corporate raiders were beginning to look at us, hoping to find a way to acquire our revenue stream. Then, in 1977, Austin's father died of cancer.

In April of 1982, I became a director, replacing Austin, whose health was also deteriorating. By then, Austin felt some of the Bass Strait income should go for a dividend pay out to shareholders, with excessive wildcatting to be discouraged. At that point, management had just run up expenses of $19 million for a single dry well in the Timor Sea. Austin also wanted a reduction in the yearly running costs the company was incurring. In addition, he kept saying he could not understand how anyone could enjoy the type of life required of us. Living in 747's, eating late meals, trying to adjust continuously to jet lag was the last thing he wanted to do.

"If we can't enjoy our lives," he kept saying, "what's the point of having any money?" Although I enjoyed much of the international aspects of our lives, I had to agree with him. Whenever he would allude to our dilemma, I never failed to think of the Spanish *conquistadores* who drowned, refusing to release their gold while fording the deep canals. Nevertheless, if I were to be on the board, I felt I should certainly try to do my best.

One of our early meetings had been in Madrid. A second was also scheduled there shortly after I joined the board. I recall flying all the way again to Spain, spending one night in Madrid, then having to turn right around and get the next flight back to New York. I'd received a call shortly after arrival that Austin had suffered a heart attack and was in intensive care at Doctor's Hospital in Coral Gables. Coming back across the Atlantic, wondering if Austin would still be alive when I returned, I had to ask myself the same question. What *is* the point of having money? It was controlling our lives, rather than the other way around. Thankfully, Austin survived, but I felt our lives were spinning out of control. The demands on me kept increasing and I began to wonder how much longer I could remain afloat.

At some point, Austin suggested we sell out. It would mean finding a trustworthy investment banker which we felt would not be easy. Also, we knew the fees would be high. A sale possibility also troubled us because we'd come to know many of the employees and were concerned about their futures. We didn't want them to be displaced from their jobs. Also, we'd had one raider make an unsuccessful takeover attempt and knew it could happen again. This was the heyday of corporate takeovers and leveraged buyouts. I can't begin to recount the politics also that were occurring then among various factions on the board. Too, I knew I was over my head and, like my husband, wanted a life.

At one point, an opportunity was presented to protect the company from raiders by changing some of the by-laws. I tried to communicate this to Austin but he would not sit down and discuss it with me. I could not understand his reluctance and did not feel it right for me to make a unilateral decision on something this important to both of us. Management was pushing for its own agenda as well which a change in the by-laws would have aided. There always seemed to be major long term ramifications to anything we did. So at times, I found it best to sit tight and do nothing. When I eventually voted against the by-laws change, due to good reasons at the time, but which later turned out to be the wrong decision, I recall someone's saying: "Perhaps God works in mischievous ways His blunders to perform."

Thumbing through a *Forbes* magazine, I had noticed an article about a Mr. Holmes a' Court from Australia. It said he was a corporate raider, and that he was on the prowl. I thought about it, but finally decided he was after much bigger prey than Weeks Petroleum; nevertheless, did send a memo about the clipping to the rest of the board saying I didn't think he would be a problem. Of course, I lived to eat those words.

On January 31, 1984, I was awakened by an early phone call from London informing me that the company had been raided on the London Stock Exchange. An hour later, a reporter from Australia also called to ask if I were aware of what had happened. In twenty minutes, Mr. Holmes a'Court had shelled out quite a few million to gain control of 46% of Weeks Petroleum. Now, with control of the Bermuda company, he also gained control of Weeks Australia. Due to our own government's rules relating to foreign controlled holding corporations, we'd been prevented from purchasing more of our own stock.

As Mr. Holmes a'Court was later quoted: "If there were any competitors," he said "if they were in America, they would have been asleep. If they were in Australia, they would have been preparing to sleep. And if they were in London, I don't think many of them would have been in their offices at that time of the morning."

His dawn raid hit hard. At first, Austin and I were both devastated. We'd poured so much of our time into that company and endured so many disruptions in our own lives. But after it was behind us and everything settled out, we had to admit to being relieved. "Homac," as we referred to Mr. Holmes a'Court, had been a white knight in a way. He'd saved us from having to find an investment banker. And over time, new avenues opened up to us we'd long ago given up on.

But standing about in the aftermath, listening to the lawyers who had called some wrong shots and who were now seriously back pedaling for fear we might sue them for the bad advice given directly related to the takeover, it reminded me of the meeting held five years earlier, the last week of January after Christopher's death. I'd felt so much worse at losing a son than losing my stake in a company that the two could not even be compared. But the experience of losing Weeks Petroleum reawakened the previous shock and it took me a while to get my bearings. But when I did, when things settled down, and after I'd had a chance to put my life into proper perspective, I realized the day had at last arrived. It was time to think seriously again about becoming a priest.

# 16

# ANTARCTICA

In the Diocese of Southeast Florida, assuming one has a college degree, it normally takes five additional years to become an Episcopal priest. There are exceptions, of course, to this pattern, but generally speaking, these are the church's requirements. The first year for an aspiring applicant involves interviews and personal conferences, recommendations from one's vestry and rector, medical and psychological exams, a personal conference with the Bishop, a screening interview with the Commission on Ministry, and then, if accepted as a postulant, application to a seminary. Some students apply to attend seminary unaware of all these requirements, only to find out later they must back-pedal to conform to the so called "process." If accepted, they enter seminary the second year. The Commission on Ministry requires regular reports on a student's progress, and ember day letters to the Bishop are required by canon law.

The third year (one's second or "middler" year at seminary,) a postulant must apply for candidacy. This involves more recommendations and interviews. In addition to the Commission, one also has to go before the Standing Committee. Because of previous painful experiences with those opposed to women's ordination, I always identified with Daniel's being thrown to the lions whenever I had to be interviewed. But I gradually learned to put my trust in God and hoped He would send an angel for me too. (Daniel 6: 22–23)

In the fourth year, as a candidate, one is required to take another medical and psychological exam during Christmas break. Then, at the beginning of the fifth year, candidates are required to submit their personal applications for ordination. Final reports on General Ordination Exams are sent to the Bishop and in the spring, candidates are interviewed again by the Commission on Ministry as well as the Standing Committee. If all is in order, one's ordination to the transitional diaconate occurs shortly after graduation. This is to be distinguished from the vocational diaconate—an avenue open to those who do not feel called to become priests.

One can be ordained to the diaconate in the Diocese of Southeast Florida by pursuing a part-time, three year study course so designed for this. To become a priest, however, one must usually attend seminary. Once through seminary, after a suitable period in training as a transitional deacon, one has several more interviews, then ordination to the priesthood occurs.

There were two things I wanted to do before taking off for seminary. One of these I considered fun and exciting; the other one I did not. The first involved a trip; the second, surgery. I decided if for any reason the foot surgery gave me trouble, that I should take the trip first. So that's what I did. I had always wanted to see Antarctica. When I heard that a Stanford University group was going, I decided to sign up. I can't begin to recount the thrill and excitement of that journey. It was an incredible experience. Despite all my pictures and memories, I still find it hard to believe I was actually there.

From Miami, we flew first to Santiago, then on to Punta Arenas where we joined the crew of the 250 ft. *Society Explorer* which took us first through the Straits of Magellan, then on to the Falkland Islands. This was an odyssey in itself, visiting some of the larger islands (there are some 200 in the Falklands), and getting our first introduction to penguins—in this case, the magellanics—which live on New Island and burrow into the ground to nest.

We spent New Year's Day in Port Stanley watching the British kelpers hold forth with their yearly regatta. This also gave us a chance to wander about and see the picturesque town. Of course, we had to observe the signs and paths; there were still inactivated mines left from the 1982 Falklands War. But I got to see the other species of penguin inhabitants—the rockhopper, macaroni, gentoo and king. The chinstraps and adelies we saw later as we progressed further south. There are no trees on the Falklands, only tussock grass; and I was amazed that nearly every front yard had a garden (the stores do not sell fresh vegetables). There were also lots of sheep and the wind blew constantly.

The trip was a bird watcher's paradise. If you weren't a "birder" when you began, you were certainly a convert by the end of the trip. There were skuas, oyster catchers, nesting black browed albatross, upland geese, kelp gulls, pintado petrels, the flightless steamer duck, falcons, johnny rooks, prions, sooty shearwaters, cape pigeons giant petrels, caracaras and cormorants.

From the Falklands we headed across the Drake Passage, crossing the Antarctic convergence. Here the water temperature changes drastically, marking the divide between the major physical and biological zones of the ocean world—the dividing point between the sub-Antarctic and the Antarctic. We then went on to Elephant Island in the western section of the Scotia Arc in the South Shetlands.

Here we became the first passenger ship group *ever* to land at Point Wild, the spot that served as a refuge for Ernest Shackleton's men after the loss of his ship—*Endurance*—in the Weddell Sea ice pack.

From fifth or sixth grade history, I vaguely recalled Amundsen's trek to the Pole and Robert Scott's death in the attempt, but never had I heard of Shackleton. There were times, however, later, after I got to seminary, when I was grateful I had, and that I'd been to Antarctica. Whenever I was tempted to get discouraged or "down" or homesick—holed up alone in my apartment—on days when I couldn't stand to read another chapter of Eusebius, or write another paper, I would look back and remember Elephant Island, not to mention Shackleton's unparalleled voyage to South Georgia. Things would then fall quickly into proper perspective. I would take a warm bath, cook a good meal, look at my lovely view of the Texas State Capitol, snuggle up with a book and a cup of hot tea and thank God for all my blessings.

Shackleton first attempted to reach the South Pole in January, 1909, but was forced to turn back within 97 nautical miles from his destination. There was a shrieking blizzard, and concern for his men, as well as lack of food, forced him to give up. But in 1913, after the South Pole had been conquered by Scott and Amundsen, he got backing to undertake "the greatest Polar journey ever attempted."[9] He planned to walk 1800 miles across the continent, cutting through the South Pole to link up with a group from the Ross Sea at the top of the Beardmore Glacier. Nine hundred miles of this trek was to be across a wilderness area never before explored. Unfortunately, this plan was never realized because in early January, 1913, his ship—*Endurance*—got trapped in the ice. By late January, it was frozen in. Then, on May 1, the sun went down and Shackleton and his men were stuck with seventy days of Antarctic winter.

By July, the ice finally began to break up; however, as it did, the currents and wind created pressure waves of sea ice that buckled the ship's hull. It was crushed beyond hope and the men were forced to take off what supplies and lifeboats they could salvage and retreat to the ice floes. From July until October, they remained on the ice, moving from one floe to another with what they could drag as the ice changed position, split apart, or was crushed by other ice. His first plan was to walk to Paulet Island 350 miles away where he knew there was a small hut and cache of food. But conditions forced him to abandon this idea. Eventually, after months on the ice floes, drifting and moving about, at the mercy of the cracking ice, killer whales and howling winds, he and his men were able to get to Elephant Island in April of the following year. Two of the ship's life-boats were salvaged;

and these they managed to haul with them on sleds. But by then, many of their supplies had been lost or used up.

Shackleton knew no one would find them, so he had to go for help. He took one of the boats with five men and left the other twenty-two men there, promising he would return. This was on April 24. There was really no other choice since the alternative was either freezing or starving to death.

I came off a warm ship with warm feet, good water-proof boots, thick socks, heavy thermal jacket, pants, hat, warm gloves, and survival gear. I knew I would be going back to a hot meal and a hot shower. Standing on that island in the howling wind, looking at that desolate god-forsaken cold place, I could not begin to imagine what those men must have gone through. They remained there for one hundred and five days huddled under the other lifeboat—now their home—hoping Shackleton would return. What an incredible amount of faith they must have had. What perseverance under such trying conditions. And what courage Shackleton had even to attempt what he did.

After all he and his men had gone through up to then, the tale of his desperate journey to South Georgia Island for help is even more remarkable. There were giant waves, one that went over their boat; salt water destroyed most of the food and it was so cold that the salt water froze continuously to the boat which necessitated having to chop it away with axes. They had to deal with fermenting sleeping bags, frostbite, howling blizzards, icebergs, and a hurricane. In an open boat in that hostile environment, they sailed eight hundred miles to South Georgia, by then out of water and food, having to make their way through a jagged reef in order to land. If they had navigated wrong, or missed landfall in the heavy east to west current, they would have swept by, unable to get back. They finally landed at a place called King Haakon Bay, then had to climb seventeen miles through deep snow over a mountain range and glacier in order to get to the whaling station on the other side. By then, two of the men were too sick and weak to continue, so Shackleton left one to take care of them and took the other two with him.

By then (now August), his men on Elephant Island were running out of food. They were reduced to digging up discarded seal bones and cooking them in sea water. When Shackleton reached the whaling station, the people in South Georgia had difficulty believing his story. No one previously had ever survived such a harrowing trip.

The day after he arrived in South Georgia, however, Shackleton sailed on a Norwegian whaler to return to his men. Sixty miles from the island, the pack ice stopped them. So he returned to the Falklands where the Uruguayan government loaned him a trawler. But he was still unable to get through. In Punta Arenas, he chartered a schooner. One hundred miles north of the island, the engine broke down. The fourth try, the Chilean government loaned him a steamer. After one hundred and five days, he finally made it and saved every one of his men.[10]

To really appreciate those early explorers and what they accomplished, one has to see for oneself. I was there in the "summer" when the sun was up most of the time. I can't begin to imagine what it must be like in the winter, in the sub zero temperatures, in the dark. When I was there, the sun did not set until 11 p.m., then rose about 3 a.m.. Our average daily temperatures were usually in the 10's to 30's—not cold at all with modern gear. We saw abandoned huts with food and equipment still there, dating back to the early 1900's, still sitting on the shelves, preserved, where long now dead and frozen explorers had left it. Those huts were holy places, shrines to the courageous people who risked their lives to explore that unknown continent. Antarctica is still the world's last true wilderness.

I had somehow always thought of Antarctica as being a flat wasteland, but it is anything but that. It is the highest of the seven continents, with an average altitude above sea level of 6800 feet. Compare that with North America's 2362 feet. The scenery is spectacular, mountains rising straight out of the sea in some areas to a height of 5,000 feet. The wide, stormy waters of the southern oceans are what separate it from the other continents and these provide an uninterrupted corridor for the circumpolar winds. Navigating through the icebergs is indescribable. Gigantic tabular bergs are produced from the Ross, Weddell and Amery Ice barriers which move down from the inland ice sheet and constantly calve off along the coasts. Although we did not see it, I was told the Ross Ice Shelf is larger than Spain.

But we did get to land on the continent at Neko Harbor in Andvord Bay, midst many seals and penguins, and in deference to arch football rival—the University of California at Berkeley—President Donald Kennedy of Stanford who was on the trip, unfurled a banner that said "Beat Cal."

We also made landings at Danko Island, King George Island and Port Lockroy, and at Deception—a volcanic island—we climbed the cliffs above Whaler's Bay, then went on to Telefon Bay and walked around a huge caldera. We also visited the various research stations—the American one at Palmer Island as well as the Chilean, Brazilian, Chinese and Polish stations. The Russians also had one, but they kept to themselves.

We were grateful for our heavy boots as we walked midst hundreds of penguins who were often squabbling and stealing rocks and pebbles from one another's nests.

My most unforgettable experience was on the way home, coming back through the Drake passage on the way to Cabo de Hornos. The seas were extremely rough with seventy knot winds so I decided the ocean waters were worth a picture. I groped my way to the top deck and had just pulled my camera out when the front of the bow pitched forward almost vertically. I looked down first into the trough of the sea, then up to see an enormous wave coming over the ship. I barely had time to shove the camera under my jacket, then cling for dear life to a nearby pole as tons of ice water plummeted over me. The boat finally righted itself leaving me half frozen and looking like a drowned rat. It was truly a miracle I was not washed overboard.

Having gotten in my trip to Antarctica, I made arrangements the fall of 1987 to have the surgery done on my foot. It was a simple out-patient procedure: a bunionectomy. The doctor told me I should be quiet, keep my leg elevated, and "try not to move about much afterwards." I followed his advice to the letter which landed me back in the hospital with phlebitis because I hadn't moved around *enough*. I finally got back home and recovered properly but not before spending a few more days in bed.

It was on one of those days, while looking at the ceiling, letting my thoughts wander, I found myself thinking about Mr. Holmes a'Court—the man who had raided Weeks Petroleum. We were still receiving various newspaper clippings and letters from people in Australia. He was also mentioned now and again in the *Wall Street Journal* or *Forbes* magazine; so we knew he was still expanding, taking over more companies, enlarging his empire.

Despite the fact that I detested what corporate raiders were doing to companies and, by extension, to many who worked for them (not to mention the stripping off of good assets and the destroying of company morale), I had Mr. Holmes a'Court to thank for extricating us from the life we had inadvertently landed in. And I had to admire the way he operated. He did his homework well, in addition to which he and several of his close associates managed to run a billion dollar empire practically by themselves.

Although he was a native of South Africa, he had become an Australian citizen; So after his raid on Weeks Petroleum, I told him at a meeting in his corporate office in New York City that I wanted him to know I felt no animosity towards him, for what he had done. I also added: "Australia has been very good to us ... to our whole family ... we have always appreciated the income we have received from 'down under'." There was no point in being bitter.

But we couldn't help but be aware of his activities, if only from a distance. Too, he still owed us a hefty bundle of money; and though we had no control over the situation, it was incumbent upon us to keep informed. But the more I read about him, the more unsettled I became. Much of his early fortune had been made due to his remarkable business acumen in acquiring poorly performing companies, then turning them into solid profit makers. Of late, however, he'd been involved in a series of unsuccessful, but highly profitable, takeover bids. He would run up the price of a stock, then bail out.

The year before he raided us, he'd made a bid for BHP—a blue chip, and one of the largest companies in Australia. Not only was BHP invested in the Northwest Shelf project and the Port Kembla Steelworks, but they also had foreign operations such as the giant Escondido mine in the Atacama Desert of Chile. He now had 28% of the parent company. And he was also dueling with Mr. Rupert Murdoch over the *Herald* and *Weekly Times* group in the country's media shakeout. I recalled his responses from an article I had read: "We begin with a policy of low risk. I like to know that if I wake up tomorrow and find it is September, 1929, I'm comfortable."[11] What he was doing didn't seem like low risk to me. The more I thought about his remark, the more disturbed I became. His earlier business dealings had all been on solid ground. Now, he was in with the *really big boys,* leveraging more and more of his empire to acquire more and more companies. Sharks are known at times to eat one another; and I began to wonder to myself if sharks might not be circling him. These international financiers—raiders, if you will—were really money-grubbing pirates, gobbling up smaller companies, stripping assets, selling off what didn't attract them. In most instances, they did not create wealth. They only destroyed people's jobs and companies in which they often had no knowledge or real interest. And not only did Mr. Holmes a'Court still owe us money; we were not even getting interest on it. I couldn't forget his comment about the crash of 1929.

Also, in my experience, the oil business has always been cyclical. And just then, among other things, "Homac" was depending quite a bit on his revenue stream from Weeks Australia Ltd. My intuition told me he was heading for trouble.

I hobbled out of bed and wrote him a letter. I can't remember everything I said now, but I do recall ending it with the admonition that "the sun is always largest just before it sets." And how right I was. But I didn't fully realize at the time how prophetic my statement would prove to be. With the trip and the surgery behind me, however, I was at last able to turn my energies towards seminary.

# 17

# BISHOP DAVID RICHARDS

Bishop Richards was—still is—my spiritual director. The role of a director is to help others discern those inner movements that are of God, as opposed to influences that are from one's self or others. He's a gracious, spiritual man who exudes compassion and understanding. He's tough too. And he's always had an unusual effect upon me.

The first time I saw him, he had come to St. Andrew's one Sunday to substitute. I did not speak with the Bishop, only saw him from across the church and heard him say a few words. But there was something about him—an aura, you might call it—that left me wishing I could know him better. Strangely, something intuitive inside of me whispered: "Someday you will."[12]

I didn't see him again until years later, this only because I was told I had to fill out a form which the Diocese sent to all prospective postulants. It required we list our spiritual director. I didn't have one, but it was then I recalled Bishop Richards. So I made an appointment to see him. He was even taller and bigger than I had remembered him to be.

"Why did you come to me?" he asked.

I thought for a bit. I could hardly say "Because of an aura about you." I should have said "Because I need a spiritual director." But I was so unnerved, I could only blurt out "Because I need a name to put on my form." He looked at me quietly and I could tell he was not at all pleased with my response; nevertheless, he agreed to take me on as his directee.

From that moment, and for years following, whenever I visited his office, I used to feel I were walking in to see God.[13] I would always have planned in advance what I was going to say, but as soon as I'd get into his office, under his scrutiny, my thoughts would all disappear and I would talk about things I never intended to discuss. All my defenses would crumble and I'd find myself talking about things I scarcely recognized at first. Being with him was like having the sun come out on a cold day. His demeanor was always warm and inviting and more than once I ended up in puddles of tears talking about things I'd never thought about discussing with anyone else.

My last visit before leaving to go to seminary, he asked how I was getting along. "I'm still trying to read the Propers," I said. (Propers were specific liturgical readings we were expected to read on a daily basis.) I wasn't sure I should tell him more, but finally added: "The characters in the Bible have always struck me as being frozen in time ... like some vast mosaic.... the kind you see in Byzantine churches ... only they don't seem like that anymore. I mean ... they're beginning to seem like real people almost." He'd just sat there quietly, waiting for me to continue. Then I told him I'd never particularly associated the Bible with love.

"Why not?" he asked.

I wasn't sure. "Maybe I've never related it to loving associations," I finally said.

The Bible had to do with religion. And religion was an awful subject to discuss. It had always made me think of the Mormons. Or maybe the Crusades. Besides, the Bible was not one of those books my parents had kept handy around the house. Certainly no one had ever read it to me. Except once, my sister had read some stories to me from the Bible story book mother had given to us, but that ended when we got to the story about Abraham taking his son to be sacrificed. We didn't understand in the larger picture that it related to obedience, so my sister decided for both of us that we didn't want that kind of God, and never opened the book again. Poetry, we both knew, held all the answers to life. Why else did our mother read Shelley, Keats and Byron? Or quote Chaucer to us in Middle English? Or talk so much about Shakespeare and Tennyson?

But even with that, I knew the Bible held some importance in our lives. I knew my parents respected it; I knew my grandmother had read it at night before going to bed. Many of our family sayings had come from the Bible. And certainly I'd been exposed to it a little during the years I'd been in Sunday School in Maracaibo. I thought about Miss Sloat for a moment. But no. That was all behind me. So why was I so uncomfortable?

Bishop Richard always just sat there. Shining.

Other stuff tumbled out I've forgotten now. Stuff I'd never much mentioned. But I know I didn't tell him about my grandmother. She had always seemed so different to me. And associating the Bible with her did nothing to help my understanding of it. When I was four though, I could recall her digging a penny out of the little coin purse she carried in her pocket and giving it to me when she saw me helping my mother dust. That was very special because in those days a penny could buy me six caramels at the little store near our home; and as I grew older, I came to associate grandmother with baked chicken and mashed potatoes, flowers, raspberries and homemade root beer; so I certainly should have made the leap from questioning to love. But I'm not sure I ever did. Those original impressions stuck. She was old, with a very wrinkled face and hands. She spoke Swedish, a language I could not understand. And she was someone who could take a chicken and twist its neck or chop its head off before plucking. Once, also when I was four, she chopped the head off a chicken at the chopping block, near where I'd been watching. The hen's headless body had gotten away and run wildly about, flopping in my direction, spurting blood as it came. It frightened and left me horrified.

Also, perhaps subconsciously, I was not sure I could depend on my grandmother. I have no recollection of the occasion, but I heard mother tell the story many times about how grandmother had taken care of me one day shortly after we had moved back to Utah from Argentina. I was only two years old at the time and what little language I knew was a mixture of English and Spanish. Most of the day spent with my grandmother, I apparently kept asking for *agua*. But grandmother did not know that *agua* was another name for "water," so by the time my mother returned, I was crying hysterically for *agua, agua*.

Gradually I came to understand what a wonderfully honest, hardworking, thrifty, yet generous person my grandmother was. But I was too young at that time to appreciate her. I am reminded now I always pick up pennies when I see them. I view pennies as good luck, angels in a way, reminding me that God is there, looking out for me, taking care of me. And my very first penny stems from my grandmother.

As I look back now on it all, especially on my life in Miami and my trek to seminary, I know it was God who sent me to Bishop Richards. Only it didn't hit me until much later why our paths crossed. A lot more water still had to go under the bridge.

# 18

# PRAYER EXPERIENCE

At first, my prayer life, after going to Bishop Richards, which of course was tied to my prayers and Bible reading, began to confound me. I might say it even got me into trouble. Not with others, but with my *self* and the way I began to view things. What really perplexed me was something I did in my capacity as a trustee of the University of Miami. Before I get to that, however, I must mention Bishop Richards once more.

The previous summer he had given me three pages entitled: "Approaching Spiritual Direction." Over a three to four month period, I was to reflect on four themes he listed, as well as think over ways wherein I genuinely experienced God. I was also to identify several major values in my life that seemed to me to be rooted in spirituality. I tried hard to work on this over the summer although I was pretty clueless as to what it all meant, but eventually got to a point where I felt I had at least brushed the surface of the four themes, these being reflections where I felt I *needed* Christ in my life, distinguishing between needing and wanting and trying to discern how I *wanted* Him in my life. Then, on the basis of needs and wants, I was to clarify within myself what it was for me to *invite* Christ into my life. And finally, I was to reflect on what it meant to *welcome* Christ into my life.

For any would-be Christian who thinks that's easy, I can only suggest they try it. He said I was to explore the overtones of each word. Some aspects would be immediately evident, but I was to keep pressing more and more deeply into the Word, seeking to enrich my understanding of its relationship to Christ and myself.

I floundered around, wondering if I were really doing any of these exercises properly, felt at one point I might even be making progress until one day, realized I was just butting my head up against a wall. I wasn't going anywhere; my prayers weren't going anywhere either. This effort was all a colossal waste of time. I even had to admit I was spiritually deader than I could imagine a de-winged angel would feel stuck in a tar bog.

Still, I kept reading the Propers for the Daily Office each morning and tried to follow Bishop Richard's suggestions. Then a strange thing happened. The Biblical characters began to come alive in a way I'd never thought of them before. They began to seem almost *real*, and at some point, I began to view my childhood and things about me from a different perspective. Though I couldn't explain how, I had the feeling that things inside me were being rearranged.

Also, from the various tests required as part of pre-seminary orientation, I knew (though I could not understand why) that I was not always in sync emotionally and intellectually; and the Graduate Record Exams reinforced what I also knew: I was more intuitive at times than analytical. So as part of my spiritual discipline, I earnestly began to ask God to help me line up my emotions and intellect. And that takes me back to what I wanted to mention.

Before resigning to go to seminary, I had been a trustee at the University of Miami for nearly five years. Much of this time had been spent on the Academic Affairs Committee. Among other things, we were responsible for reading the files of professors coming up for tenure. These included recommendations on reappointment and promotion and took into consideration their teaching evaluations by students and peers, as well as letters attached from well-known persons in their fields who often analyzed and critiqued their publications. Files on the faculty always included educational background, employment history, published papers and books, awards and grants, conferences attended and manuscripts in progress.

Trustees of many institutions are not this involved in the tenure process. I guess they assume administration is doing a satisfactory job and give tenure decisions a rubber stamp. But this is not always the case at the University of Miami.

In the process of trying to tighten up my spiritual life and in praying for various people, one situation kept coming back into my thoughts that disturbed me. This concerned a professor denied tenure, a situation (from the evidence at least presented to the committee) I did not find fair. I brought this to the attention of the committee chairman and gave him my thoughts on the subject. I also intended to speak to the matter at our Academic Affairs meeting. It happened, however, that the day the meeting was scheduled, I had another appointment that could not be changed and had to leave early. When I later was able to return, this particular case had already been discussed and the tenure denial stood.

Trustees, besides being expected to give money, I realized, were given selective information from which they were expected to make large, important decisions relating to the overall health of the University. The "nitty gritty" details were left to administration. And that's as it should be. Trustees are not supposed to be bothered with the every day running of an institution. But I was used to being more involved. I wanted to be in the middle of the action. When I heard about something on the campus that needed fixing, I wanted to see it fixed. If something was wrong, I wanted to put it right. If I heard a student was in trouble, I wanted to help. But I knew this was not the role expected of me. Also, the old boy network was so strong and overpowering at times, I was afraid to open my mouth. When I did come up with a good idea, I was almost afraid to express myself and what should have been a good experience for me was not that at all. And I couldn't explain it. Finally, I resigned from all but Academic Affairs and the Ad Hoc Committee for Black Students.

Part of my discomfort I know now was the result of my own hesitancy in coming to grips with my vocation, but it was also a result of something I had not begun to recognize, each of which was affecting the other. After leaving the board, I went one last time to visit a university women's group where I had been a member. During the meeting, one of the women, understandably upset, mentioned the fact that her husband had been denied tenure. Of course, I already knew, because this was the same decision I had questioned earlier.

It was the following morning, while trying to pray, that this all came to the surface for me. There was no vision certainly, no voice (unless you can call it my inner voice), but God's presence was there telling me here, in this instance, I might make a difference. Perhaps I could help this family. I can't explain it. I can only say I was overpowered with a tremendous sense of joy and recalled one of the letters in the professor's file had been critical because he had not brought much funding to the University. But this had been from a person not living in Miami who had no idea of the deplorable conditions of the labs.

Early on, in my role as trustee, I had acquainted myself with the various schools within the University and I well recall the day the former Dean of Arts and Sciences had shown me around and said: "Marta, it's almost impossible for our professors to get research grants in this department, the working conditions are so deplorable. Would-be donors come, take one look at the building and refuse to grant the funds. The morale here is terrible."

It was not hard to see what the Dean meant. It was raining that day. After dodging drips from leaky roofs and walking around buckets half filled with water, I tried to open one of the doors into a lab. The door came off one of its upper hinges and fell on us. "The mystery," the Dean told me, as he stood holding the door, "is why the city of Coral Gables has not condemned this structure."

I called a friend who let the professor know an anonymous donor wished to make a gift to his research program; but I imposed the condition that the professor be the one to decide where the money would be spent. Indirectly, this meant the University would have to consider this in his tenure decision. I understood from things his wife had said, he had appealed and it was now up for review. What I hoped for was to get the president's attention so he would be forced to revisit the professor's file. I guess I hoped that my intuitive feelings would be borne out by facts that would eventually surface. I knew the president and provost would not recommend tenure if the professor were not tenure material, but I also knew them to be fair people, who, once their attention had been captured, would investigate and see to it that the professor be given a proper hearing. In retrospect, I should have gone to the president directly, but by then, I was no longer an acting trustee. So my main concern was fair treatment for the professor. There was no question in my mind that I was doing the right thing and I felt good about it all—until the next day.

While trying to pray, my rational, analytical faculties came into play and part of me began to accuse another part of me of trying to play God. I dismissed that. It wasn't true. With God's grace, I'd been trying to *help*. I hoped so anyway. But having been a trustee, I knew this situation posed a dilemma for the University. The administration needed funding badly for some of the other labs, and maybe other research had priority just then.

Too, the politics that week, much that had been going on between some of the faculty and the provost, had not been very positive. I knew my action would not make the provost's job any easier. Also, the dollars and cents of tenure for a professor meant any other professor the provost might have in mind to bring in could be affected. Tenured professors stay until retirement and cannot be dismissed or replaced, except for reasons of moral turpitude, incompetence or financial exigency. And there was the president too. I admired and respected him, and knew how much he was in need of unrestricted funds. If he determined who was making this offer, he could see this as a personal betrayal of his goals.

So I promptly began to feel guilty, agonizing over all the pros and cons of what my good deed might set in motion. I was never so miserable in my life; had to admit, finally, if only to myself, perhaps I had jumped in where only angels fear to tread. I began to worry that the Dean or Provost would assume I was the anonymous donor and wonder why I was meddling on their turf. A weight like a heavy, black cloud descended upon me. Psalm 30 best expressed it to me:

*While I felt secure, I said, "I shall never be disturbed.*

> *You, Lord, with your favor, made me as strong as the mountains.*
> *Then you hid your face, and I was filled with fear."*

For a while, I was afraid I might run into the president; then, for awhile, I was afraid I wouldn't! I wanted in the worst way to explain my actions, to straighten out any possible misunderstandings that could arise if he suspected my involvement, especially since I would be leaving soon; but I wasn't sure how to go about it. On one occasion, I had to call him about something that concerned the Rosenstiel School, but it was all business. There was no way to hint at what was going on inside of me. I knew too, even if he suspected, he would be too gracious to bring it up. In my stress, my mind began to visualize running into him and figuring out what I could say if I did. Soon, the University, the president and his family, the professor and his family, and the provost (I didn't know his family) began to fill up my prayer life. I scarcely slept for a week, dreaming when I did of running into the president and having him ask me unexpectedly: "Marta, do you know Dr._____?" There would be a long pause and I would say "I can't say I know him exactly, but I've met him." There would be another long pause, then I'd say: "Why do you ask?" And he'd look at me with a deep, honest expression and there would be another long pause. And suddenly I'd wake up and discover it was a dream and I'd wish he were there so I could tell him why I'd done it.

With the psalmist, I too found myself asking:

> *"Why are you so full of heaviness, O my soul?*
> *And why are you so disquieted within me?"*

But I knew also that I had to put my trust in God,

> *"for I will yet give thanks to him,*
> *who is the help of my countenance ..."*

Through all this, I came to realize I cared about that young professor and his family, as well as the university. And in the process, had to admit I had been out of line, that God was showing me very clearly where my intuitive and my rational selves were not at all in sync. I had no way of knowing what transpired at the university. But I know what transpired within me. God answered my prayers—in spades! In retrospect too, He was trying to get me to slow down and take a look at other things just then in my life. Things which badly needed attention.

I only mention my experience with the university because it shows how unsettling prayer can be. One has to be willing (psychologically and spiritually) to go out on a limb at times, not knowing whether it might break, and if and when it does, trusting God will be there to hold and support us. One learns a great deal about oneself during these confrontations. But one can also learn that God eventually leads us out of the pit with a better understanding of who we are and what He wants us to be. In Urban T. Holmes' book, *Spirituality for Ministry*, he says: "A fundamental measure for evaluating genuine movement in the spiritual life is the presence of strong, *mixed* emotions—joy and horror, fascination and fear, delight and desolation—which are typical of the inner wilderness."[14]

At that point, as a possible future priest of the Episcopal Church, I was just beginning to understand about the inner wilderness. I didn't like it at all. At the same time, however, I found I could not wait to embrace it.

Holmes' book also quotes from Edward Hays, a Roman Catholic spiritual guide: "Among the numerous duties of a disciple, two are essential: to embrace a discipline in life not only in theory, but also in daily practice, and to fall in love with death!"[15] A rather tall order if one takes being a disciple seriously. But once I'd caught a glimpse of what it could mean, I came to realize, it was the one thing in life truly worthwhile.

# PART III

# 19

# PREPARING FOR SEMINARY

I finally got through all the required preliminary hoops and knew I would be leaving for school the summer of 1988. By then, the Rt. Rev. Calvin O. Schofield, Jr. had been diocesan bishop for nine years. Of a possible ten, he offered me a list of five seminary choices, so I visited one in Virginia when they held an open house for prospective students. It seemed like a nice place, so while there, asked to be interviewed. When they accepted me, I decided that's where I would go.

After returning my deposit and other required forms and papers, the school sent me information about living in Virginia. I would be subject to taxes which raised a red flag for me. This was because Mr. Holmes a'Court was scheduled to pay back Austin and me for our shares he now controlled, and I would be in Virginia when this took place. I didn't want the State of Virginia taxing me. This would no doubt be the largest financial transaction of my life. It did not seem fair the state of Virginia could take part of it away. We were already paying what I thought were exorbitant taxes to the federal government. Although the seminary responded that I would not be considered a legal resident for major tax purposes, I felt it incumbent upon me to check further. After more investigation, one of our tax people said "just to be on the safe side, we suggest you find another seminary."

By then, it was late spring and I was scheduled to be in school in just a few months. I wasn't sure what to do. The Bishop, however, told me there was a seminary in Texas, one he had not included on the list. Like Florida, the state of Texas did not have state income tax.

"I've met the Dean at ETSS,"[16] he told me. "Let me call and see if there are any openings." There were. The Dean called me personally and invited me for an interview; so I flew to Austin, Texas. Three professors interviewed me and I was accepted.

"Maybe God works through the tax laws," the Dean joked.

As it turned out for ETSS, I think perhaps God did.

Once the seminary problem was resolved, Austin and I made plans to go to Utah. But there were so many things to bring closure on first. Besides having to meet all the diocesan requirements, I had to prepare for our daughter Leslie's April wedding, house guests, an Episcopal Church Women's luncheon and several other social events I'd been committed to doing. When that was all accomplished, I was exhausted. Not only that, I was unsettled and did not understand why. My prayer discipline was certainly improving, but accompanying that was the concomitant feeling that maybe I wouldn't make it. After all, I'd been out of school—*serious* school—for thirty-seven years, and was beginning to get cold feet.

We were also still receiving and reading various clippings and articles relating to Mr. Holmes a'Court. Oil prices had begun to drop the previous year, falling from $34 to $28 a barrel. Six months after the slide in oil prices began, west Texas intermediate crude eventually hit a low of $10.25.[17] Of course, the oil business world-wide was affected and this included Mr. Holmes a'Court.[18]

After raiding Weeks Petroleum, he had been involved in a great many hostile takeover games and had by then tried five times to gain control of BHP (Broken Hill Proprietary)—the largest steel and resource company in Australia. At one point, he managed to acquire 30% of it. But BHP foiled his raid with a cross holding arrangement, a deal wherein it and Elders—a brewer and farming concern—bought 20% of each other.

According to the financial press, "Homac" had a credit line of $2 billion in February, 1986. Now, in 1988, with oil prices falling, he was cash short. As I had unwittingly predicted, the sharks began to move in. By then, he owned Australian newspapers, radios and TV stations, transportation, entertainment and oil and gas exploration interests. But, like the proverbial house of cards, it began to tumble. From having his Bell Group listed as being worth $4.55 billion Australian (a little under $4 billion American) at its peak, Mr. Holmes a'Court now had to start selling off holdings in order to meet his commitments. Mr. Bond, of Bond Corporation Holdings, worth some $5 billion Australian in June, 1988, began to circle with the sharks. By July of that summer he managed to purchase in excess of 50% of the shares in the Bell Group. This gave him control of "Homac's" company. So now we had to deal with another shark. Would Mr. Bond honor the commitment inherited through Mr. Holmes a'Court? We hoped so. Other than reminding him through the usual legal channels, there wasn't a great deal more at that point we could do. So I tried hard to focus on seminary.

In order to establish some kind of routine, I began to go through eight of the eighteen books that had been suggested for pre-seminary reading. By early summer, my days resembled a catalogue of prayers, exercises and books to read.

I also heard about the professor. My friend from Miami called me in Utah. "The professor's tenure was denied," he said. My first reaction was relief. At least the suspense was over. But that was followed by a deep sense of sadness for the professor and his family. For a while, I prayed for them; and for Tad Foote and the provost as well. They all just kept showing up in my prayers. I think I still wanted to justify myself to someone, for what I had done. And why.

Several weeks later, I received a letter from the professor's wife. I had asked her to let me know the outcome of her husband's tenure review. She may have guessed I put up the money for his research, but this was never mentioned. But it was interesting hearing things from the faculty side. I can't go in to more detail, but suffice to say, one of her last comments to me was: "Someday I think I should like to write a book. It will be a mystery. And I might call it: *Who Killed the Provost?*"

By the end of the summer, I was getting bored, really bored with the Psalms. I'd told Bishop Richards once I loved them; but after spending every morning with them for over four months, some were beginning to irritate me. Those of praise, of course, I liked. But it was all those about the oppressive and wicked enemy that I didn't care for. I couldn't decide if they referred to Israel's enemies or one's inner self. And those calling for revenge bothered me too. Despite my two years in the Theological Education Program, I still had very little background in Biblical history.

In my Bible reading too, I was disturbed how the Israelites—the people of Yahweh—could march into Canaan and take over the land, killing all kinds in the process. They seemed to justify it by saying Yahweh said it was theirs as long as they were faithful to the law given to them by Moses.[19] Of course, this was all written some 600 years after the event, and the redactors were writing it to explain God's relationship to his chosen people. But I didn't know that. I just knew it didn't seem right. And perhaps I was relating the idea of being "chosen" to what the Mormons believed they were. It's just that some things were historically accurate and some were not. My educational background had been too scholarly to gloss over all the inconsistencies that kept turning up. Later, once introduced to the three versions of the creation stories, this explained some things, but at that point in my journey, I didn't know about the Judean,

Ephraimite and Priestly literary traditions in Genesis. So I read, and prayed and struggled through the summer, still trying to hold on to the phrase from my previous life in academia: "With all thy getting, get thy understanding."

As the time drew near for me to leave for Texas, Austin also began making life difficult. Certainly he wasn't supportive. At times, I felt he was taking every opportunity to lambaste religion. He never came outright and said I was stupid, but the inference was always there. After thirty-seven years of supporting him in all the things he'd wanted to do, I couldn't help be a bit miffed. By then, I was having second thoughts myself about going and really needed a cheering section. But Austin was beginning to equate me and the church with the Iranian fundamentalists, the Catholics and Protestants fighting in Ireland, the Tammy Baker scandal, the Jonestown people who drank poisoned Kool-Aid, along with every other lunatic group he could think of. Utah is also a state which has been widely influenced both for good and bad by the predominance of one religious faith and Austin was only too happy to point out the negatives of all this. It seemed to me we were always comparing apples and oranges. Austin prided himself on his scientific approach to everything. But I could never seem to get across that one cannot approach faith in this manner. Science deals with provable facts, experiments that can be set up and repeated, theories that can be tested. At best, religion deals with faith and relationships. And how can these be put in a test tube?

I had to agree with him on much of what he said, but also did try to point out that I found much of these situations he brought up to be a *lack* of good religion, not religion per se. I could also see he was going through his own personal adjustment to my decision to go, so tried to brush off most of it. Still, I could not help but take some of it personally. Years later, I heard a clergyman say that some of his congregation were "Four years old, married, with a beard," the implication being they had never progressed far in their spirituality. In dismissing the religion of their youth, they had ended up with a neurosis of their spiritual worlds because all they wanted to do was argue over beliefs.[20] That described Austin just then, but I wasn't perceptive enough to see it. I also was ignoring something seriously affecting our relationship that I should have been paying more attention to and hadn't.

The rest of the family wasn't very supportive either. At first, my mother mostly ignored what I was doing. Being chronologically gifted (by then she was 91), she had her own problems. I think mainly she was embarrassed one of her daughters had chosen to do (at least in her eyes) such an unusual thing. My sister was more to the point: "Why are you going into a dying profession?" she asked.

And my children, for the most part, shrugged it all off. To them, their mother was just "doing her thing."

In spite of this, and before school began, I had a good time in Utah playing golf, puttering about on my valley property and enjoying the mountains and raspberries. At times, I didn't want to think about giving up any of it. Still, I knew I would be going to Texas and that I wasn't going to change my mind, not anymore than Austin was going to change his mind suddenly and embrace golf or the church! But the thought of backing out crossed my mind occasionally. And paradoxically, the idea of becoming an ordained priest ceased to interest me at some point. By then, I had come to agree with the words of Joseph Campbell that it wasn't the destination, but the quality of one's journey that really mattered.

On June 17, 1988, the contractor hired by the Utah Department of Transportation knocked down the old home my grandfather had built for my grandmother's parents. With it went the oldest visible remaining signs of one hundred and thirty-six years of my family's history in Utah. One minute it was there; a few hours later it was a pile of rubble fifteen feet high, waiting to be scooped into waiting trucks and hauled to the dump. This section of the Newman valley property was condemned, all for the sake of progress for a freeway off-ramp. They didn't try to save anything. They just moved in with a bulldozer and ran over the fence, the gate, the trees, the grape arbor, the pond I'd put in several summers before, the plums, and the old house and all the memories I'd had from that property as a child. The land had belonged to my blind uncle who died intestate, so I purchased it after the neighbors refused to allow the first buyer in line to have a zoning change for a wedding chapel. The land adjoined a piece of property I already owned next to it, close to my sister's place, also part of the original family homestead secured by a deed signed by Ulysses S. Grant. I bought my uncle's additional land in order to keep it in the family, and also to be a buffer in the event we ever decided to build a home there.

It was that same day at Snowbird, after promising me weeks earlier he would quit, I discovered Austin was back to drinking. Quite by accident, while vacuuming, I heard some glass clink when moving his suitcase. Inside were one empty and two full bottles of vodka. In my heart, I should have known, but I always liked to think the best of him. I knew I'd been overlooking little things I should have been paying more attention to.

Drinkers can be very sneaky. It can be devastating to live with one. I reacted in I guess the way most spouses react when they feel betrayed or let down. I got really angry. Then I cried. Then I got angry again. Finally, I sat down and tried to pray about it. As a future priest, I suppose I should have tried to pray first, but I couldn't. I felt more like throwing the bottles out the window, or at him. In many respects, just then, I felt my marriage was that pile of rubble I'd seen earlier, waiting to be hauled to the dump.

After some deliberation, I calmed down enough to put the vodka in the cabinet above the stove. I thought about pouring it all down the sink, but knew he'd just go out and buy more. And I hated to waste things, even alcohol. I could always clean the windows with it. What struck me at the time as being so ironic was that I had just the previous month sent a large contribution to *Informed Families* in Miami, so they could fight drug and alcohol abuse! I'd known all along Austin was a nicotine addict, but I'd been too focused on other things even to consider he might be addicted to alcohol. And not only that, I didn't have the foggiest notion how to deal with it. That's probably why denial had been the easier route.

I tried to tell myself that God was showing me how to understand problems that a lot of other people had, people whom I might someday be involved with in a parish, perhaps. "I'm just getting some experience that will help me get through seminary," I told myself.

But I was grateful Austin hadn't been there when I found the bottles and I did confront him with my findings when he returned, when I was more in control. I also told him I was working hard at having a good marriage and I expected the same from him.

"I don't see that having a little drink now and then can hurt anyone," he said.

"One little drink before dinner probably doesn't," I responded; "it's those *big* drinks before dinner.... and the ones before lunch, followed by the *bigger* drinks perhaps.... That's what worries me," I told him.

He promised me again he would cut down and probably stop all together. And the next week or so, he did. Like the fool that I was, I believed him and forgot the incident. More classic denial on my part.

The edges of summer began to fray finally and I knew it would soon be time to go. Already at the higher elevations, temperatures were slipping into the 40's, and varying shades and patches of orange were beginning to appear out of nowhere. With careful observation, we could see the soft shadows of yellow creeping into the stands of aspen that mingled midst the pines blanketing the slopes. As I packed, I couldn't help remember an anniversary card someone had sent us years before. It had been a picture of a frog on a lily pad catching flies, with the caption under saying "Time's fun when you're having flies." I wasn't a frog certainly. I didn't like flies; but I hoped I'd have some fun.

On my return to Miami, there was a note in my mail from a priest. Among other things, it said: *"My concern is that you may expect to be part of a Christian institution at seminary. I did, and only the intervention of a great professor kept me on my course. The pettiness and jealousy and the defensiveness and closed minds of the students drove me to say 'forget Christianity,' so expect the worst."*

Under other circumstances, I would have laughed this off. But I needed encouragement just then. I later offhandedly mentioned the letter to Bishop Richards and was relieved when he said: "I suppose if you go looking for that, you'll be able to find it. But what does that letter tell you about that priest?"

Despite his opposition to women priests, Bishop Duncan wrote me:

*I may not approve of the ordination of women to the priesthood, but I do approve of you. My opposition to women's ordination comes from the belief that the church has misused all three orders and that the Church is confused as to what it is trying to accomplish. This step further confuses the situation. You know how much I admire and respect you, that I'll support you right along."*

He gave me the name of a professor to look up when I arrived in Texas and told me he would be in touch with him, that he was happy for me. I know he meant it. For someone who had campaigned so against women's ordination and later again, against having women in the episcopate, I had to admire his ability to separate his relationships from his personal beliefs. I believe this is one of the marks of a good priest.[21] When I saw him several years later, I had occasion to ask: "Bishop Duncan, if you were still the bishop of this Diocese, and I were presenting myself to you for ordination, would you ordain me?"

"Considering it's you ... I'm not sure ... I'm sort of...." But we were interrupted at that point in the conversation and I never heard what he might have said. He didn't say "yes," but I didn't hear him say "no" either. Regardless, I liked the Bishop. I always felt I knew where I stood with him. And I liked to think because we'd played golf together, this had helped put us on an equal footing. Christianity is so much like golf. After hitting some bad shots or messing up, there's always another chance. That's when God's grace and forgiveness come into play. He helps you pick up your ball and start over at the next tee. And yes, Bishop Duncan came to my ordination. But it wasn't until five years later that he told me he'd come to terms with women in the priesthood. "I just didn't like the way it was done," he said, referring to the early irregular ordinations held in Philadelphia back in the 1970's before the vote to include them was passed. [22]

Before leaving Miami for Texas, I went once more to see Bishop Richards. He gave me the results of a test I had taken before going to Snowbird. It had to do with an inventory of values, something I guess the diocese required for future seminarians. This had been a long involved questionnaire, the results of which were supposed to provide insights into issues relating to personal direction and growth, career development, faith and ethical concerns. It also talked about time management priorities and asked questions which the taker was to reflect upon over a period of time. I took it with me in my suitcase on my drive to Texas and tried to review the entire contents the first night on the road. That, coupled with the stress of getting ready to leave, saying goodbye to my children and a husband I couldn't seem to understand anymore, plus the two days of steady driving alone, was too much to think about all at once; because the third day of driving through Louisiana and Texas (in dense fog and heavy rain), it's all I had to think about; and by the time I finally reached, Texas, I was mighty depressed. But it was then I recalled my complaints to Bishop Richards about the Psalms and how they were so irritating at times. I had specifically mentioned the 69th Psalm. "That's a good one to read when you're depressed," he'd told me. I hadn't realized how soon I would need it!

I was also reminded how, during other visits for spiritual direction, Bishop Richards had been helpful in explaining to me how someone with paranoia looks out and blames others for his or her problems, the idea being if *they* would change, everything would be all right with *me*; whereas metanoia is a looking within at oneself, with the idea that maybe there's something wrong here and that if *I* could change, then I would not see the world in the way that I do.

I eventually arrived safely in Austin, Texas; looked up some friends from the oil business days; got moved into an apartment overlooking the state capitol and told myself to be cheerful. I soon found another girl as lost as I was and invited her to go to a swim meet with me. Eventually the black cloud I'd felt under since my departure from home lifted, aided by something from Lawrence J. Crabb and Dana B. Allender's book—*Encouragement*. Among other things, it said: "During moments of deepest loneliness, abandon oneself to God, depend on Him to minister to us and this is where we shall meet God."[23]

# 20

# GETTING ADJUSTED

Although I had not envisioned anything in particular, still, seminary was not at all what I expected. That's because I only had past experiences of other schools to go by, and the Episcopal Theological Seminary of the Southwest was not like any of them.

I felt like a complete outsider the first few weeks. I didn't fit with the married students because my husband wasn't there. And I didn't fit with the single students because I was married. I couldn't seem to get a handle on much of anything. Too, after thirty-eight years out of serious school, all the unanswered questions I'd had buried for years began to surface. Havelock Ellis once said: "A person should not swallow more beliefs than he can digest."[24] I had filed away more beliefs than I could ever digest. Now, I was having to sort through them all, trying to digest only those that made sense. I was in a time warp in a way, jumping back and forth from the past to the present. For a while, I was quite sure there was no God and kept asking myself "What am I doing here in seminary anyway?" Then, I would alternately find myself trying to pray to a God I could believe in, or avoiding a God I did not, or at least the one I thought the seminary expected me to believe in. And although I could no longer recall how to set up the syllogism, I kept remembering from sophomore logic at Beloit how we had shown Anselm's argument for the existence of God to be fallacious. Many of these questions had never arisen during my TEE (Theological Education by Extension) experience with Father Masterman, I guess because those class meetings had never really reminded me of college.

At first, seminary seemed like a never ending quest for answers that never presented themselves. Like an early scene in Boris Pasternak's *Dr. Zhivago,* a woman—always out of reach—can only be glimpsed occasionally, because she is always disappearing in the crowd. That's the way seminary was. I would begin to get a handle on something, then it would all change, or disappear.

The seminary had what they called the "August Course"—a pre-school session for entering students to acquaint them with the rigors of seminary. This extended over a period of eleven days during which time we were to read Werner Jaeger's *Early Christianity and Greek Paideia,* George Steiner's *In Bluebeard's Castle,* and Jose Bonino Muguez' *Doing Theology in A Revolutionary Situation.* We were also given handouts to read from Guthrie's *Anglican Spirituality* and Bellah's *Habits of the Heart.* Half way through this short course, we were expected to hand in an essay describing Jaeger's views of how a relationship developed between the Christian religion and the Hellenistic cultural ideal of paideia over the course of late antiquity. Even after I'd read Jaeger's book, I wasn't sure I was defining "paideia"[25] properly, so writing a paper on it was a bit pointless. I had studied and loved the Greek dramatists in college, but that was about all I could recall from my earlier formal education, and this didn't relate at all to any of that.

We were also told we had to follow Turabian's guidelines to research papers, along with the comment that if any of our papers had more than three errors in grammar, punctuation or spelling, they would normally be returned unread once "real" seminary began. Although I'd had a short beginning class in computers the previous summer, I was still woefully ignorant of their operation and still didn't even know how to print a footnote on my word processor; so I spent much of the night before the paper was due trying to decipher the instructions. And my memories of the honor code at Stanford, which I had always heartily subscribed to, did not improve my predicament. I was afraid to ask for help because I thought someone might think I was cheating. I had never felt so inadequate or so stupid.

My paper was finally returned with the comment that at least I had all the tools in order (proper grammar, etc), but that now I needed to concentrate on understanding assignments. Not an auspicious beginning!

The course ended with a retreat at the Moye Center, a place founded by the Sisters of Divine Providence who had come from France in 1868. It was located twenty-five miles west of San Antonio in Castroville, Texas.

In retrospect, that weekend was what George Lindbeck would probably have defined as an experiential expressive dimension of religion: God makes himself known through others, and often, it is through their joy, or sorrow, or pain that we come closer to understanding God at work in ourselves as well. I was mostly lonely and depressed but tried to put on a cheerful face. I even invited several of my new-found female student friends to ride down with me. During some of the services we had during that retreat, total strangers hugging one another unnerved me a bit, but I gradually began to adjust. I guess what I still recall was when someone asked to sing *Morning Has Broken* [26] at one of the services. It was all I

could do not to cry. But I couldn't let myself do that in front of all those strangers, so I finally made it outside and found a tree and sat behind that and cried. It
was the song my sister had asked to be sung at Christopher's funeral. It would be
nearly three years before I could sing that song without breaking down.

I was pretty much in shell shock that first month of school. I could not deal
with finding answers because I could not understand the questions. I could not
even formulate the kind of questions I thought maybe I should be asking. I knew
a lot more about formulating questions in the business world than I did in the
theological world. In the latter, there was no bottom line, only an endless pit
filled with unintelligible rhetoric. What came through very loud and clear, however, was the fact that if I were to survive this seminary experience, I would have
to change my entire manner of thinking. This period of "deep plowing" as some
called it began a process of rearrangement in my intellectual and emotional subconscious which caused a lot of psychic pain and stress. And particularly painful
for me at the beginning was the fact that I could not identify the causes.

One priest had told me before I left home that going to seminary was like
entering a tunnel. I didn't mind that if I could be sure there would be a light at
the other end. But I wanted some assurance I wasn't going to get lost. And I recall
one professor's saying: "Seminary is analogous to flying. The faculty is here to see
that none of you crashes." As far as I was concerned, it was more like treading
water. And it was so deep, we could never put our feet down. Nor was there anything at hand to hang on to.[27] An entry from my prayer journal from that period
said:

> *Being here so far has been an experience in never never land for me. A sojourn*
> *in a foreign country where I do not speak the language. And I do not possess the*
> *remotest idea of how to go about learning it. This is so discouraging. I know my*
> *heart's in the right place. But I don't know how to get from where I am to where I*
> *envision seminary wants me.*
>
> *And later: A dream I had last night says it all. I was in a large room and there*
> *were lots of people and we were all celebrating Christmas. I was happy, busy, con-*
> *tent, then looked around and realized I was the only one without a Christmas tree.*

At the beginning, there was so much required reading we all began to feel we
were trying to dig out of a sandy tunnel. And the sand, in the form of assignments, just kept pouring in whenever we'd get close to the top. A letter from
Father Len Brusso, a rector in Miami, dated September 20, 1988 confirmed this.
Said he:

*"I remember from my seminary days that it was calculated that
in order for a student to do all the assigned reading, it would
require twenty-eight hours a day."*

I dutifully read all the required assignments until I reached a point one day when I was only reading words with no meaning. I suddenly could not assimilate any more. Some of this was partly because of the ancient vocabulary, but it was also due partly to my meticulous study habits and in thinking we were going to be tested on it all. It was total overload. In some respects, seminary recalled to me the first time I'd tried to play golf. I could not believe people were expected to *pay* to do this.

In desperation, when sitting at my computer, when words would not come for a paper due, just to get started, I would type whatever came to mind. It was the only way to overcome the morass of near unintelligible assignments and readings required of us. And no matter what I wrote, I discovered this would eventually get my intellectual juices flowing. The following turned up in some notes (never turned in, of course) along with one paper I had to write:

> *I am feeling so much resistance to school right now, I can
> hardly stand it. I absolutely <u>hate</u> theology. It's so miserable.
> What can all this gobbledegook possibly have to do with love?
> I guess I am worried about my marriage. School right now is so
> irrelevant to real life. I don't know if I'm going to last the
> year. I hate all this stuff we have to read; it makes so little
> sense. It's ridiculous. I could be sailing, or trekking in Nepal,
> or maybe skiing somewhere right now. How am I ever going to get
> four long papers written before the semester ends?*

Then, as an afterthought, I had written:

> *Perhaps you should pray some more.*

I had naively thought seminary would be a place where we could learn to love others better. And in the overall view, I know we did learn that. But seminary also helped me realize I needed—for God's sake—to learn to love myself too. That took a while.

In retrospect, it wasn't so much that I was denying God. I was denying the way God had been packaged and presented to me by others. Most especially, through experiences learned through my parents and my husband as well as my early years in Utah, much of which related to organized religion. I had as many questions as Austin, only I hadn't been recognizing it. In some form or other, seminary was going to have to help me come to terms with all that, or I knew I wasn't going to make it.

Much of my early education too had been spent learning what others thought. Now, I was being forced to come to terms with what *I* thought, and that was not always easy. But I was grateful for Dr. Floyd's statement: "Jesus came to take away our sins, not our minds." That gave us permission to question aloud, something I privately did all the time anyway. Once in a conference with him (he taught Bible among other things), he told me I was part of an interesting class. "There seem to be extremes among you," he said. "For example, you have trouble believing *anything*; on the other hand, some of your classmates take much in the Bible literally."

One evening, while studying in my apartment, trying to make sense of an assignment, I had an incredible sense of Ceako's presence. This was the boy I'd known some forty years earlier in Venezuela. It was such a real experience, I could not ignore it. I've always been somewhat psychic, but this really amazed me. Could Ceako possibly be near by, I wondered? Finally, to satisfy my curiosity, I went to the telephone directory and looked up his name which, though we never called him that, I knew was Charles. And sure enough, there it was, so I dialed the number. It was Ceako all right and he still remembered me. Talking to him made me feel as though we'd never been out of touch. We had a good chat. He was married with a family now, living in Austin, Texas. I couldn't help marvel at this coincidence. I saw it as God's way of telling me that a good part of my past was near by, so not to let all these assignments wear me down.

It would take too long to write about the first two weeks of pre-school orientation, or the weeks that followed. Suffice to say they were confusing, humbling, exhilarating and full of anxiety. But there was love there too. My classmates (41 of us) were all undergoing the same pains of transition as I, so we tired hard to cope, and reached out to help when we could. In the course of that week, one student lost his mother and another girl's husband had to have a biopsy (thankfully not malignant); and one girl, who had just been married three weeks earlier, was trying to adjust to both married and seminary life! We were a cross section of America—students, ex-military, ex-teachers, ex-business types, an ex-nun, a rancher, broker, veterinarian, one lawyer, with a sprinkling of students from other denominations (mainly Methodists and Lutherans). We also had three clergy (Catholic, Anglican and a Baptist minister) returning for "re-spraying" or "re-treading" as it was called, to update them on Anglicanism. We were a real hodge-podge of people, our only denominator being our faith which had some-how landed us there.

After school started and the real grind began, I had to laugh when people would write and ask me how I was enjoying seminary. If and when I had time to write back, I usually said that one really *survives* seminary. That's because to me, first semester was awful. Despite all my preparation, I, and everyone else, arrived at least six months behind in the reading. There was no possible way of ever catching up; there was never enough time to do all the assigned work. The pressure never stopped. We decided this was purposely done, to see how we would make use of our time, and whether we would be able to take the stresses that obviously went with our vocations. But it seemed more like training for burn-out to me. Either that, or I was overly conscientious. There were days when I would equate all those required papers and reading assignments, services and classes, to a piece by Stranvinsky: discordant, only out of control.

I totally subscribed to the strong intellectual requirements, but it was tough when there was so much to condense and understand and retain in such a short period of time. I decided my younger days at Beloit and Stanford had been a breeze compared with my graduate experience at ETSS.

One mistake I made was thinking we would be tested and graded on factual information, only in a subject like theology—the science which treats of God, his attributes, and his relations to the universe—where is the yardstick? Who determines what is factual? Of course, theology is also the knowledge of God and the supernatural, but how was it all supposed to fit together? I found it difficult at the beginning trying to study about something I could not see, measure or even prove existed. We had hundreds of assigned pages sometimes which made it virtually impossible even to finish the readings. And often the readings were impossible to comprehend. I would first read through, then underline what I thought were the salient concepts in an assignment, then I would usually have to go to a Dictionary of Theology and read what it said, this to find out if I was even close to understanding what I had read. Then I would try to write some notes about it.

The vocabulary at first was impossible. I spent hours looking up words that made little sense at first—words like homoousios, parousia, eschatology, ontology, anamnesis, immutability, monophysitism, prolepsis, soteriology, subordinationism. Even when I read what they meant, I often had to look up what the words describing them meant.

We had readings that discussed Henry Schillebeeckx and Friedrich Schleiermacher and Wittgenstein. The latter questioned the nature of philosophy and drew a line of demarcation between philosophy and the sciences. This intrigued me so I read on, then looked up something relating to the latter's "Verificationist Thesis" that said: "It is worth noting that the positivists monistic conception of the world as a logical unity of experiential data and constructions out of them is at explicit variance with Wittgenstein's view of the anumerical multiplicity of logical forms."[28] (!!) How did this sort of thing relate to Jesus' admonition to feed the poor, I wondered? At that point, I was more inclined to think with Austin and Voltaire that theological religion was the "enemy of mankind."

Friends who lived in the complex where I was renting an apartment encouraged me to attend the opera or symphony with them on occasion. This was wonderful and at least got me beyond the confines of seminary life. But often, when they left town, they would ask if I'd mind visiting one of their parents afflicted with alzheimers who lived in the same building. I was very happy to do this, but trying to carry on a conversation with her transported me right back to school. I imagined I was Alice taking tea with the Mad Hatter, being asked the same questions over and over.

But it wasn't just the studies. It was the emotional, spiritual, physical *and* intellectual all compounded into what I began to feel was a movie sped up to go five times faster than normal. It was like going from flying a Cessna to reaching Mach 1 in the Concorde. I was getting up at 5 a.m. and going to bed at midnight, squeezing a swim or dinner or a chance to write a letter in between ironing while trying to watch the news so I wouldn't feel completely cut off, because the seminary world is one all to itself. "You resign from the world when you enter seminary," my sponsor told me on arrival. And she was right.

We had chapel every day and were expected to attend a church service of our own choosing on Sunday as well. Along with all the assignments and chapel duties, I also had to shop for food and get the laundry done plus deal with my mail and any other reality that happened to hit. Austin came to visit for a week in late September. I had missed him and could not wait until he arrived, but after three days, found myself sinking so far behind in the reading assignments, it was a relief to see him return to Miami.

In one course, a handout was given to us that showed how to measure people's levels of stress. It had a long list including such things as a recent move, financial difficulties, divorce, marriage, change in job or location, death in the family, having a baby, losing a close friend, etc. It then gave points for each category to which one answered "yes." Some categories received more points than others. It then showed a chart depicting the numerical total and where one fit on the chart. Above a certain category (sixty as I now recall), one could expect to become ill or have other serious problems if some way were not found to reduce the stressful environment. Many of us, if the scale were one to one hundred, with stress at the top, registered eighty-eight or higher. We were all of us grappling with, and trying to balance, so many factors in our lives, in addition to seminary, that it's a wonder to me in retrospect that any of us made it through the three years. (Of the forty-one in our entering class, seventeen of us were there for the entire three year program. Of those seventeen, fifteen of us graduated.)

Time was a valuable commodity, so how it got used was very important. This resulted, after Austin left, in the best ways I could think of to take short cuts. I started with the huge oversized double bed furnished with the apartment. Since I only slept on one third of it, it seemed like a waste of time to change the sheets every week; so I learned to sleep on one side of the bed the first week, in the middle the second week, and on the opposite side the third week. That way I only had to change the sheets and pillow cases every three weeks. (I was proud of this until I heard that one student only changed his sheets twice each semester!)

But it was my class work where I found the most challenge. I was constantly trying to sort out Austin's arguments with my own beliefs along with what I was learning in class. This generated much confusion and anxiety. I realized in going over my notes one day that I was exhibiting the characteristics of a radical.

"The fundamentalist and the radical share the same concern—to go to the foundations or roots. But it is not accidental that the one uses an inorganic and the other an organic metaphor. Digging around foundations can have a very different effect from digging around roots: dislodge one stone and the entire building may collapse."

I wasn't in fear of having my foundation collapse, but I was having problems rearranging my philosophy to fit everything I was having thrown at me. I was badly in need of having my roots watered and nourished. But I had such adventitious roots, no one recognized them.

One day in Theology, something came up relating to Plato and Aristotle's ideas and whether God had stood outside of creation or had been an intrinsic part of it. Before going to seminary, I had read Stephen Hawking's book entitled *A Brief History of Time, From the Big Bang to Black Holes,* and it seemed to contradict what I was hearing. I guess I wanted some assurance because at some point, Dr. Sugeno said: "Mrs. Weeks, it's all right to disagree." I was so relieved. Despite the openness of the faculty, all along, I know I'd been afraid the seminary (certainly according to Austin) was going to ram something unpalatable down my throat. "By God, don't let them brain wash you," he'd warned. But he needn't have worried about that. It was a relief to have it affirmed by others that the Bible was not necessarily factual, much was symbolical, and that its myths and stories primarily related to creation, sin, judgment and redemption.

A prayer written out which I found later in my notes said a great deal about where I was at that time:

> *You gave me my mind, God. You know I'm not the type to accept everything on faith. It's my nature to question. That's the trouble, God. It's this trying to understand who you are, and who I am, that's making life so difficult right now. But it's good too. The more I doubt, the more you seem to tell me it's okay. Sometimes this doesn't make a whole lot of sense, God. But that's the way you're leading me right now. And you know I'm trying hard to follow.*

Denial, or questioning just then, seemed to be the only entree I had in being able to relate to God, or to what I perceived as God. Yet, it's said one of the main reasons for sending people to seminary is not to enforce or change their beliefs. It's to break down any prejudices they might have.

One week, our class was invited to Dr. and Mrs. Sugeno's home for a dessert and coffee evening with some of the other students. Dr. Sugeno taught history and was one of my teachers that semester for HTS1 (history and theology). He was also the professor Bishop Duncan had told me to look up. While we were talking, I found myself saying all kinds of things to him I normally kept to myself. He's one of those kind, quiet, understanding types that seems to elicit things you'd never think of saying to anyone else. A bit like Bishop Richards. I recall telling him how difficult my first week at school had been, how I was certainly questioning God's existence, not to mention lots of other things. And I remember him smiling his inscrutable oriental smile and saying: "It takes a leap of faith to deny God."

Half way through the first semester, I found myself under a lot of tension. Whenever I tried to study for mid-term exams, I'd end up crying. This didn't make any sense at all and I couldn't understand what was happening to me. I just knew I was under a lot of stress. By the time I went to take my first test, I could hardly function. I know now I had all the classic symptoms of hysteria. I tried to write my name on the paper and could barely make a mark with the pen. It took me five minutes before I could write anything at all, even though I had plenty of recall of much of the information I'd spent weeks learning. But I couldn't get my fingers to move. I just sat there like a dummy, all the while listening to everyone else around me writing furiously, which made me feel even worse. Finally, I managed to write a few things on one question and made a stab at the other. But I knew I was doing a terrible job and couldn't seem to help it. In a desperate gesture finally, I wrote at the bottom of the exam: "*I feel like Polycarp must have felt on his way to martyrdom.*" By the time I got home, I was close to being a basket case.

I should have gone and found someone to talk to, or maybe I should have had a stiff drink. But I seldom drink, and never alone, so I finally took an aspirin. Then the crying began again. By then, I decided maybe I was in trouble and determined to see my advisor. Once I had made that decision, the tension eased up and I was able to study a little more for my next day's exam. But I had the same experience the following day also, only to a lesser degree. And by then, was beginning to get a glimmer of why this was occurring.

When I had been at Stanford studying for exams, my cousin had called me from Utah and told me my father was dying and that I should come home. It was the second most traumatic thing I'd ever experienced up to that point in my life, the first being when I'd been six years old and my music teacher had thrown an epileptic fit during my piano lesson. Much of the trauma of that experience plus the flying home and watching my father die, I'd also buried away. My entire childhood had been geared to the day my father would come home and we would get to do all those wonderful things together as a family we had never been able to do. With his death, much of my future disappeared and I'd had no one to talk to about it. There had been so much pain connected to his death, I'd just buried it all. And being back in school that fall of 1988 had been a constant reminder of those days at Stanford.

Likewise, when Christopher was killed, I had been studying for my first canonical exam in the Bible when someone called me on the phone to say he was missing. Now, studying for an exam, I was subconsciously relating all that shock from the past. If it hadn't been related to the Bible, perhaps this would not have happened to me. Whatever, the Bible reading and cramming brought back all the trauma from the week Chris had been killed. And I know now I was also subconsciously relating it to my experience in college. I had never properly worked through the grief from either of those two shocks in my life. What concerned me was that reading the Bible and dredging all this up again was upsetting me badly. Yet, I was totally aware too that part of me was able to look at myself in a detached way. This somehow held out the promise I was being healed, that the past and present would eventually come together. The inner rearranging I'd experienced as a result of my prayer life and my visits to Bishop Richards was still continuing, only at a much faster and more pronounced speed. I was being re-formed and re-molded internally in ways I couldn't always comprehend.

My advisor was an astute woman and suggested I go to a "Beginning Experience" seminar. One was coming up in November which dealt with just this kind of thing. I decided it couldn't hurt and made plans to go. That somehow helped me survive until after mid-term break.

But flying home, I couldn't help wonder if I would ever make it through first semester. Many of my long cherished beliefs were being blown out of the water. Too, my lack of intellectual knowledge regarding Christianity and theology was appalling. Though grateful for the two years in TEE class with Father Masterman, I still could not get a fix on just what I was supposed to be learning.

Essentially, I'd always felt it more important to *be* a Christian and had never thought much about Christianity in intellectual terms. I had always equated it with my spiritual grounding which I thought was adequate. At least until I got to seminary. And this reminded me of the time I'd been asked to teach a class at St. Andrew's to the 7th and 8th graders. I recall how woefully ignorant I'd been. No one gave me a lesson plan or any information on what I was supposed to teach, so I wandered around with ideas, like a bull in a china shop. I learned early that most of the students, as far as Bible stories were concerned anyway, knew much more than I did. My one and only visit to a Unitarian Sunday School when I was six years old had dealt with Darwin's Theory of Evolution, and I could not recall anything about Bible stories from my few Sunday School experiences in Maracaibo. All we'd done in that class was memorize Bible verses. Realizing I would not make it as the usual Sunday school teacher, I took the kids to Planet Ocean and told them about God's being our Creator, what a gorgeous planet He had given us to take care of, and how we shouldn't muck it up with pollution and defoliation. I was big on field trips that year and it's the only way I got through the class. Thankfully, no one ever asked me to teach it again.

Once in seminary, I had to keep reminding myself the way scripture had been combined with the Hellenistic philosophy of the day to explain the faith Christians practiced. I should have absorbed all this earlier in TEE if it was discussed, but if so, I couldn't recall any of it. I couldn't understand why we had to study Plato and Aristotle at all, but one day a light finally came on and I began to understand some of what the professors were saying. The Logos was not a Christian idea. It was borrowed from others. Heraclitus (c. 500 B.C.) had conceived of the Logos in a pantheistic way as the universal reason governing and permeating the world, then the Stoics popularized this idea. Later, Philo of Alexandria combined the Greek and the Biblical concepts. He interpreted Greek OT in terms of Greek philosophy, depicting the Logos as the intelligible element in God's mysterious being; the means of God's self-disclosure to the world. It was how Christians would eventually describe their incarnate God—Jesus. The Prologue of John describes the Logos as God from eternity, the Creative Word, who became incarnate in the man, Jesus Christ. The author of John was the first to identify the Logos with the Messiah.

Having been brought up in Mormon Utah, where local religious history began in 1847 with Brigham Young's entrance into the Promised Land, I had a lot of catching up to do. But how could I have arrived at the venerable age of fifty-eight and never understood this about Christianity?

Basically, what came through to me was the fact that no one spoke my religious language; and I was having a tough time understanding theirs. My spirituality was grounded in non-Mormonism, non-Catholicism, poetry and a little Chinese philosophy, none of which related much to what I was reading in seminary. I'd always had my own little spiritual rooms with a set of air locks that kept out what wasn't meaningful to me.

Also, even though I had earned a degree in political science, it was a revelation to me to discover that Marxism was a secularized form of Biblical eschatology.

The day we took our second mid-term exam, the professor met the class afterwards to treat us all to a beer. That was the morning I had to see my advisor, so was late getting to the "Posse." This was a snack and beer joint near campus. But there were a few stragglers, and a few who remained after the rest left, and these I got to know much better that day. To put it another way, I should say they got to know me better. I stopped being a listener, had two beers, then told them how little I had understood on our first exam. I had thought we were to learn all the reading assignments. But the questions we were asked didn't seem to me to relate a bit to the readings; so seminary had me perplexed from day one. I also added I thought I was coming unglued. There was no point in pretending. The student I thought I was, the one I remembered from college days, no longer existed. So I swallowed my pride and believe that's where my first real sense of community began in seminary. I recall one student, putting his arms around me, giving me a big hug and saying: "We're all in this boat together." Indeed we were. I didn't find out until much later that he and his wife were having difficulties and were subsequently divorced.

There was so much going on those first few months, it's hard to narrow it down. I guess one thing that stood out to me was the contrast of my previous life to the one I found in Texas. When I began to hear all the sad stories of how broke many of the students were, I was reluctant to let anyone know I was well off. I felt really bad going to lunch one day with one of the women seminarians whose husband did not have a job. She'd received a check from her diocese and had allowed herself $2.00 to spend. "First time I've splurged in a long time," she told me. There's not a whole lot one can buy for $2.00, so I offered to pay for both our lunches. "Look, I can afford it," I told her. But seminary was not short on hubris. She wouldn't hear of it. Her husband did eventually find employment, but not before she'd lost eighteen pounds.

But seminary had its light moments also. The mail room had a bulletin board for notices and messages. One day I found this pinned to it:

> **Dear Abby,**
> **I have two brothers. One goes to the Episcopal Seminary in Austin, Texas. The other was sentenced to death in the gas chamber. My mother died of insanity when I was three years old. My two sisters are prostitutes and my father sells narcotics.**
> **Recently I met a guy who was released from prison where he served time for smothering his mother to death. I love this guy and we want to get married.**
> **My problem is this: Should I tell him about my brother who goes to that seminary in Texas?**
>
> **Signed: Wondering in Wisconsin**

The mid-semester October break could not have come at a better time. I got back to Miami, to Austin, my kids and my dog. It was such a relief. I was able to relax, be more philosophical about this entire experience and even accept the fact I might not make it. Meanwhile, I decided since I had a lease on my apartment until the following August, I should definitely return to see what the next semester would also bring. And in most respects, it was a good vacation, even though I had to spend much of the time reading a book for a paper I had to write. But too soon, it was back to Texas.

I returned with the idea that I would not let exams worry me in the future, that I could leave if I wanted (I knew by then I wouldn't), and that I would try harder to relax. My good intentions lasted about four days until the tension began again. By the end of the first week, however, I sensed everyone else was as stressed out as I and thankfully, we had time out for a quiet day. It came the day after we had our HTSl exam returned which, for some, was traumatic. I already knew I hadn't done well, so it was no surprise. Still, it was awfully depressing, especially after all the studying I'd done. So I had to re-do it. This, on top of a ten page paper that had to be handed in for Theology based on the following assignment:

"Imagine that you were educated in Plato's Academy and have become committed to the Platonic teaching regarding the mind, the soul, eros and the will. You have also accepted the Platonic notion of the proper relationship between the individual and the polis. Write a lead editorial for the Academy's official publication on the 1988 U.S. presidential election. Then criticize your editorial on the basis of your understanding of the relationship between philosophy and theology."

This, of course, presupposed we had read and mastered the concepts in *Plato's Republic* and *Symposium*. So I struggled with that, along with trying to re-write my patristics exam which still made very little sense.

Our quiet day was led by a priest from the outside. He made himself available to us; so I went, told him nothing was making much sense.

"In seminary, you are dealing with true reality," he said.

Thinking of some of my classmates, worried over how they were going to feed their kids and pay their bills, I felt they had a better handle on reality than he did, and told him so.

"That really isn't important," he told me. "Not in the long run." We talked a little more, but I couldn't get on his wave length at all. So I gave up and went back to the chapel.

The next day, I was in the SAC (Student Activity Center) which was an old house across the street from the seminary. It was available to the students and housed the bookstore, as well as a pool table, coffee pot, drink machine and refrigerators. Essentially, it was a gathering place to relax between encounters with the stressful academic world across the street. If I wasn't too wiped out trying to finish an assignment, I would often go there and sit and listen to the conversation before chapel. This particular day, one girl dragged in and announced she'd just had a third paper returned. Then she screwed up her face and said: "I guess I must be making progress. This time I didn't cry."

Another student commented: "My computer barfed up my theology paper ... since it's two pages too long, I'm going to have to rewrite it."

The analogy to theology and what one generally barfs up said it all to me then. There were days when we all detested theology. Yet, most of us ended up with a Master's in the subject. How, I'll never know. I just know God works in very mysterious ways sometimes. And for sure, the Almighty has a sense of humor.

An ex-colonel, there to study for his General Ordination Exams continued: "They can shoot us and they can kill us, I guess, but the bright thing is they can't eat us. Cannibalism is out. It's illegal." He than added "But when they stomp all over our cadavers, I just wish they'd take the spikes out of their golf shoes!"[29]

I remember his expressions because they really did reflect the way we felt at times. I can only speak for myself, but as earlier mentioned, I'd honestly thought seminary would be a place where we would learn to love people better. In the long run, I believe it was. But at times, it seemed like they beat us up first. In their zeal, the faculty showed us the way. And no matter how much it may have hurt, with few exceptions, we were fond of and respected our professors. They cared that we learned. They were paid to teach us. And by God, that's what they were doing. For us learners, however, it was difficult.

I re-wrote the HTS1 exam question and handed it back in. A few days later, Professor Green asked me to come to his office. I knew I hadn't done the question well. I'd just wanted to get it behind me. So I sat down and he began to go over my paper. Before he'd even read through the first paragraph, I recall saying: "Please stop. Please don't go on." I couldn't bear to hear him read that stupid paper. He stopped, and we sat there through a long, pregnant pause.

Finally, I said: "I didn't really want to mention any of this ... but maybe I should ..." Then I blurted out how Chris had been killed the week before my first canonical exam in Florida which was to have been on the Bible ... how studying the Old Testament had brought it all back ... how seminary reminded me of college ... how my Dad had died when I was in college ... how awful I felt ... how it was like trying to put two identical maps on top of each other.... only they wouldn't fit somehow.... I said a lot of other stuff I've forgotten, then wished I hadn't spoken at all. I was terrified of Dr. Green and braced myself to be told to shape up; and quit making excuses for myself. At the least I expected to be reprimanded, or told I was failing. Something like that. Only nothing like that happened.

Dr. Green, in a very slow, concerned way, made me realize he had listened. He told me to forget a Tillich presentation I'd volunteered to do, and not to worry about re-writing the paper until January. "You'll have time later," he said. "Forget all this for a while."

I could hardly believe my ears. Everything stopped spinning. I remembered to tell him how I'd liked his sermon on angels, how it had transcended where I was at that point, and how it helped me relate to good things. Then I vaguely recall, I got up in a daze, thanked him, and walked out of his office.

# 21

# A REVELATION

I never knew when I went off to seminary that many people were there because they had some kind of problem, or were recovering from some kind of difficult experience in their lives. At least that's the way it seemed to me. Only I really didn't know what my problem was until I'd been there awhile. Plain and simple, besides trying to deal with grief—the loss of my father and Christopher—I was in total denial over being married to an alcoholic. To me, the word *alcoholic* had always been synonymous with the occasional drunks I'd seen at parties, or the *winos* that sat in doorways nursing a bottle along the streets on Salt Lake City's west side. My husband didn't answer to those descriptions. To think of him in those terms bordered on the absurd. He was a polite, sensitive, educated, decent, caring man who, besides liking jokes, music and photography, I'd come to realize also had some kind of problem with his father. And yes, Austin drank, but only on social occasions. Or so I thought.

When I could finally admit his situation to myself, I was so mortified and ashamed that I could scarcely talk about it to anyone else. For ten years my life had revolved around pretending things were "okay." And in suppressing what wasn't "okay," I lost much of myself in the process.[30]

I don't know if it was that way with everyone, but I gradually began to understand over time that becoming a priest was not something I really chose to do—like choosing a profession. It was something I *had* to do, (you might say I was *called* to do) because there was no other way out. I could live my life no longer the way it was.

Bishop Otis Charles told me he once interviewed a young man who had come to him for postulancy who told him: "I only seem to have three choices: drugs, suicide, or Jesus."

I wasn't interested in drugs or suicide and I didn't know a whole lot about Jesus. But there was something about church, about worshiping in a community, that gave me a sense of peace I could not find elsewhere. When I had applied to become a postulant years earlier, I knew my life needed to go in a different direction and that this was one way to accomplish it. Later, when I left Miami for Texas, I certainly knew I had a rocky marriage but had no idea what was wrong, or what had gotten it to that point. In many ways, I blamed myself for this predicament, all the while not understanding its cause.

Perhaps everyone in seminary was not as dysfunctional as I when they arrived, but looking back, I recall the tension and the loneliness and the wondering if I really belonged. And I know others also had those thoughts. We did not have "how to do" classes in the sense of learning to make or do anything, but were immersed in a way of thought and surroundings that could be sometimes frightening. At the center of it all, of course, was the Bible—the Scriptures—the Word of God—encompassed in the liturgy of the church and presented to us in every conceivable way.

But Jesus, per se, had never consciously been part of my spiritual life. When the nuns in the boarding school I'd attended said we should "do things for Jesus," that had never made sense to me. And as far as behavior was concerned, my Mother had always told me and my sister that we should "be good for goodness' sake." Being good had nothing to do with Jesus. Being good was the way we should act because it kept us out of trouble! Life was better when people were good; it was worse when they were not. And there were all kinds of examples mother went out of her way to show us. Recently, in some old notes of hers, I found something that expressed much of my mother's philosophy when I was growing up:

> "..... .I find myself telling the children that God is not
> a fairy but a principle, perhaps a super human something that dominates nature
> and preserves order."

Jesus was not anyone my mother ever spoke about to me or my sister, though we did celebrate Christmas. But I didn't recall Jesus' ever having anything to do with this wonderful holiday. And as for Easter, she did hide some chocolate eggs for us once or twice; but there was no connection with Easter and religion as far as I can recall. Mother scoffed at the resurrection, since it dealt with (in her mind) the resuscitation of a corpse, and since that was impossible, there was no point in believing *that*. Hope came to me through the poetry Mother often read to me and my sister, along with the promise that someday our "Daddy" would come back from South America.

God was nothing I could describe or comprehend. He was beyond understanding. Certainly I did not relate to Him as a person. It's no wonder that much of the readings we had to cover in seminary seemed so *pointless* at times, at least from my viewpoint, and so *boring*. I wondered too if I'd ever have reason to tell a congregation about Pseudo-Dyonisius or Clement's *First Letter*, or Theodore of Mopsuestia, or Ratramnus, or Oecolampadius or Polycarp or Eusebius. Possibly George Lindbeck, or Tillich or Brueggemann and maybe St. Paul and Jesus would fit in eventually, but they all seemed so far removed from my real life. Although I didn't realize it at the time, I was operating out of a different paradigm from everyone else, only no one understood that, least of all me. But eventually, we got to the Enlightenment, and that's when I think I began to relate to the readings.

But to return to the problem mentioned. When I left Miami for seminary, I truly had no idea I was married to a *real* alcoholic and that my marriage was falling apart. Of course, I knew Austin drank at times and I knew we weren't communicating well, that something was wrong, but I could not articulate what was happening between us. Austin and I had married "till death us do part," so divorce was never part of our vocabulary. We'd always assumed, no matter what, that we would stick together. We were not so naive as to think there might never be problems, but under-girding our relationship was the acceptance that there was nothing we could not overcome. It was that basic. After all, hadn't we weathered tough times of unemployment and the loss of one of our children?

At some point, however, we reached a jumping off place and neither of us seemed to know what to do. I only knew I was experiencing a great deal of unexplained anxiety and was scared in a way that I could not fathom. So I left. I had to. The longing, the terrible longing for God (as I knew Him) that had come into my life would not let me do otherwise. I was in a great deal of denial over my own life, just as Austin was over his. But we could not recognize it for what it was. Intuitively, I knew I was doing the right thing, but I could not for the life of me have told anyone why.

One of my final desperate attempts to help my failing marriage occurred quite spontaneously a few weeks before leaving Florida. I was at the home of the dean of the music school of the University of Miami and in the course of our conversation, the needs of the music school were discussed. These included everything from new practice pianos to more space, and more specifically a new music building and recording studio. I made no commitment then, but said I would look in to it. At the back of that comment was a final grasping at straws. Austin enjoyed music. "Could I do something to honor him, give something in his name?" I had asked. I believe I thought this might draw his attention, keep him occupied and give him some kind of purpose. In a sense, I was entrusting him to the safekeeping of the university. I couldn't entrust him to the church very well. He detested the church and all that went with it. English boarding school had seen to that. The dean and his wife had no idea what was going on inside me. So I just asked them to look after Austin with the vague promise that I might be able to make a donation to the music school in his name; perhaps they could get him involved, and I would get back in touch with them when I could. They graciously agreed.

By the time I returned to Miami in October, I had changed in many respects. Getting away from the house and being immersed in a different existence had seen to that. But what really hit me when I got home was the way I related to Austin. He was my husband; I really loved him, but I was able to be much more objective now. I'd never been looking for it; had never detected any alcohol on his breath, but it finally occurred to me one day why he'd always chewed so many mints! Prior to then I would never have associated this habit with a desire to conceal his breath. But I'd been away now long enough around others who *listened* to realize just how little we actually communicated. It was not hard to see also that he was in serious trouble. I still was not ready to admit he was an alcoholic, though I'd openly told Bishop Richards once that I was concerned about Austin's drinking.

The second or third day home, I had a meeting with Bishop Richards. He asked me all about seminary, my prayer life, what I'd been doing. So I told him, about my studies, the pain of being away, the people I'd met. When I couldn't think of anything else, he asked: "Have you told me everything? Is there anything else you'd like to bring up?"

I thought for a long while. Finally, I just said: "You're my spiritual director, not a marriage counselor. But I don't mind telling you my marriage isn't all that great." For the second time, I told him I was concerned about my husband's drinking habits and that I didn't know what to do.

By now, there was no way to step around what is proverbially referred to as "the elephant in the living room." The bishop asked me how much Austin drank. Conveniently dismissing my earlier experience with him in Utah, I told him I had no idea. Dr. Metcalf, the psychologist, whom I had to visit also as part of the "process," had asked the same question. I'd given her the same answer.

"Have you discussed his drinking with him?" asked Bishop Richards.

"Yes," I finally admitted. "And he tells me he's cut way back."

"And do you believe him?" he asked.

"Yes," I answered.

On the way home I kept thinking of our conversation and I kept wondering: *Do I believe Austin?* And I finally decided: *No, I don't really believe him. I can't anymore.* The only thing to do was to check and find out for myself. I went home with an awful sense of dread, feeling like a sneak going into my husband's den, looking through his closet and drawers. Austin was a private person and I'd always respected this. Nevertheless, I searched all over the house, marking any bottles found. What turned up over the period of several days was devastating. There were bottles in suitcases, bottles in sacks, bottles in the liquor cabinet, bottles stashed away in his closets. I marked them all. It was not only true that he was drinking more than he admitted to; he was drinking more than I dreamed possible. He was drinking <u>lots</u> of vodka, then glibly telling me, whenever I asked, that he was only having one cocktail before dinner. On one occasion, I gave him five opportunities to level with me, and each time, he lied. I could hardly believe this. However, the Bishop had given me some information on alcoholism and denial to read, so at last it all began to make some sense. I'd known, of course, that he drank and often I'd thought maybe a little too much, but I'd never in my wildest thoughts believed him to be an alcoholic, nor understood what this entailed. If I had entertained the idea, I would have only dismissed it. Now, here I was, faced with information I did not want to believe, but clearly had to.

Bishop Richards called and asked me if I'd like to come back and see him once more before returning to school. Of course I said "yes." When I returned, he discussed the possibility of an intervention. This, however, takes time and careful planning. I had to get back to school but at least could alert the children. So I got them together; Leslie with her husband and Kermit with his girl friend, and told them what was going on. They didn't believe me.

"Oh, Mother. Daddy doesn't drink that much.... .you're exaggerating," said Leslie.

"Dad's fine," said Kermit.

Austin had been so good at hiding it from me for so long, it was no wonder the children, who no longer lived at home, had trouble believing me.

"Your Daddy is putting away a great deal of vodka a day," I insisted.

Their denial was just as great as mine had been. An intervention would be hard to pull off when no one except me, and possibly the secretary, could document any of his drinking habits.

"He's destroying himself," I insisted.

They at least promised to keep an eye on him and include him more in their lives.

I was still in shock, having trouble believing all this too, yet terribly relieved at the same time. But it all hit me the day I was to return to Texas. On the way to the airport, Austin mentioned that Kermit had told him he and his girl friend were having some difficulty. "They're getting counseling," I told him.

"I wonder why?" he asked.

"Because they need it," I told him. "Kermit comes from a dysfunctional family, as does his girl friend. But at least she recognizes it ... she's the one that's insisted on the counseling."

"What do you mean 'dysfunctional'?"

"If you have to ask, you'll never understand," I answered.

"I don't see anything wrong with our family," he said.

"Well, I do," I told him. "Maybe you're happy with it, but I'm not." And that was the note I left him on when we got to the Miami airport.

He called me in Texas that evening, and tried to come to some understanding. But there was no point to the conversation. As long as he couldn't see that his drinking might be creating problems, there was nothing I could do. I felt bad I'd been so sharp; at the same time, I knew I was never going to go back to that situation; not unless things improved. And if they didn't? At that point, I wasn't ready to think about an alternative.

It was the next week in class that I found a possible solution. I asked one of my classmates, who by then I had discovered was a recovering alcoholic, what I might do.

He told me when things had been unbearable between him and his wife that he'd written her love letters to "keep the lines of communication open. Maybe it can work for you."

I reminded myself of something said by St. Bernard: "*In matters spiritual, not to long for progress is to fail*" and realized I could write to Austin. Not gushy, sentimental letters, but powerful, prayerful letters. Over the following ten days, I wrote him seven. I'm not sure if Austin ever read any of them. But almost immediately, within myself, I began to see very positive results.

I won't go into all the ramifications of co-dependency. There are probably as many definitions of the term as there are people who write about it. But to me, at first, my reactions to Austin's drinking had been simply normal reactions. When he didn't do things, I assumed he didn't have time, so I picked up the slack; thing left undone, I did. If he said he didn't feel well, I thoughtfully accepted it and did double duty. When letters should have been answered, but weren't, I took care of them. At some point, however, my "normal" reactions began to accommodate

Austin's somewhat irrational, abnormal behavior. That's when I crossed the line to co-dependency. Gradually, without even knowing it, I became an enabler.

It can take ten years for this to occur. Ours was a classic case. I was terribly confused that he could not be logical. But I never asked myself "why?" We often got into arguments that never went anywhere. This I couldn't understand. He could be charming one minute, impossibly maddening the next. Denial is part of an alcoholic's disease; so they don't—can't—admit to being ill.

Co-dependency, by extension, is the same thing. Co-dependents might not drink. But they are in denial. They don't want to admit they live with someone who does. And even if they do, they don't know how to deal with it. And sometimes, like me, they don't recognize they have a serious problem until years have gone by. The worst of it is that a co-dependent often experiences a loss of a sense of self. Personal boundaries can become blurred or exaggerated and personal defenses become apparent only to others.

Denial of feelings is extremely harmful to co-dependents also, because they lose touch with themselves. That really defined me at that point. I'd always been good at burying my feelings anyway. It was easier to bury them than to hurt. And not grieving fully after Chris' death was a case in point. It is a myth that grieving feeds pain. One has to fully experience grief before one can be fully healed. I'd never gotten that far. The whole purpose of grieving is to help a person reach the point where they can remember without feeling pain.[31]

After the brief mid-term break, when I got back to seminary, I spent the weekend at the "Beginning Experience." It was another world. Conceived as a program to help people overcome grief in their lives, it was an intense, emotional weekend. There were only two of us experiencing loss from death, me and a young college girl who had lost her mother, so we were put in the same group with three others. The rest were trying to get over broken marriages.

By this time, I had already begun to come to terms with the emotional confusion in my life; I was also well aware that I too was grieving my marriage. However, it was emphasized that we grieve one loss only. So, though I knew my marriage was in serious trouble, I grieved for and concentrated on a lot of still unexpressed feelings about Christopher. One thing still stands out for me from that weekend.

The seminar was organized around large discussion groups which included everyone, and small discussions which involved one's own group. These would be interspersed with recreation, meals, and chapel. No one was allowed to wear a watch. There was one man in my group whom I did not really relate well to at all. He had a beard, reminded me of the kind of person one might meet at *Alabama*

*Jack's* [32]and was a bit strange to my way of thinking. I suspected he'd been on lots of drugs, either in the present or in the past, because he seemed a little spaced-out to me.

One of the exercises we were expected to do in this program was to share our feelings with one another, in addition to other types of experiences, depending on the particular exercise. The entire weekend was very structured and intense, the whole point being (at least to my way of thinking) to wear down our defenses so we'd let go and really say how we felt. I had my defenses up as high as they would go at first and certainly wasn't about to share my feelings with any strangers. At some point, however I began to feel like part of the group and by the end of the second day, when it was my turn to share if I wished, when I was supposed to read something I had written, I recall that I began to cry. I didn't really want to, but I couldn't help myself. The point I want to make is that of all the people in that group, the one who really related to me and knew what could help just then was this great big, hairy, lumberjack type of a man whom I had not wanted to get near. As I started to talk and then cry (we were all sitting on the floor in a circle), he crossed over to me, picked me up in his arms, and just hugged me and said "It's okay to cry. It's okay to cry. You must really miss your son." This great big man, whom I had been so averse to getting near to, had a heart of gold. He radiated comfort. He just held me and hugged me.

Nowadays, of course, if that man had been a priest, he wouldn't have done that! The Church Insurance Corporation definitely frowns on such behavior. Nevertheless, sometimes being touched and hugged by another human being can be a very necessary part of healing. Intellectually I'd known it all along, but I had to experience that to truly comprehend.

Of course, I was behind in assignments by the time I returned to school, but so glad I'd participated in that group, out there in the hill country of Texas.

# 22

# REFLECTIONS & LETTERS TO GOD

Before Christmas break that first year, the seminary sponsored a night of caroling, followed later in the week by the Dean's candlelight supper at Rather House. It was a wonderful party that put me into the holiday spirit, so I was really excited about getting back home, putting up the tree and celebrating Christmas.

When I returned to Miami, however, there was no one to share my excitement. Leslie and her husband had gone skiing; Kermit and his girl friend were still having problems. I couldn't even get them to commit to coming for Christmas dinner. And Austin didn't even want to put up the tree. It was such a disappointment. I couldn't believe how negative everyone was. After one day at home, I decided I was not going to have a miserable Christmas. I'd already had four trying months at school and this was my vacation. I was upset at first that Austin didn't care about the tree, then had to admit finally that he'd never cared for holidays anyway. But while being removed from the Miami scene, I'd been pulling up all my wonderful feelings and memories about Christmas from earlier times, expecting my family to share them with me. This was obviously not going to happen. I also had to deal with the fact that Austin was still drinking. So, after thinking about things for a few days, I called up some of our friends. These included Austin's cardiologist and his wife as well as the Dean of the music school, Bill Hipp, and his wife, Frankie. They all came to dinner and helped trim the tree.

At the Christmas Eve service, those prayed for included "Marta, our seminarian." It seemed as if they were talking about someone else. Even though St. Andrew's was my sponsoring church, and I still pledged to it, I didn't feel like part of the congregation anymore. From my conversations with the Texas seminarians, I knew this was not the case for them. They were closer to home and were included in many of their church activities. But many of the out-of-state students, like me, often said they felt they were in limbo. I could identify with that, but came to realize to my surprise I didn't mind after a while. My life, my community, my friends were all changing. In many ways, God was changing for me too. I think I was becoming a "process theologian." [33]In most respects, this was a welcome, positive change.

Later, I would view my seminary interlude as an in-between time, like after the Ascension, before Pentecost, when Jesus has gone, and the Holy Spirit he promised to send had not yet been realized in people's lives. But I didn't equate anything in my life just then to the rhythmic cadences of the church's liturgical calendar. I only knew I had to hang in for the long haul and hope things would get easier. Too, I think I was experiencing what my liturgics professor would have called "limenality," a somewhat unclassifiable state of transition that exists between separation and integration.

The plans for an intervention still had not materialized, but I was hopeful something would happen. Leslie and Ed were coming back later in the month. And I planned to return after exams before January term started on the chance something could be worked out. I think that's when God arranged His own intervention.

A few days after the tree trimming, Austin went to see his cardiologist for his annual physical exam. George suggested some tests be taken. He then called me with the results and suggested Austin return to discuss them. One test showed his liver enzymes were up, signaling reversible liver damage. "Unless you take immediate steps and do something," George told him, "you're heading for serious trouble." That got through to Austin. Show him a scientific reason for something and he'll usually listen. He came home and told me he had a problem and that George was checking him in to the hospital for a few days. (It ended up being six weeks.) Austin would not tell me it was because of alcohol, but did suggest perhaps he'd been smoking too much! I didn't care what he told me. Whatever it took to get him there was all that mattered. The rest of that vacation is a blur now, but I know I went back to school relieved and grateful.

I'm sure God's hand was involved in all this, because it's hard to believe it was just a coincidence that the apartment I had rented in Texas belonged to the lady who had started the Falkner Center. This was a drug and rehabilitation place, named after her husband who had died of alcoholism. Since I was unable to attend any of the family sessions Austin was doing in Miami, I found out I could attend similar sessions in Texas. And did. I also began to attend Al Anon. I couldn't believe there were so many addictive people in such a small city; decided if Austin, Texas were any barometer, then the USA was in deep trouble. Drugs and alcohol were something I knew very little about. As a child, I came to realize

I'd been pretty protected. It was quite a revelation to me to discover there were so many people involved either <u>as</u> or <u>with</u> addicts. I dutifully went to Al Anon for a while and also continued writing love letters to Austin, and, occasionally, to God.

*Dear God,*

*How would you have me be? I know how I want to be. But I'm not sure that's how you want me to be. And when I get a glimmer, I'm not sure how to get from where I am to where you are.*

*Deep down, I want to be like Bishop Richards, God—the part of him that's so loving and understanding and accepting and discerning. He's holy, God. At least the part in him I've been able to see. I think you'd like that goal for me too.*

*I want you as a friend, God. That means I have to be a friend to you. That shouldn't be too hard, should it? Of course it means I have to be honest. Please help me be that.*

*I'm married right now to an alcoholic. But you already know that. So you know how it hurts. I guess that's a good place to start.*

*When I went to my third Al Anon meeting, the girl next to me said: "I'm Cindy and I'm a grateful Al Anon."*

*When it got to me, all I could say was "I'm Marta." I didn't feel grateful, God. I felt it was Austin's fault that I had to go to Al Anon. I'm not the one who's been drinking. I feel like I'm being punished for his behavior. I don't think that's very fair. It's like cursillo. I was always left out because Austin wouldn't go.*

*Our marriage is a shambles. I'm not denying that anymore. And I'm not denying Austin is an alcoholic. I've written Sandy and John and Bill and Frankie and Jim and Shirley and Macon and Ginny. And I've told Len and many of my friends here. I'm trying hard to face that reality in my life.*

*What else have I been running from, God? Will you help me face up to the other things I must be doing wrong? I know seminary has been an escape for my failed marriage, but it's been a life-affirming escape. I couldn't bear to leave seminary right now, regardless of how much I dislike it at times, and return to Florida. That's all pride, isn't it? After going off to become a priest, I wouldn't want to return and admit I'm such a miserable failure.*

*Last Thursday after classes, I got talking with Dr. Coke. And I told him I thought people really invented you. The part about Your Son, I mean. By that, I was trying to say that man made Christ—God—in man's image, rather than your sending a Son in Your image. That idea makes more sense to me than the other, but Dr. Coke was rather surprised. He suggested perhaps I not tell that to the examining chaplains if the subject ever came up.*

*But then the next evening I was reading something by Alan Jones and he said it's hard sometimes to believe in God; so the important thing to remember at a time like that is to remember that God believes in us. And that made a lot of sense to me. That's helping me to put you into the middle of my prayer life at last. Whenever I get really down, I stop and consciously tell myself that <u>You</u> believe in* _me_, then everything starts looking brighter. That's sort of like you are already in my life, so I don't have to go looking for you. By way of extension, that's putting you, God, first and mankind second; which contradicts what I told Dr Coke. So that's been a peculiar paradox in my life this past week.

A few weeks later, I wrote God another letter.

Dear God,
    Touch my heart. Please keep touching my heart. It gets so constricted with every day chores and cares and concerns, usually unimportant things, so that I miss the times that I should be there for others.
    Why am I so many "me's"? Why can't I always be grounded in you?
    Watching the news this evening.... .all those poor kids in that orphanage, left to die, in a "warehouse" situation in Europe. It made me cry. I never used to cry when I saw suffering like that. But their potential has been taken away from them at such an early age. And all those people murdered and tortured in South America. There are so many awful things going on all over the world, right now, God. Wouldn't it be wonderful if we could all learn to love each other better? Why do people treat one another so badly?
    I'm feeling ashamed I was complaining to you today about my marriage. Austin's come such a long way. And I think I have too in some respects. Please guide him, God, to know you better in his life, just as I ask the same for me.
    I think you've been telling me to go back to Al-Anon. I haven't felt the need until today. But perhaps I need it now.

It's difficult to explain all that happened to me my first semester in seminary. But all the reading, studying, writing papers and praying forced me to come to terms with the denial I'd been suppressing over Austin's alcoholism. And at last it explained the discomfort and confusion I'd experienced on the University of Miami's Board of Trustees, and why I'd approached some things in an unorthodox manner. I think too the denial over Austin's drinking had also suppressed other experiences in my life into a tight ball which began to unwind slowly, coming to the surface as I struggled through the following semesters. Intellectual recollections turned into emotional memories. It was like being in a geologic time scale. Some of the earlier periods of my life began emptying into the present, like volcanic magma pushing up and surfacing through accumulated strata previously laid down.

I knew I was in a healing process, but things were going on at such a deep level, there were times I could only get brief glimpses of what was really happening. Professor Spong emphasized in pastoral theology that what people told us initially were usually only the surface ripples of their lives. So I could very much relate to that.

Too, there were days when I felt I was hemming a black dress with a black thread in a dark room. Still, underneath it was the assurance things were improving and that the light would come back into my life. And it did, eventually. The study of family systems opened up a whole new world to me. One did not have to stay in the same rut as dictated by family, or culture, or community. One could *change*. And not like a mobile out of balance, but by design. There were choices available I'd never thought about which began to hold promise.

After first semester, it was like a twenty thousand foot drop in altitude, tapering off finally into a gradual descent to normal life again. I recall the joy of having an entire morning, just to clean my apartment and do the laundry. That sounds rather mundane, but after being under constant pressure for five months, it took me a while to make the transition into everyday activities. I can remember standing a long time at the window one morning, just watching the sunrise, thankful I did not have to dive for the elevator and hurry to class. Time had become such an important commodity.

Besides sleeping for three week stretches on the sheets in my big bed, I determined the next best way to save time would be to install a FAX machine. Despite the statement that "seminarians have to resign from the real world," there were a lot of things from my other life that I could not totally shut out. At least once a week, a packet of emergency mail arrived, so called because I was the only one who could deal with it. I still had involvements with charities, long term gift commitments, partnerships, other business ventures and investments. I hadn't realized when I'd become so involved in things a decade or so earlier that it would take years to extricate myself from some of these activities.

Also, since I left my apartment very early each day, various people were always having difficulty getting hold of me, or I with them. So I solved that problem with the FAX machine son Kermit had sent to me. It sat on the floor on an upturned waste basket next to a dresser near the big bed. It was an inexpensive FAX without a paper cutter. So, often I would return home to find rolls of paper all over the bedroom floor with information from all kinds of people. That funny little FAX was my lifeline to the more sane world. That's because there were times when seminary and the process towards ordination made so very little sense to me. But it was nice coming home to that empty apartment to find occasional messages of cheer on the machine. It kept me in touch with my community in the outside world. It also informed me one day that the New York offices where I had once lunched with Mr. Holmes a'Court were now closed. I hadn't had time yet to wonder much about Mr. Bond. We had a few months still before he was to pay us back. But I wondered now and then about Mr. "Homac" and how he was adjusting to his precipitous downfall.

Upon my return to seminary after Christmas that first year, Austin went through de-tox at South Miami Hospital and stopped drinking for good. After that, my life began to brighten as well. Having a place to be while he was working through this experience was literally a Godsend for us both. I'm not sure our marriage would have survived had we been living together then. While he was coming to terms with his life, I was coming to terms with mine, as well as my reactions to his changing. Though we communicated by letter or phone, we spent little time together. But each time we did see one another, it was a good and positive experience. I know at times he felt I had abandoned him. But leaving home when I did was what saved our marriage. Certainly it became stronger and more meaningful.

Seminary helped me come to the realization that much of what I had previously believed still made sense. It validated my spirituality, only with a different vocabulary. It helped me dump a lot of needless intellectual baggage I'd been toting around for years, and it also helped me distill out of the matrix of learning what was really important to me, and what was not. Seminary enlarged and changed some of my views; it also affirmed me. Early on, once I'd managed to hand in a required essay that didn't get sent back for a re-write, I felt I was finally launched in a positive direction. Apparently my professors thought so too, because I never had much difficulty with any subsequent assignments.

The remainder of three years went quickly and I tried hard to fit into the community. For the most part, I think I did. Still, Texas never seemed like home to me. I was more like a migrating bird sitting precariously on a telephone wire, waiting to fly on.

When Austin and I finally got back together permanently, it was on a different footing, at a very different level. And what made me realize how much he really had changed was the sensitivity and support he showed for me when I returned for good to Miami.

But before that, there would be two and one-half years more of school, and training, and traveling, all of which, God willing, would culminate in my ordination. In retrospect, once I sorted out what I believed—what the Christ of faith and the Christ of history were all about—and that no one was going to be upset if I subscribed intellectually to Vawter's Theory of Resurrectional Retroactivity, the remaining years of seminary went really well.

# PART IV

# 23

# TRINITY INSTITUTE

The Episcopal Theological Seminary of the Southwest was intentional in exposing its students to as many experiences as possible. Especially did they want us to have an overall view of the Anglican Communion and the operation of the entire church. I guess that's why for January term of our first year, all students signing up for the class in Mystical and Ascetical Theology were required to attend the Trinity Institute in San Francisco. When it was discovered the seminary would be paying our air fares, nearly everyone signed up.

I was accustomed to traveling; the fact I was getting credit for something I normally loved to do anyway made it a plus. It was a surprise to me that several of the students had never been out of the state of Texas, and it was on this trip I was first able to see the impact seminary was beginning to have on my classmates. At the outset, I saw these changes only in others; it was not until later that I began to recognize them in myself.

The Institute did not begin until Sunday, so the seminary told us we could go west a few days early, stay there at our own expense, and explore San Francisco. Most of us did not have classes late in the week, so that's what we did.

One of the students made arrangements in advance for us to go to a hotel all could afford. By the time we got to San Francisco and found our luggage, it was dark. As we rode into the city, the driver of the van I was in pointed out various landmarks to the inquiring students. Said he, as he dropped us at our hotel: "If you do any walking around here at night, don't go out alone, be sure to stick together, and above all," he cautioned, pointing out the window, "don't walk in that direction."

We dragged our bags into the lobby. After looking about, it was not difficult to see why we'd gotten a bargain on the room rates. When we got to the desk, the hotel clerk informed us they didn't have enough rooms, "but we'll put you in our sister hotel a few blocks from here."

We were all upset, but there was little we could do except go to the other hotel. Since most were on tight budgets, no one even suggested more transportation. We asked where the second place was and proceeded to drag our luggage out of the lobby.

When we got outside and followed the directions given, several of us recognized we were heading in the direction we'd been warned to stay out of. At first, it wasn't bad, but soon we passed two run-down looking bars. A strip joint showed up in the next block followed by some advertising about transvestites. This was followed next by an "adult only" movie house, then several more bars. The sidewalks were rough cobblestone which made it difficult to walk on with suitcases, and those fortunate enough to have luggage with wheels found it almost impossible to drag them across the uneven surfaces. Mine possessed wheels that rapidly got out of alignment; so every time I came to a large cobblestone, my suitcase tipped over. The farther we walked towards what we hoped would soon be our hotel, the more people we saw sleeping in alleyways. We also had to keep stepping over an increasing number of empty or broken bottles. After the third block, we saw several more people stretched out on the pavement. After five blocks—each one raising our apprehension level considerably—we reached the second hotel, which was locked. We tried to read the instructions on the door in the dark, finally succeeded in finding and ringing the bell, and after an interminable wait, were let in. The clerk said they had not been expecting so many of us, that we would have to make do with what was available.

I eventually ended up in a room with one queen sized bed and five women. The men had somewhat similar arrangements. By then, we were all exhausted.

I didn't feel right, however, with what the clerk had told us, so while my roommates tried to figure out how to arrange the sleeping accommodations, I told them I'd go in search of extra pillows and blankets. I was thinking perhaps one of us could sleep in the bathtub. By the time I got to the front desk, I was angry. There was no excuse for this. It reminded me of the time Austin and I had ended up in a hotel in Lima, Peru, with prepaid reservations, only to be told they didn't have space. We'd finally had to sleep in a small room with another man, with two twin beds, a sheet strung up between us, the stranger in one bed and Austin and I crammed into the other.

"Why aren't there any more rooms?" I asked. "We had reservations. The other hotel told us you had space." I tried to be polite. Then something prompted me to pull out my American Express card. "Isn't there a chance you might have some more rooms with several more beds, one you may have overlooked? And some extra blankets and pillows so we can use the bathtubs to sleep in?"

The night clerk eyed the card, hesitated, then became all business. "Well, there might be another room." And what a coincidence. There was, and it just so happened to be right next door to the one we already had. "You can have it for an extra fifty dollars."

I should have raised the roof and questioned why he hadn't offered it to us originally, but it was late and I was tired. I agreed to pay as long as we got the extra pillows and blankets. Luckily, the second room had two beds.

We awoke the next morning to a strange scene. Our rooms looked out on an open area totally covered with newspapers. It took us a while to realize there were people sleeping under them. The damp January air in San Francisco can be very chilly. How good our rooms looked to us then! We had ended up, unwittingly, in the tenderloin district of the city where many homeless try to get by. I had to laugh, thinking what a great experience this was for seminary students. The Dean could not have done better if he'd planned it.

As soon as hunger finally forced us to band together to look for breakfast, various panhandlers approached our little group asking for help. One asked Kenny (though that was not his real name) if Kenny could give him some money. Kenny turned pale and did not know what to say or how to relate. We all knew Jesus had said to feed the poor and the outcasts. Could he have been talking about *these* people? Kenny was not naïve by any stretch of the imagination, but he'd never envisioned himself being in a place such as this. And he admitted later to being horrified that someone might touch him. But by the end of our stay in that section, he began to relate. He was able, when approached, to say honestly he had no extra money to share, but that he did care about their plight and hoped it would improve. We all learned to ask if there were not places they could go to for shelter. Were there any soup kitchens in the area? Did they have families?

All our readings and discussions to that point in our little community suddenly began to come into play. And I think for the first time, we became fully aware that our formation for priesthood had begun in earnest and that it would invariably come from unpredictable situations.

Having spent some of my early life in South America, I had seen lots of poverty. That's the way life was there. Some were rich; some were poor. There wasn't much of a middle class. And the Roman Catholic Church helped keep it that way. Education and improving one's lot were not high on the agenda. The church was better at getting people to accept their poor station in life as "God's will," rather than helping them to rise above their poverty. And my mother, even though she sympathized with the down-trodden and often went out of her way to help people she considered less fortunate, did not expose me to the sad or sordid things in life around us. Once in Maracaibo, going home from the market some distance away from the oil camp where we lived, I could not help seeing an unusual person begging on a corner.

"What's the matter with that lady?" I asked.

"She must have elephantiasis," my mother observed, trying to get in front of me so I would not see more. But I looked anyway, the lady was so different from anyone I had ever seen. She was in fact so grotesque that she appeared almost inhuman. But Mother whisked me away without more comment. I never saw another person like that in my years in Venezuela, but I saw many other things to remind me that other people were not like us, nor did they live the way we did. So, when my class ended up in the skid row area of San Francisco, what I saw did not surprise nor repel me, as it may have some of my friends. It was just another aspect of life that society in general tries to overlook.

When the Trinity Institute eventually began, we moved "uptown" to pre-arranged homes of parishioners from Grace Cathedral who had volunteered to let us stay with them. These accommodations were a great improvement after our hotel. My hosts lived not far from a bus line; I was able to ride or walk to the cathedral as time allowed; and my bed was conspicuously comfortable.

That off-campus long weekend was a wonderfully stimulating experience. Bishop Tutu was there, as were Stanley Hauerwas, and Margaret Farley. They lifted us all intellectually and spiritually to a realm we were only just beginning to explore gingerly. It was exciting, heady stuff.

Several things Hauerwaus said have remained with me. One of these was his insistence that only by membership in a non-violent community can violent people be helped. A second was his statement that it was absurd to let children make up their minds about faith when they got older. Said he: "I want them to know the truth. If you give them choices, you are controlling them by pretending to be tolerant." And last: the greatest idolatry in his mind was the statement that "the family that prays together stays together." He told us that the Christian community is not about togetherness. It's about disciplining our wants and needs in congruence with the true story which gives us the resources to live truthful lives. And in the process of living that story out, togetherness happens, but only as a by-product.

This was during the time of the anti-apartheid movement in South Africa, so much of the content of Bishop Tutu's sermons and lectures dealt with peace and justice. He very much impressed me by the way he was able to weave Scripture in and out of his talks. In addition to meeting him, I had an opportunity to meet and hear the Dean of the Cathedral—Alan Jones—whose books—*Soul Making* and *Journey Into Christ*—I had been reading just prior to arrival.

And as I walked about the city, I could not help recall my days at Stanford when I had come there on dates for dinner or to parties, or to the Cal/Stanford Big Game. Back then, part of me had been very much in touch with the spirituality discovered during high school days, and though buried, it had never left me. Now, it was a matter of sifting through the past and uncovering and incorporating into my beliefs those kernels of love and truth that still remained. So much had lain dormant since my father's death. And happily, seminary was giving me the opportunity to reawaken those lost dreams.

# 24

# CLINICAL PASTORAL
# EDUCATION

On the twenty ninth of January of 1989, our family was expecting the pay off from Mr. Bond. The gentleman we retained for these negotiations reported that Mr. Bond's representatives did not want to honor his commitment and tried to stall the proceedings. Anticipating in advance that problems could occur, legal work to file papers in circuit court had already begun. Our representative told them that we would begin charging 17% interest if they did not ante up on schedule, then surreptitiously let their attorney see part of a paper he was keeping in reserve under his briefcase. When they understood there was little room for posturing and that we were preparing to fight, they agreed to wire the funds. It wasn't any too soon either. Shortly thereafter, due to his questionable business practices, Mr. Bond's financial assets were frozen and he eventually ended up in an Australian jail. He (and others) were charged with offences in relation to the use of Bell Resources Ltd. funds in 1988–89 following the Bond Corp. Holdings Ltd. takeover of Holmes a' Court's Bell Group of companies. [34]

After this, I was happy to be a student and returned to Texas for my next semester. I found some of it tough, but not as difficult as first semester had been.

My second off-campus excursion was the following summer during Clinical Pastoral Education. This is a course required of anyone on the track for ordination. It's usually done either in a regular hospital, a prison or a psychiatric hospital and can be a good or a bad experience, depending on one's supervisor. I was fortunate in that I had an excellent supervisor, a priest named Lincoln Ure. There were a great many stories floating around about the horrors of CPE, just like the horrors of the GOE's (General Ordination Examinations), so I was anxious to get CPE behind me. My reason for applying to the hospital in Utah was because we had a condominium in the area so I would have a place to stay. Not only that, my sister lived in Salt Lake City not far from the hospital, so on nights when I would be on call, I could sleep at her house. By then, she had also been diagnosed with cancer and I wanted to spend as much time with her as possible.

Clinical Pastoral Education is a very intense program and, like seminary, leaves one absolutely no time for anything else. It's difficult to describe, but for me, it was a painful yet liberating experience, dealing primarily with illness, dying and death on a daily basis. We were all required to write a learning contract which we monitored in our reports, and the course essentially covered two areas of learning: the didactic, which included lots of lectures and seminars, and the clinical, which included verbatims, case studies, conferences and ward work. Besides the 400 required clinical hours, we were also on call one night each week as well as two weekends each.

At that time, St. Mark's had a 305 bed hospital, so all of us had opportunities to experience different areas. Included in our studies were IPRs (interpersonal relations), pastoral didactic meetings, understanding transference and triangulation, required reflection reports and evaluations, role playing, dreams and their analysis, AIDS information, drugs, alcohol, required books to be read, and home visits. Essentially, we were there to learn to minister to the patient's immediate needs and to guide them in the use of their spiritual and emotional resources.

Besides the tutorials of every possible description, there were services, prayers, our turns in the emergency units as well as being with families who were experiencing the deaths of loved ones.

The first few days were spent learning our way around the wards and preparing for being around various types of patients. When they walked us through the wards with the newborn infants, it triggered the remembrance of Christopher who had been born at the old St. Mark's hospital years earlier. I thought I had dealt with all the grief I could dig up at the Beginning Experience, but this had all related to his later years. Despite dreams about him as a child, I'd never dealt with the memory of him as a baby. The other students could not understand at first why the tears came streaming down my face when we walked through the obstetric wing the first time, but by then I didn't care what people thought. By then, I'd developed enough trust in the church as a community to know it was okay to cry.

But you never forget your babies. Just seeing those little people wrapped in blankets in all those bassinets brought everything back which I thought I'd left behind. Had it not been for my CPE training, however, I could never have coped with ministering as a chaplain at Jackson Memorial Hospital later, especially to those women who had lost newborns. You must deal with your own pain before you can be helpful to anyone else.

Seminary was rife with stories about CPE. One classmate, a year ahead of me, told me he'd had a pretty tough time. This was because he could not stand the sight of blood. The first time he was confronted with an accident patient, he told me he became hysterical and ran out of the room. The second time, he fainted! However, he said he finally was able to be around sick people, though he never would volunteer to make hospital calls unless it was forced upon him. But he was really the exception.

Our first week, just to see how we reacted, we were asked to watch minor surgery. After rearing three children, seeing someone's hand sewn up didn't seem very intimidating to me; so then I was given a choice of one of several operations I could watch. I chose the open heart surgery which one of my patients would be having the following day. I was told to eat protein for breakfast, wear comfortable shoes, and to take deep breaths before entering the operating room. As an afterthought, the nurse said: "Please leave if you think you might faint."

At the appointed time, I was asked to stand by the wall until the doctor had sawed through the patient's breastbone, then braced open the rib cage. After that, I was invited to watch the rest of the operation. I stood next to the anesthesiologist, directly behind the man's head, looking down in to his chest cavity the entire time. It was all so fascinating I never even thought about getting sick or passing out.

There were six in my group. Three at St. Mark's Hospital and three at the Holy Cross Hospital. We alternated our seminars between the supervisors in the two hospitals where we had intense discussions relating to our verbatims (written papers from our conversations with the patients) as well as our reactions to what we were experiencing. I think it's safe to say all of us went home most nights physically and emotionally exhausted.

Two of us were Episcopal seminarians. Four were Roman Catholic, two of whom were male seminarians, one an Irish nun, the other a Catholic lay woman. One of the RC seminarians was adamantly opposed to the ordination of women priests, so we had some good discussions. The young man told me very seriously that the only time a woman should be allowed near the high altar was with a vacuum! I determined if ever he got ordained that I would send him a vacuum for his ordination gift. The poor kid was so hung up on sex and celibacy, however, I'm not sure he continued with his studies. I tried to suggest that one way out of his dilemma would be to become an Episcopal priest, but he was not amused. I never heard if he ever got ordained. Certainly he did not send me an invitation. But I would have sent the vacuum (along with something he would have liked) if he had!

Even though St. Mark's hospital had been started by the Episcopal Church in Utah, quite a few of our patients were Mormon. Normally they preferred the L.D.S. (Latter Day Saints) Hospital, because that's the Mormon hospital in Salt Lake City. However, some came to St. Mark's because their doctors sent them there. It was a large, growing hospital, moved from the northwest part of the city to the south part of the valley and built under the administration of the Episcopal Bishop (Richard Watson) who had become Bishop of Utah in 1951. I had worked one summer at a part-time job in the nutrition department at the old St. Mark's, and since our two sons had been born there, felt very much at home in my surroundings.

A chaplain is supposed to attend to the spiritual needs of a patient. It was always interesting to me to see how the Mormon patients reacted when they discovered I was an Episcopal chaplain. One could almost see the shades pulled down inside of them. Many Mormons are brought up to think only they have the real "truth" and that everyone else is wrong,[35] so it's their duty to try to convert people to their way of belief. They would immediately think I was there to proselytize, since that's how they operate. But I always asked if they wanted me to call their bishop or ward teacher to visit if there were a chance they might not know they were in the hospital. This usually surprised them. They interpreted this as a sure sign I might be a potential convert! Consequently, I had many offers to receive a copy of their *Book of Mormon.*

The Mormons are gradually changing, but slowly. A few years ago, if one did not live in conformity with their many rules and regulations, members could be hauled before a kangaroo court and soundly excoriated. They still practice shunning members who fall away from what they consider to be the "true church." And they very much discourage the questioning of their faith. Despite their emphasis on family, an Episcopal deacon told me one day he'd always loved to attend his family reunions, but had discovered recently that because he now attended the Episcopal church, his Mormon relatives had intentionally left him and his entire family out of their recent annual gathering.

It came as a real surprise to me during the summer of 2001 to hear Gordon Hinckley, their current leader and prophet, say that other world religions also had "truth." They did a superb job of turning a tolerant face to the world and to the many outsiders who went to Salt Lake City in 2002 to attend the Winter Olympics. I was personally impressed by the outpouring of many Mormons who helped and for their genuine courtesy and graciousness to all who attended.

For years, the Mormons have claimed to be the fastest growing church in the world, but recent figures show that since 1990, the Seventh Day Adventists,

Assemblies of God and Pentecostals have far outpaced them. One reason given for this is that the Mormon Church is now requiring its young people to be better trained and equipped before going on a mission. There used to be approximately 62,000 active missionaries throughout the world but this has dropped now to a figure more like 51,000. Whether this will remain at that number remains to be seen. I've been told there are upwards of 5 million Mormons in the United States and approximately 12 million worldwide.

From a wider view, of course, in times of turbulence and change, many people want to be told what to believe. They want a faith that will make them comfortable and always right. Anything that threatens this meets with rejection. The right wing fundamentalists in America are just as scary to me as Osama Bin Laden and his ilk. God gave us minds and I think he expects us to use them.

Many members of the Utah legislature are descendants of the early polygamists (who think of themselves as "True" Mormons), so it's taken years for the laws against plural marriages to be enforced. Even now, unless abuse can be shown to be present, the law tends to look the other way. Political conflicts and challenges to the Mormon's separatist communal and theocratic venture led the United States to dispatch troops to Utah in 1857 and assert federal authority. Brigham Young was notorious for his many wives, a practice taught as a religious principle by his predecessor, Joseph Smith. The latter sanctioned polygamous marriages back in the 1840's believing one could attain the highest levels of heaven by conceiving as many children as possible so they could bring more souls out of the limbo of pre-existence. Even though Utah could not become a state until polygamy was outlawed, it's estimated today that 2% of Utah's state population (or about 40,000 people) still practice it. There are various polygamous sects, but the one most in the public eye of late goes by the title of Fundamentalist Mormons (FLDS) whom the Latter Day Saints (LDS) Mormons do not recognize.

Many of the FLDS (estimated at 6,000) have been living in Colorado City, Arizona or Hilldale, Utah, where enforcing anti-polygamy laws has been difficult. That's partly because half of the police force practiced polygamy. But this particular group headed by Warren S. Jeffs finally forced the legislature to do something about the sect's practice of assigning under-age girls to marriages with older men. Child abuse was finally brought out into the open and they were forced to act.

The African Church, which is part of the worldwide Anglican Communion, also includes polygamists. But it's not against the law in Africa. I'd hate to be part of a polygamous marriage, but recognize also that this is a matter of culture in some areas of the world, just as it once was in Biblical times as well as Utah's early history. Changing the law doesn't necessarily change the culture, however.

A group of women in Utah, former members of polygamous situations, who are members of *Tapestry*, offer self-help to women who are stranded and want to get out of polygamous relationships. They give them support and help if they want to leave with their children in order to build a different life. *Tapestry* firmly believes that male manipulation and exploitation are what keep the practice of polygamy still going. Sadly, the two towns in Arizona and Utah, with their large pockets of plural marriages, show that many of the large families have to be heavily subsidized by Utah taxpayers.

It's my belief that whenever one group holds the power in a community that there will always be some forms of discrimination. But the programs of regular Mormons for their young people are very good and they are to be commended for their work ethic and dedication to family and community.[36] Sadly, however, their insistence on reparative therapy for gays and lesbians, rather than help, tends to tear some families apart. An article in the *Salt Lake Tribune* in December, 2006, however states they are now openly discussing this issue as are many other churches. On that same subject, one of the issues in the Episcopal Church at present is over the ordination of bishops who are homosexual. This has yet to be resolved amicably within the wider Anglican Communion. Hopefully, science will come to the rescue of the outdated theology in so many of our churches. For me, it's a no brainer. God made heterosexuals and God made homosexuals. Who are we to pass judgment?

# 25

# RUSSIA

CPE (Clinical Pastoral Education) finally ended August 16th the summer of 1989, just barely giving me time to get my life in order and suitcase packed before leaving for Russia. The trip was sponsored by Trinity Church parish in New York City where I met up first with other seminarians who were going. The Rev. James C. McReynolds, who directed the program, was accompanied by Dr. William Green, our mentor, chaperone and theology professor. As a member of the International Anglican-Orthodox Joint Doctrinal Discussions Committee, Dr. Green was adept at explaining the orthodox views. There were twenty-six of us in all, eight of whom were from my class.

The evening before our trip officially began, we students were invited to the apartment of Canon Edward West who lived behind the Cathedral of Saint-John-the-Divine. St. John's is an enormous, beautiful, Gothic church in the throes of what appeared to me to be under continuous renovation. It was disconcerting to learn it costs $23,000 a day just to keep it open.

After a brief look at the cathedral, we walked to Canon West's museum-like apartment filled with icons, pictures, and a veritable assortment of Russian mementos and treasures. Here, his five exuberant dogs—a cocker spaniel, some retrievers and an Irish setter—greeted us. They had the run of the place, including all the leather chairs, so one had to stake out a chair and keep the dogs off, or else stand! But he served us a tasty dinner that included Ukrainian borscht, black bread, salad and cheesecake.

In addition to his icons, the Canon's showcases included crosses inlaid with amethysts and topaz from the 14th-17th centuries, a Roman coin with Caesar's head on it (the same type Christ purportedly held up when he said "Render unto Caesar the things that are Caesar's") and some intricate looking eggs. The Canon removed a gold tiara from one of the cabinets and placed it successively on all the women guest's heads. In Russian history, these were used at wedding ceremonies.

All of the Canon's godchildren, we were informed, had used these at their weddings.

Canon West had been described to me as "eccentric." I found him to be a delightful conversationalist, full of fascinating bits of information. He sat at the end of the coffee table and held court all evening in a long eggshell colored robe. Around his neck was a chain that held a cross inlaid with mother-of-pearl.

The next day we met at Trinity Place, across from the Gothic-spired Trinity church designed by Richard Upjohn. It was here Dr. Green gave us an overview of Anglican-Orthodox relations which began in 1920. This was when the Orthodox first visited the Lambeth Conference. At that time the Archbishop of Canterbury and the Patriarch of the Orthodox Church appointed a commission to come together to explore areas of agreement as well as areas where the churches differed. The agenda had included such items as scripture, creeds and councils, ecclesiology, dogma, theological opinion and the veneration of the Theotokos. The first conference was held in the early 1930's. Since there appeared to be serious differences, the Archbishop felt a permanent working group was needed. Although interrupted by World War 2, dialogue was reestablished in 1948 at Lambeth and they have been meeting ever since. There are still areas of disagreement, especially regarding the ordination of women, as well as the Filioque clause[37] but in time, it is hoped these dialogues with the Orthodox will eventually restore Eucharistic communion. Our own *Book of Common Prayer* already incorporates much of their liturgy.

Our flight to Russia had a five-hour layover in Helsinki that gave us time to explore. I loved the clean lines of the Finnish architecture—Finlandia Hall as an example—and the lantern held by large stone sculptures overhanging the entrance to the railroad station. I found a lovely spot along the water at Toolonlahti Lake also where I enjoyed visiting with a girl from Lapland studying to be a lawyer. It was a wonderful, sunny break that gave us an opportunity to take pictures and stretch our legs before continuing.

Not only do Russian subways run on time, so do their airplanes. We left Helsinki for Leningrad on schedule aboard a Russian Aeroflot plane. Although quarters were cramped, everything was done with efficiency. These planes are set up so they can be converted into troop carriers at a moment's notice. For this reason, comfort is not a consideration. There were no emergency instructions, written or verbal, and though we arrived safely and on time, I vowed I would never again fly Aeroflot. Unfortunately, I was seated next to a man very much opposed to the ordination of women. The entire flight consisted of having to listen to his views. He was a terrible bore, but likable nevertheless. But he never once allowed me to state any of my views. It was at least a relief to discover he was not Episcopalian. I was also grateful for my previous weeks of CPE training. It was quite easy, I discovered, to let his words float over me like so many hot air balloons.

In Leningrad, we hooked up with a Cadillac of guides—Mouza Makousheva—who was totally unflappable. No matter what happened (and a lot did), she always found the bright side. Of course, we got to visit the usual tourist things—Petrodvorets (the winter and summer palaces of the Tsars), the Palace of Count Stroganoff, the Admiralty building and the old harbor of St. Petersburg, as well as the Hermitage Museum. The latter had wonderful art including works by Da Vinci, Rembrandt, Raphael, Titian, Michelangelo, Matisse and Picasso. Unlike many museums, one could get as close to them as one wished. But what really amazed me was the absence of any protection from the sun on some of these priceless paintings.

This was at the time when *glasnost* (opennes) and *perestroika* (reconstruction or rebuilding) were coming into vogue and Russia was just beginning to open up to the churches. It was also the anniversary of the introduction of Christianity into Russia one thousand years earlier. Officially Russia is an atheistic state with Lenin its "patron saint," but when we visited, six hundred churches had by then opened up as a result of *perestroika*. Prior to that, under Kruschev, the churches had all been closed and many Christians persecuted.

Memories of my Russian studies from college days began to come to life. It was fascinating to see the castle where Rasputin had been offered poisoned cakes. And there was a long University building with barred fence casting shadows over its walls and flowers. We visited one section called New Holland, saw Theater Square and the monument to Russian composers. There was also the conservatory where Rimsky Korsakoff had worked, and the fortress of Saints Peter and Paul where Peter the Great is buried. And there were the cathedral of St. Nicholas, Hay Market Square (where Dostoevski had lived), the Swan Canal and the Neva River, which we crossed many times over the Kerof bridge. We went through many of the twenty-one districts that make up Leningrad, and in the Tar pit area, visited the Smolmy nunnery, a beautiful blue and white building in the Russian baroque style. There was a drama house named for Pushkin. And one evening, along with many Japanese tourists, we attended a performance by Russian Cossack folk dancers.

Our academic part of the journey began with a visit to the Leningrad Theological Academy and Seminary, one of the three seminaries and two graduate theological schools of the Orthodox Church. At that time, I doubt we could have visited as regular tourists. Our own clergy among us wore black cassocks, and a liturgist—Professor Bronski—showed us around. This particular day, the students were taking competitive entrance exams which involved four subjects: oral prayers, a proficiency in church Slavonic, an ability to sing with a good sense of pitch and a knowledge of scripture and the sacred writings. My classmates and I all wondered how many of us would have made it in under equivalent requirements! Only one of four Russians who apply is accepted. But once in, the church provides for all a seminarian's needs. Morning prayer is required of all students and each day ends with prayer. Those already ordained take part in the liturgy; the un-ordained sing and read, and on major feasts, local people often participate.

Russian seminaries get all their monies from tithes and offerings; there is no such thing as a tax credit in Russia, and anyone receiving a salary from the church pays a higher tax. The Council for Religious Affairs is the link between church and state; they do not have the separation to which we in the West are accustomed.

In their beautiful chapel, Professor Bronski explained the iconostasis—the wall that separates the sanctuary from the main church. The iconostasis here had three levels and on the second level one could see all twelve feasts of the Orthodox Church. The third level contained the icon of the Last Supper. Normally the icon on the left is the Mother of God; on the right is the Savior. This seminary's icons included Our Lady of the Sign from the 17th century that belonged to the family of Tsar Peter the Great. It was used at his coronation and later moved to the academy after the war. They also had another beautiful one from Kazan.

I had never thought about icons until introduced to them through the orthodox faith. Icon means "image," and more specifically the holy images used in worship. They serve as a window to the divine and many Russians have an icon corner in one room of their home which plays a vivid role in their daily lives. They are living scriptures in a sense, painted (or written) by those who closely follow the rules of iconography. These painters must be Christian, and in Russian iconography, the face and hands of an image can only be painted in canonical times when the painter is fasting.

The librarian—Alexander Alexandrovich—a very gentle and sensitive man—told us they had the richest theological library in the USSR with 200,000 books and journals, some dating back to the 16th century, including sixty Bibles in various languages.

After this, we visited St. Isaac's Cathedral which at one time was the main Orthodox church for the entire country. It has a capacity for 14,000 people. The church, including the ceiling, is utterly fantastic. I recall a dove visible at the very top of the dome. The under structure was a beautiful example of 19th century architecture. It had lapis and malachite-faced columns, a gilded dome, bronze doors and a white marble iconostasis. The exterior had huge columns made of granite brought from Finland and our guide impressed upon us the "hot process" which used gold and mercury necessary to accomplish the gold work. The chief architect—Montferrand—had begun the church when he was 32, completing it at age 72. When he asked to be buried in it, he was refused, so because of this, left Russia. St. Isaacs is currently maintained by the Soviet Ministry of Culture as a museum.

Our next stop was Novgorod, meaning "new city." This was one of the few areas that survived the Tartar invasion. The Swedish later invaded in the 17th century, and in World War 2, the Nazis destroyed it. Of a population of 240,000, only 30 persons from Novgorod survived the Second World War. We visited this area because of their icon painting school that dated back to the 12th century.

On the three hour bus ride from Leningrad, we passed large collective farms of wheat, cabbage and sunflowers. There were many really quaint cottages alongside the farms with small gardens where the workers lived. We saw apples and peaches as well as many greenhouse type plastic covered frames for new plants. It was a nice three lane highway. Once we were stopped for a road check by a policeman ("a little man with a little authority," said Mouza), but when a bus goes beyond its normal district, the driver must show that his papers are in order. The cemeteries we passed were well kept. There were lovely stands of birch, evergreen, poplar and mountain ash. Often I spotted yellow flowering shrubs similar to the gorse one sees in New Zealand. There were a few rest areas, although we never "rested," and occasional signs showed deer crossings. Sometimes we saw men cutting weeds with hand scythes. There were also periodic gas stations and many haystacks.

We passed trucks carrying huge loads of cabbages and potatoes and every so often large apartment complexes would suddenly loom up on the horizon. There were few private autos in this section of Russia, only buses and many old trucks. We were told there were television, furniture, and porcelain plants near Novgorod and that one factory produced bells for cows and horses. Many of the women I saw were very stocky.

After Novgorod, we departed for Odessa, Russia's seaport on the Black Sea. We did a lot of sight-seeing and shopping about, but what I especially remember was the morning we participated in the Holy Eucharist in a private dining room of the hotel. Dr. Green led the service and gave a short sermon on the eastern Orthodox and how they view their faith. "Important is the fact that Christ has risen. He has risen indeed!" he said. The Orthodox believe in raising earth upward to heaven. They also believe in the communion of all the saints. Their icons symbolize this in that they represent all who have gone before. I could not help think how I'd read somewhere that some Christians worship a crucified Christ who has risen, while others worship a risen Christ who was crucified. I still think about this.

The seminary in Odessa was primarily to train seminarians, although they also had a small ecclesiastical and archaeological museum with a wonderful display of iconography. Many icons were from different parts of the country, from different centuries, with some showing as many as five saints on one icon. Even though all the rules of iconography were followed, one could see the progression of changes through time as old styles became less acceptable and new styles came into vogue. Some were even embroidered.

There was one case filled with crosses from the 11$^{th}$ century going up through a 19$^{th}$ century folding cross—used by people who traveled. There were models of churches, coins from the time of Constantine, medals from international conferences and Gospels in many languages from various centuries. There was one exquisite three dimensional construction of the Last Supper, all done in inlaid mother-of-pearl. And one icon—three in one—showed the Father, Christ and a dove, which changed depending on the direction it was viewed.

I somewhat expanded the idea later in an Anglican Studies class project to show an enlarged picture of Thomas Cranmer behind a vertical series of hanging slats (like a vertical venetian blind) which when opened one way showed the *First Prayer Book of King Edward VI of 1549,* then when reversed, showed a hand in the fire, reminiscent of Cranmer's final act before being burned at the stake. I guess it raised a few eyebrows, but I thought it was neat. It was one of the more fun, creative assignments I did in seminary. The reversal of the blind was symbolic of Cranmer's life who, at the end, revoked all his recantations saying he had not believed them but had signed in the hope of saving his life. Facing his martyrdom, plunging his hand that had signed the recantations into the flames, he said: "This hand hath offended." And it is said as soon as the fire got up he was very soon dead, never stirring or crying all the while. Possibly my idea was too subtle for some, but I liked it! At the end, it was Cranmer's loyalty to truth, though it cost him his life, which saved him from a betrayal of the best that was in him. His monument, of course, lives on in the *Book of Common Prayer.*

In Odessa, most of us attended the two services celebrating the Feast of the Dormition of the Theotokos. This title, meaning "God bearer," was attributed to the Blessed Virgin Mary around 4 a.d. The evening service, which lasted three hours, was beautifully sung, ending with candles passed and lighted.

The following day we returned for the Eucharistic liturgy which was the highlight of our trip here. Since we had arrived in plenty of time to be seated, our hosts invited the *men* in our group to see the sanctuary behind the iconostasis. Women were not allowed. All of the men went with the exception of one priest—the Very Rev. Hollinshead Knight—who was at that time the Dean of the Cathedral in Honolulu, Hawaii. He and his wife—Ann—had flown from London to join our tour. When I noticed him still sitting with us, I finally asked why he hadn't gone with the others. "I couldn't. It wouldn't be right," he said, "not when you aren't allowed to go too. I prefer to remain in solidarity with you women." *What a neat man,* I thought. We all wanted to hug him on the spot.

Knowing we were westerners accustomed to sitting for services, our hosts arranged chairs placed on either side of the altar for each of us. Everyone normally stands through an orthodox service. From this fantastic vantage point, we had an opportunity to view everything. The orthodox liturgy is a beautiful blending of incense, colorful vestments, singing, candles, crosses, icons and banners. It is certainly not something one forgets in a hurry. This particular service also included the ordination of a priest.

When it was over, the Metropolitan processed through the throng of people and motioned that we follow directly behind. As we did, people (mostly women) grasped our hands and kissed them and asked the priests amongst us for blessings. There were tears in the eyes of some, as well as warmth and joy radiating from their faces. There was so much love directed towards us that it would have taken a hardhearted person indeed not to have been swept up in the moments of that experience. The three hour liturgy passed so quickly that I had difficulty believing we had been there that long. Clearly too, where there is love, there are no language barriers. I can still see those beautiful faces and hear the choir singing the *Gospodi Pomilui.*

Our next stop was the monastery of the Dormition, founded in 1824 with 50 monks. Connected with it was a seminary where 300 boys were studying. They related well to our male seminarians, but when they discovered some of us females were also in the same class, they had difficulty handling that. Not just for their cultural and theological reasons, but perhaps because once one is ready for ordination in Russia, one is expected to grow a beard! When we asked why, we were told that "Discipline has to be alert" or "A beard gives a priest away."

The Orthodox see the question of women's ordination, as well as the ecumenical movement, as a purely western phenomenon, based on western presuppositions and determined by a specifically western agenda. This is because the Orthodox have a pre-scholastic experience of the church, just as we have a post enlightenment perspective. The Reformation, Counter-Reformation and Renaissance were absent from the Russian Eastern Church which is one reason they were ready for the communal ideas of Marx. They do not have the concept of doctrinal development or, as the Roman Catholics have, a Magisterium, to decide which developments are legitimate and which are not.[38]

We were told they had 25 professors who taught 25 subjects, their task being to "prepare pastors for the church who could worthily represent the church anywhere." After four years here, some of the students would go on to study at the Moscow Theological Academy or the Theological Academy in Leningrad. They encouraged us to ask questions. I was told a steel factory had asked for a priest to speak to them about religion, the surprise result being that the workers stopped swearing!

Since *perestroika*, approximately 400 persons a day were visiting this monastery. Someone asked if the church was prepared to grasp the moment as presented by the current political changes occurring in the Soviet Union. Through our interpreter we heard him answer:

*We believe our 1000 years old tradition will help us do this. We do not differentiate between believers and non-believers. The average person gets a Christian education either at home or at a seminary. We have recently opened Diocesan Institutes and schools.... We are like a big pool with big fish. If you lower the water level, the fish might die. So we want to keep our conservatism. We have words and deeds ... our tradition comes from the Greeks in the $4^{th}$ century. We do not wish to take any bricks from the wall. We are not always sure what the church is. Is it teachers? Seminarians? Theologians? People? We are not sure. But we know we don't want to be up-to-date. The symbol of epiclesis is important to us ... our icons began in the first century a.d. and they are not going to change ... they are what will help us through the hard times ... we will be very cautious regarding women in the priesthood. People do not change quickly."*

The example he used for this was that they still use the Julian calendar and are having trouble getting people to use the Gregorian calendar. [39]The reason for this is that Roman Pope Gregory used it!

Before dinner, His Eminence Metroplitan Sergius of Odessa had us as a captive audience and spent time telling us about the Dormition of the Blessed Virgin and the traditions and beliefs of Eastern Orthodoxy. He also said they were anxiously awaiting the new law code for religious cults and hoped when the new session met in the fall that it would pass.[40]

Moscow was next. We settled into a hotel that sold us tokens for the drink machine that had "Senalco" in the lobby. This was a sparkling citrus crush canned in West Germany. It was disheartening that the hotel would only take dollars from us. They refused any offers of rubles for the tokens and likewise refused to accept our rubles for Russian stamps.

And we found lots of lines in Russia. We had to wait to purchase things, then wait in another line to pay for them and get a receipt, then back to the first line with the receipt where we got to wait for the purchase. There were few cash registers and no one seemed to have figured out a better way to do things. Only on the streets and in the open markets could we pay directly for purchases.

One of our first shopping stops, our guide took us to a place called *Faberge*. The entrance resembled a warehouse, and the store was small and dark. They did take rubles but there was not much to buy—a little amber, a few pieces of jewelry and some lacquer boxes. We had dutifully changed our American dollars into rubles upon arrival in Leningrad but soon discovered whereas the official banks gave us 1 ruble for .64, the black market gave us 10 rubles for $1.00. Few stores would take our rubles, so we were left either spending U.S. money, or getting very little for our exchanged money. And the Russians said we could not take out more than we had brought in! They had all kinds of rules, but we quickly learned no one was enforcing them. It was madness to go to a *Berioska* shop (where by law tourists were supposed to shop) and be expected to pay $100 for something that could be purchased for $10.00 on the black market. That's if it could be found, of course.

But capitalism, on a small basis, seemed to be growing and thriving in Russia. We were approached everywhere by people wanting to change money and sell us various articles. This usually involved purchases like T-shirts saying "Spy for the KGB" or *Glasnost* or *Perestroika* on them. There were also military watches, Russian caviar, nests of wooden dolls and lacquered boxes. We were, of course, supposed to get receipts of anything purchased to be taken out of the country, but this was not possible when purchased on the gray or black market, so we all bumbled along, hoping for the best.

I thought my moment of truth had arrived when we left the country and I had to show my passport before being allowed in to the departure lounge. The line had been moving along steadily until an official went to stamp my passport. He suddenly disappeared and I waited and waited for him to return, while everyone meanwhile behind me was agitating more and more to get moving. I was beginning to harbor visions of ending up in Siberia when he returned smiling, with my passport stamped. It turned out he had been so intrigued by the Antarctic stamps in it (which apparently he had never seen) that he'd taken my passport off to show other officials.

Our final trip 44 miles north of Moscow was to Zagorsk. It was here we visited the Holy Trinity/St. Sergius Lavra, a monastery founded in 1340 by St. Sergius. Brother George, a monk with a PhD from the Moscow Theological Academy, showed us around. He began by pointing us to a picture of the cosmonauts and directing us to the visitor's book. I noted Cyrus Vance and Jimmy and Rosalyn Carter had written their names in it when they had visited in July of 1987.

As far as monasteries go, this is the most important center in Russia. That's because this is the spot where the forces of the Russian nation first gathered. The first major victory of their troops occurred here in Zagorsk in 1380 after receiving Sergius' blessing. He is the patron saint of Russia and the Holy Trinity church was constructed over his relics.

There was an ecclesiastical museum here that included art of the catacombs donated from Alexandria. These had Byzantine icons showing Mary as nurturer, as well as 15th century icons of St. John Chrysostom and St. John the Baptist. The first icon on the entrance was 1000 years old and near it was a model of the catacombs. There were also the wooden patens and chalices used by Sergius and the sandals he wore in his grave before being exhumed.

One room was filled with different types of icons of the Mother of God (700 in all we were told). If gold covered, an icon symbolizes the divine light. Silver is used as a symbol of grace. Some icons are covered with pearls which symbolize that in Jesus and Mary, all good acts were fulfilled or complete.[41]

One icon had 160 types of icons on it representing the Theotokos. One of St. Lea of Rome had been painted by an artist with his teeth since he had no hands. The face and hands normally must show in an icon, but in this particular one, the rules of iconography had been broken.

Until this trip, I had never thought about icons, or venerating relics, I guess because I viewed it all as superstitious. I didn't disapprove of the practice certainly. It was just something *other* people did. As I came to understand more about icons, however, and the meanings they had for the orthodox, I also began to understand more why they venerated the relics of their saints.

Visiting in the chapel where St. Sergius was venerated, I suddenly found myself in a line that was moving towards his sarcophagus. A priest from our group in front of me opted not to go, but something caught me and I found

myself thinking: *I've come all this way to Zagorsk and here are all these Russian people who have come a long ways too to venerate their Saint, and I don't think I want to
miss this.* So I followed the line, past the candles to the sarcophagus of St. Sergius.
His remains were under a tapestry-like cloth. I knelt first, crossed myself, then
approached the coffin. Part of me was saying: *Can you believe you're doing this?* At
the foot of the coffin, there was a cloth on top which I kissed, then crossed myself
again as I had seen others do. Part of me by then was saying: *You crossed yourself
wrong … maybe you should have done this the orthodox way … cross from right to
left, not left to right.* By then, I'd gotten to the center and repeated the kneeling
and kiss again, then moved to the head of the coffin (which was glass) and kissed
that. Here I could see into St. Sergius' resting place which contained a protuber-
ance under a cloth, which I guess was part of his remains—a skull, perhaps.

Part of me kept asking why I was doing this; still, I did, and was glad. I was
touched by this action in a strange way. I had gone first out of curiosity, and
partly because Professor Green and my classmate—Francie McNutt—had been
ahead leading the way, but I partly went also because I'd begun to like what I'd
been reading about St. Sergius; about his ascetical life as a hermit in the forest. I
didn't know about being a hermit, but I knew I liked trees and forests. And
maybe in time, I hoped I could learn to be more like St. Sergius. In tune with
God.

On our return to Moscow, we made one last visit to St. Danilov's Monastery.
Here we met with the Director of External Church Relations which was established in 1942. Seventy people worked in this department and its policy is to
maintain relations with other churches working in the field of peace. This
includes non-Chalcedonians as well as non-Christian groups. It was interesting to
be told that there are as many Moslems in central Asia as there are Christians.
Alcoholics Anonymous was first established in Moscow by an Episcopal priest
and the army we were told had recently asked the church to send men to serve as
chaplains. Indeed, Russia was changing.

Our final activities in Moscow included a fun tour of the underground subway
system. It was very clean, modern, had lovely art, and only cost the equivalent of
a nickel to ride. We also got to visit the Kremlin and Red Square, Lenin's Tomb,
St. Basil's and the circus.

Walking in front of the Raisia Hotel—one of the largest in the world which I
was told contained 3000 rooms—I was surprised to see walking just ahead of me
the University of Miami's baseball team. I was no longer a trustee, but after being
immersed in such a different world, far from home and family for so long, I
somehow found those green and orange jackets comforting. They brought back a

nostalgic touch of Florida to me that I'd not had a chance to think about for a really long time.

# 26

# ST. LUKE'S, ATLANTA

After the Russian trip, it was back to Texas to begin my second year of seminary. After the first year when they "killed" us, this is the year we got "buried." It was a good year as far as seminary was concerned.

In December, I had an opportunity to go to Utah for four days. This was partly to be with my sister who was having a rough time with her chemo and radiation treatments, but also to be with my daughter and her husband who were planning to spend Christmas at Snowbird before going on to the South Pacific. Of course, I also wanted to ski.

It's difficult to relate how I felt after that second fall semester in school. Basically, I have to say it was like being a teenager all over again, except that I knew more this time around and could really appreciate being in love with love—and life—all over again. I guess I was so aware of being fifty-nine, that time was running out for me, that I just let out all the stops and decided I should really live what I believed. (In my paper on Tillich, I had told my professor that I believed in life *before* death, certainly not all that stuff on the bodily resurrection *after* death,) so when I got to Utah, I skied better than I'd ever skied in my life, certainly better than when I was eighteen or nineteen. And I chased my daughter one day down the steepest runs on the mountain, attacking the deep powder with gusto. I reveled in the cold temperatures, the wind blown snow, the fresh powder up to our knees. I don't know what happened to me, but it was like being in a time warp in a way, surrounded with memories and dreams and wonderful feelings that hadn't been mine for years. It was pure joy.

Of course, I wanted to be in Miami with Austin for Christmas and had to be there for the Commission on Ministry meeting also later in December, so I headed for home happier than I'd been in years. The holidays were wonderfully special, and then it was back to Texas.

Field Education placements for our January, 1990 term included working with people with AIDS, helping battered women, involvements with hospice,

Hispanic ministry, Junior Helping Hands and alcohol treatment centers—these all located in Texas. Others included Covenant House and St. Joseph House in New York City, St. Luke's in Atlanta, Georgia and the Church of the Savior in Washington D.C. I went to Georgia.

Prior to leaving for our assignment, my group attended a soup kitchen in Austin preceded by orientation meetings and discussions. Some of our reading included an article entitled *Helping and Hating the Homeless*, a second dealt with transcendence and a third with economic justice.[42] It was interesting and challenging background reading.

I liked the story our professor—Charlie Cook—told us: Someone wealthy had given Dorothy Day an expensive diamond ring which they expected her to sell and use for money to feed the poor. Instead, she gave the ring to a bag lady. Everyone was horrified, whereupon Dorothy Day said: *Who are we to decide how that lady will use her things? She can wear the ring and enjoy it; she can sell it and maybe use the money to feed herself for a few years, or she can go to the Caribbean on a three month cruise. It's her decision, not ours.* Charlie's point of course was to insure we would know where we were coming from with our own "stuff" before dealing with street people. "Know your biases," he stressed.

When we got to Atlanta, there were terrible cross winds. As our plane bounced around, I heard Charlie say: "This is bound to improve our prayer lives!"

I found it interesting that the transportation system into downtown Atlanta was called MARTA. When we arrived at St Luke's, the rector—Charles Bennison—met us and took us on a tour.

St. Luke's was a large, inner city church operating on a budget at that time of $1.6 million. They had 90 Sunday school teachers, and their outreach program included a soup kitchen, post office/mail room for 2000 homeless, a street academy and television ministry. They also had a CPE program and choir and housed the national headquarters for the Daughters of the King.

We were then shown around the city; stopped at the house in Auburn where Martin Luther King, Jr. had been born, saw Ebenezer church where Martin Luther King Sr. had preached and went to the MLK Center for Non-Violence. We also saw Atlanta University, passed Georgia Tech, and drove all about the outskirts seeing good as well as not-so-good areas. At one point, the rector's car lost its oil plug (and oil), so we had to get that fixed. When we went further, I noticed he was nearly out of gas. When I mentioned this, he said "Martha Martha, you are anxious and troubled." It took me a moment to realize he was quoting from the Bible! (Luke 10:41) However, fresh from Miami and thinking of our secretary's nephew who had been shot and paralyzed in Liberty City, I felt my concern over his cavalier attitude in a not-so-good area was justified.

For dinner, we ended up at Pascal's—a restaurant that had been a meeting place for many of the leaders of the civil rights movement in the 1960's. Then it was up at 5 the next day in order to be ready by 6 so we could get to early morning Eucharist, then report to work for kitchen duty. I was first given the job of unwrapping sandwiches to put on trays, then was assigned to dish out ice cream and cookies. We served over 400 men that day, mostly young and black, though there were a few whites and a few women with children. One lady had a five-day-old baby with her. I felt overwhelmed at first dishing out ice cream, until I finally realized I should *always* be giving out the bowl first that could be seen with the largest amount in it. That precluded its being traded back for one with a larger portion.

We next met Dr. Reynell Parkins, a black Panamanian priest. There was a great deal of wisdom in his comments and I only wish I could recall everything he said. I do remember he told us St. Luke's originally had the only soup kitchen in the city, but that there were more now. Reynell was concerned, however, that a woman was in charge because he felt this gave a wrong image to black men. In the early 1980's, we were told those in the soup lines had been predominantly white and elderly. Now they tended to be black and young, primarily due to the down-turn in the construction industry. But soup kitchens were really band-aids because basic causes were not being addressed. This is why Rev. Parkins had started SLEDCO (St. Luke's Economic Development Corp).

He went on to say they saw many now who were mentally ill, were on drugs, had AIDS, or were often physically ill with other problems. And he mentioned the modern hobos, there to rip off a system they refused to support. The problem was how to move them from the soup kitchen to the stage of economic self-sufficiency. It was fine to create jobs, but not if they only paid $4.00 an hour. People could not pay for rent, food or transportation on that, so they had to go to a soup kitchen. Having food would at least alleviate things so they could perhaps manage to pay the rent.

He addressed the need to understand fund-raising and to know about 501C3's. He was concerned that volunteer programs were usually for the convenience of the volunteers, not for the people they addressed. People looking for jobs needed to be out in the world being interviewed at 11a.m., not standing in line for a meal ticket.

In SLEDCO, Georgia Power had donated materials so they could insulate many low-cost homes to help people. He also stressed with the homeless it was very important to be able to identify those willing to work, and that one had to learn to be "wise as a serpent" yet "gentle as a dove." He told of a young man who had asked for a job, then murdered the couple who had taken him in.

At St. Luke's, they also helped people fill out forms, though most were not interested in full-time employment. The biggest problem was the mental attitude of the homeless who often did not want long term work but preferred to be paid the same day. The biggest issue they dealt with was self-image and the questions of worth and frustrations that accompanied this. It was important for them to believe Christ (or some higher power) was at the center of their lives so they could keep hope alive.

With its large budget, St. Luke's dealt with the upper levels of society on Sunday and with the lowest levels Monday through Friday. A number of parishioners we learned came to St. Luke's so they could live off the reputation of the involvement of the church with the poor, even though they themselves were not involved. Only about 25 of the 200 volunteers that attended the church were involved with poor people. But they did support the programs financially. So should a rector preach involvement or contribution, we were asked?

In Atlanta, the political power is held by the blacks; the economic power by the whites. And kindness can be interpreted as weakness depending on which side one is coming from. Basically, Dr. Parkins thought the Episcopal Church had to become more political in the future in order to make any impact.

He also reminded us that Judaism says society should be organized so that no one should have to become the object of charity. Though we don't have to become poor in order to help the poor, we can certainly help out of our surplus. And in his view, what we call racism is really classism. "That's where the cross hits the fan."

Tensions are raised when there is the issue of being responsible *to* and responsible *for* people. When people use the idea of entitlement like "you owe me," it ruffles feathers. We need to ask: "Whose responsibility is it?" I liked his story about changing a flat tire. Someone asks you to help and you say you will. So you start to help them change the tire and they go sit in the car and listen to the radio. You can then say to them: "Look, I love you unconditionally, but I sure don't have to be manipulated." At which point, you should leave them to change their own tire. When helping the poor, we have to keep asking ourselves if we are working *with* or *for* people.

He told us the most effective groups in our society were those who made demands, like the Black Muslims and the Mormons. This included political, economic as well as religious demands. The Muslims are effective because they require the entire family to come to the temple once a week. They insist on male responsibility and say "no guns" (unless it's to fight a war for Allah.) They also say "No drugs or alcohol" and expect their members to tithe.

It seemed strange to me viewing the civil rights history. Though I'd read extensively on it and kept up with it in the news, those were the years Austin and I had been trying to rear three children. So this was like deja vu in a way. Martin Luther King, Sr. had answered my letter when his son was killed, so I felt a certain kinship visiting his church.

But what really hit home to me that trip were the contrasts in my life. It was like being at the far end of a yo-yo string viewing the world in one way, only to be snapped back to another dimension, all the while spinning. Had I been in Austin, Texas that week, I would have been using my opera tickets to *Madame Butterfly*. The week before in Miami, Austin and I had been chauffeured by friends in their Rolls Royce to a party where we'd listened to the Yale Whiffenpoof choir and sipped cocktails around a pool that overlooked a vast, beautiful lawn leading down to a private yacht. I had returned to seminary to eat at El Buen Samaritano with the street people. And now I was working in a soup kitchen. No matter which world I was in, it was always the thought of the other that kept me going, though I couldn't say I was ever comfortable in either for long. But it all seemed right. So I just shrugged and continued on.

(Some years later, when back on the University of Miami's board of trustees, I was surprised how forcibly the Atlanta experience crashed in on me during discussions about low wages being paid to some of the university's cleaning employees. It involved a company the University had contracted with to hire those people for us and a union that was trying to organize the workers. All I could think of were the homeless I'd often seen and the nagging fact that I was quite certain I could not survive on the wages they were being paid. The University did the right thing and raised wages and arranged for health care. Still, it took forever to get the company and the union to work things out. Of course, each group had its turf to defend.)

Our first Sunday in Atlanta, we were introduced to the congregation, then had an opportunity to hear the vestry candidates up for election. I was very impressed with the caliber of those people. St. Luke's had a vestry of 21 with 667 pledging units in its congregation. We also watched the 11 a.m. Holy Eucharist from the television room where the service was broadcast live. And that evening, Charles and his wife had us all to dinner, then took us to see the play *Fences*.

We were really busy January 15th when we served 730 people for lunch. It was a special meal due to its being Martin Luther King's birthday, so some people came who would not normally have been there because they were on their way to the parade. I was assigned to serve rice on all the plates. Clyde, the cook, was impressive. A real ball of fire. The way he pulled that kitchen together was amazing. I was told he'd been a cook in the army.

After our KP duty, we went to the parade. I loved that almost as much as the first Orange Bowl parade I'd ever attended on New Year's Eve in Miami a few weeks earlier. I was out of touch with many of the public figures in Atlanta and could scarcely identify any of them, but there were two delightful black families close by who seemed to know all the TV personalities and rock stars. Actually, there were really two parades. The glitzy, marching band, celebrity one with floats, then the people's parade that followed. The TV crews packed up and left before the people's groups got going. The latter represented those supporting various causes. The theme, of course, centered around Martin Luther King and non-violence. The onlookers were mostly black. Charlie steered us to a Burger King afterwards for lunch and I had to chuckle recalling I'd lunched with Jim McLamore (the founder of Burger King) just two weeks earlier. It was just one more contrast in my life.

A vestry dinner followed later at St. Luke's to which we were all invited, and the next several days, after kitchen chores, we heard from the other priests at the church. Rev. Pat Merchant, an assistant, was concerned that women were often interviewed, but very few were being called as rectors. The stained glass ceiling was alive and well.

Isaias Rodriguez was involved with Hispanic ministry. He'd once been a Roman Catholic Carmelite priest. But "the Vatican has lost control due to its unchanging policies," he told us. There were about thirty Hispanic families at St. Luke's and he said he supervised a soccer league that had eleven teams.

The following day, I couldn't help reflect on the fact I'd spent most of my adult life working in a kitchen in one form or other, but this was the first time I was getting any credit for it! And I had to chuckle at one classmate's remark that one could go to seminary and see the world. So far, we'd been to San Francisco, Atlanta, Helsinki, Moscow, Leningrad and Odessa together.

By the following week, I was beginning to recognize some of the people who came through the soup line. And I was beginning to see how one fellow worked the system. He'd slip in, have some soup, then slip out, get in line again and come through, then eat something, leave and get back in line a third time and come through again. I had seen him do this the previous Friday also. I watched him trade up his smuggled out sandwiches with others in line for things they had that he apparently wanted. He was a survivor and I'm sure would have done well in the business world had he had a different background. We were asked not to call attention to this kind of behavior, even though there were signs saying eating had to be done in the dining hall and food was not to be taken out. But many broke that rule. They arrived with coats with large pockets which often received many rolls and flasks of hot soup. On days when there were extras served, thermoses would often appear from nowhere and they would pour the soup or drinks into the flasks when they thought no one was looking, then ask to have refills. I'm sure this was desperation on the part of many who would get nothing more until the soup kitchen opened again.

The lady in the mail room often said loudly: "John Jones," (or whoever) "you have no mail today," whenever someone had no mail. I would prefer her to have said it quietly. She was a volunteer and had been helping a long time so it was not my place to criticize. But it troubled me. There was often such a sad look of disappointment on the faces of those who did not receive anything. These people used the P.O. Box set up by St. Luke's so they could have an address since they had no homes. Without addresses, they could not get food stamps.

When I first started in the soup kitchen at the beginning of our stay, I'd felt a certain distance between myself and the street people, but by the second day, it had disappeared. By the third day, I felt very much like one of them and was totally at ease and comfortable in my surroundings. A few "guests" would look at me and try to communicate in some small way, but most did not. They were for the most part in their own worlds, some on drugs or alcohol, some lost in their own thoughts, some obviously embarrassed even to be there. But there were always surprises and each day was different.

One day when I was working the tables, pouring soup and handing out rolls, I saw a very tall black man approaching me. He had his eyes on me and I began to feel a little nervous as he kept coming right at me. Many of our clients spent the nights on the streets, seldom had an opportunity to take a bath and had to be reminded every so often that no guns or knives were allowed in the soup kitchen. So there was a certain undercurrent of insecurity for those of us out on the floor. When the young man got to me, he just stood there hovering and when I looked up, said "Do I get a hug … like my old ma used to give?" I was so surprised, I blurted out "I'm not sure that's supposed to go with the food." He just kept looking down at me and I realized then that he really meant it and that he was very lost and lonely. So I put the rolls down, then put my arms around him and gave him a big hug, all the while thinking: *Boy, if the chairman of the Board of Trustees could see this, or more to the point, what would Austin think?*

Here I was, hugging a not-so-sweet-smelling man. But in retrospect, that was one of the high points of my Atlanta sojourn. I'd been given an opportunity to pass along what I had received from the Beginning Experience. If one of my children were ever that down and out, I would hope to think someone would respond charitably to them. After I'd hugged him, I saw tears in his eyes, he said "Thank you" and went back to his table.

One morning we met with a man named Rico from St. Luke's Street Academy. Here they followed the same curriculum as the Atlanta Schools. For whatever reason, students who did not fit into the public school were allowed to come to this school. They were expected to work. And if they couldn't fit in, they were asked to leave. They received much individual attention which was a big help. Two girls, one black and one white, showed us around and explained the program to us. I recall a sign on one door that said: **If you think school is boring, wait until you sit around an unemployment office.**

Their subjects covered English, math, science, social studies and computer labs coupled with sports in various programs. There were four groups labeled something like "Laws," "Achievers," "Can Do's" and "Mind Advantage." Students moved from one group to the next as soon as they had mastered required materials. This school was part of the Exodus program consisting of five separate academies in Atlanta. The student body was 50% white and 50% black and received monies every year through fund raising campaigns.

The black girl named Kadisha told us she had a Swahili name meaning "African Goddess." The white girl, Lorie, said her name came from the Greek meaning "Famous." Rico told us he played a game with all the students, had them look up the origin of their first name, then asked them if they were living up to it. He pointed out to them that Adam and Eve's last name was "God," that persons got their names from their fathers; consequently, he tried to tie in the universal concept of creation, pointing out that they were all God's children and part of His family.

Kadisha told us she hadn't been able to make it in her previous school because she was always fighting with the students (and with her mother at home as well) and she'd "smart off to the teachers." Lorie, the white girl on the other hand, had been unable to get along in a predominantly black school, felt picked on all the time and said "They goin' to make you black or they goin' to see you be dead."

Rico said they got reviewed every 40 days and once a week someone came to the school to discuss drugs. It was pointed out to the students that they had to answer to God, their own bodies and those who loved them. I gathered Rico was Muslim which he defined as "someone who wishes to do the will of God." He pointed out that prayer meant "plan" and that they tried to inculcate this into their students. He also compared gold, frankincense and myrrh to faith, prayer and fasting.

One day in the kitchen, I was confronted with a volunteer who wanted to know exactly what my seminary taught on the issue of homosexuality. He said the Bible was the only authority and referred to Romans. He was very big on St. Paul. What intrigued me was that I realized seminary had never told us what to believe. We were expected to study, make our own decisions and develop our own theology. This man had a definite agenda and wanted to argue. But I didn't wish that. He told me he'd been a Presbyterian minister and said he'd been against women in ministry but had changed his mind when he found himself in the minority. I suggested he might view homosexuality differently some day if he found himself in the minority on that as well.

One day I realized I had become so focused on ideas, character and personalities that I took little notice of people's color anymore. But I also realized I did not feel I fit at times into my peer group at seminary. So many of the students seemed so anti-business, anti-republican or anti-establishment. I guess I was too in varying degrees, but I found myself sensitive to many of their comments because my experiences had been so different from theirs. I also had gotten through college before many of them had been born, so age I'm sure had something to do with it. And being a product of the depression gave me a decidedly different viewpoint. What I gradually realized was that I was an economic conservative that had turned in to a social liberal of sorts. A strange mix. But the Christian faith does affirm what can be viewed politically at times as irreconcilable contradictions.

The next day, after putting in seventeen hours, we were exhausted. Time did not ever hang heavy on our hands. But I enjoyed hearing various comments in a discussion group we attended. They ranged from "seeing Christ in our guests" to some who said this had been a "life changing experience" for them. Carol Jean assured us this experience would fade rapidly and would be merely a memory unless we made a point to keep it alive within.

We next visited the Food Bank. Bill Bolling (a dynamo of a man) showed us around. The food was stored in a large warehouse with cartons piled everywhere. They had a large walk-in refrigerator and we were told the food bank received funding from various community agencies, as well as businesses and private foundations, with food coming from corporations, caterers, restaurants and farmers' markets. He said some companies who couldn't market all their products donated the food. They were able to do this because marred cans are now returned to vendors who can donate them.

They also received time-dated goods such as yogurt, and government food like peanut butter was free since it was a subsidy. The government buys the peanuts, then contracts for someone to produce the peanut butter.

Mr. Bolling had twenty-six full time staff with sixty to seventy volunteers. I couldn't believe what a big operation this was. Included was a program designed to pick up surplus food from hotels as well as from restaurants and caterers, their primary mission being to distribute it to the needy. Because of the disproportionate high cost of housing and the low paying jobs in our society, hunger is not going to go away. Housing, education and jobs are the country's biggest needs.

Our host also pointed out that one should not get too attached to this kind of work as it could "do you in." He said he'd been working at it fifteen hours a day for fifteen years and thought things were getting worse. (He obviously had not followed his own advice.) He felt when our elected leaders started talking "quality of life" and not "how much you have," then progress might happen. He also said this type of ministry had to be processed within oneself and that there was a need to balance it out. "We can't be judgmental but we need to know what our real role is."

I was very impressed by the dedication of every one I met in the various Atlanta programs. They were for the most part terrific, dedicated people; but I came away especially impressed with Bill Bolling. He both angered and energized me. Angered, I guess, because of his remarks about business people who say: "There may be all these homeless and jobless people, but I sure can't find anyone willing to work," implying business is at fault, when in reality business people are just as caught up and frustrated by the system as everyone else. It's one thing to deal with volunteers who may be incompetent. It's another thing to deal with people who expect to be paid and are incompetent. A person in business has a right to expect the best! Just as a person buying a product has a right to expect the best. It surprised me that he pushed so many of my buttons.

I was energized because his remarks helped me to feel right about what I was doing outside of seminary, about my role in other activities. I'm sure my background influenced my reactions just then too. I could see Mr. Bolling was doing a super job trying to help people get back into the system. My concern was that our society with its ever increasing sophisticated technology would not be able or willing to train and hire these people, even when they opted to remain within the system.

We saw shelters for the homeless too, and I was touched one day when one of my classmates sat down, put his head in his hands and remarked that "waves of existential angst" kept passing over him.

It's usually been difficult for me to get excited about statistics. They have always been so impersonal. But now when I hear about the homeless or the hungry in the world, it translates into real people. I can only recall one homeless person growing up near me as a youngster and he wasn't really homeless after moving in to my Uncle Roy's old shack. But the man was a derelict and I wonder how he managed to survive. Certainly it was not on the occasional soup or the homemade caramels my mother used to take him at Christmas.

There was a lady named Ruth dubbed the "Iron Magnolia" of the soup kitchen. And there was Edythe—a Jewish lady—who invited us all to her synagogue to celebrate Martin Luther King Week. I found that fascinating. We first saw their shelter, then went to the service and returned for dessert. This was all part of a week long interfaith celebration. I had never participated in a Jewish Shabbat Shalom service so it was educational for me. And I was surprised to find some of their prayer book was much like ours. The Methodist choir sang Jewish hymns, as did we, and the preacher—Rev. Walter L. Kimbrough—was a black Methodist pulpit thumping, arm waving, very tall man with a booming voice. He used Exodus 3:1–12 for his sermon and began it by saying "The word of God to the people of God, praised be to God." He used words like "oppressed," "abused," "misused," in different ways and compared Martin Luther King to Moses who didn't want to be chosen for a job but "whom God chooses, he qualifies." They both gave excuses, but got the job done.

There was also a lady rabbi for part of the service and some beautiful solo singing. The church was impressive, the same one bombed back in 1958 as in *Driving Miss Daisy*. It was a lovely building. There was a circular ceiling with the 12 tribes of Israel represented and a beautiful Tiffany chandelier that hung from the ceiling. There was also a Menorah representing the seven days of creation and an eternal light which hung from the Great Seal of the United States. Between two Menorah were two tablets representing the Commandments. The Torah was housed in a special area in front.

I loved the Israeli version of *Hine Mah Tov*, the music was so lively, and they read a Litany of Rededication—things said by Martin Luther King. We then saw a shelter they supported that housed twenty-three couples. It had a poster saying: "Kids are dying to live."

The final Saturday we visited the Carter Library, Cyclorama and Stone Mountain, and the following evening we were invited out again. One lady talked a lot about her job as a development officer at Emory where she was fund raising for the school. She said the only way to raise money was to be around it, so I presume that was one reason she attended St. Luke's. She expressed her reluctance ("being amongst so many conservatives ... doctors are extreme conservatives ... and lawyers run a close second") to express her political beliefs and leanings. She saw herself as "a Democrat in a den of Republicans." That tickled me because I always felt like a Republican in a den of Democrats at seminary, though I was beginning to realize that western Republicans were similar in some ways to southern Democrats, depending on the subject being discussed.

During one of our last discussions with the rector, he said: "God calls some to ordination, perhaps because he does not trust them to minister as laity!"

And in his last sermon, he mentioned that Miami and San Diego were border towns, as was Capernaum. He spoke of contrasts and ambiguities that spoke to me then, and about the shepherd and the sheep. Who is the shepherd? Was it Christ? Or someone Christ spoke of? Or is it you and me?

The first thing I had seen in the chapel at St. Luke's when we arrived was a painting behind the altar of a shepherd boy with his sheep. So his sermon came full circle for me and it seemed like a proper way to end my January experience.

Flying back to Texas, thinking about it all, I decided cynics would not last long at St Luke's. To work in a soup kitchen with the homeless and hungry, one definitely needed an Easter faith. Certainly a faith with hope.

# 27

# PANAMA

Time passed quickly. It seemed as though following semester ended almost before it began. Sometime early in the year, my advisor called me to her office and asked if I would like to participate in the seminary's summer program in Panama. Since I was fairly fluent in Spanish and thus eligible, I decided it would be a good thing to do. I felt this would open up new avenues and teach me about other aspects of ministry in the church. Besides, I'd always wanted to see Panama since that's where my parents had been married. I'd never been there, except in an airport on the way to somewhere else.

After getting all the required shots, Kathy Glenn and I, along with students from four other seminaries in the United States, flew to Panama City to take part in what was called "Proyecto Panama." This project had been started four years earlier in the mid 1980's by Bishop James Ottley, then Bishop of Panama, with the idea of helping Panamanian students better understand the Latin American church, to see where it and they fit into the Anglican Communion. It was also to help foreign students understand Panama in its contemporary cultural and political context. This was an on-going program sponsored by the Council of Deans of the Episcopal seminaries of the U.S. and the Diocese of Panama.[43]

We were not only immersed in the culture of the country, but also had an opportunity to study and live with students from El Salvador and Colombia. The deanery house in Panama City was our home for the first two weeks where we took classes (in Spanish) taught by a Sandinista professor—Jorge Pixley—from Nicaragua, along with professors Ingwersen and Floyd from our own seminary. A local American priest—John Kater—served as our mentor and shepherd throughout the summer.

Our courses included the Bible (often seen through the eyes of liberation theology) as well as a variety of lectures from local officials which dealt with the culture, history, church, problems and politics of Panama. Some of our class time included field trips to the Panama Canal, The Afro-Antillano Museum, visiting the *damnificados* (those left homeless after the bombing and burning of El Chorrillo by U.S. forces) and learning first hand why so many in the Latin American countries embraced liberation theology.[44]

Visiting and talking with the *damnificados* left an indelible impression on me. Being in seminary hadn't left much time for keeping up with American foreign policy, not that I ever felt I could do anything about it anyway, but what I saw in Panama compared with what our American TV, radio newscasts and papers had told us left me thoroughly dismayed and disillusioned. We certainly had not been told all the truth.

I was on break in Florida when I recall seeing our President (the elder Bush) on a television newscast saying that hardly any Panamanians had been killed in the bombing of Panama City. Only Noriega's headquarters had been attacked, he said. Maybe that's what he'd been told and believed. Yet, I found myself in Panama talking and visiting with many people who had lost members of their families, had lost their homes, then been forced to live in an unbearably hot abandoned theater, entire families in ten by ten foot square areas, with stinking facilities, trying to survive. For some, sons, daughters, fathers or mothers had disappeared, and our government was no help in letting them know if they were dead or alive.

At some point after the invasion, a feisty, Panamanian woman managed to raise enough funds to hire a bulldozer which eventually uncovered a mass grave. Our American soldiers had dug it, dumped in the dead, then covered it up. By then, however, "Desert Storm" was brewing and Panama was not considered newsworthy, so the press never got it straight. One story said cocaine had been found strewn all over Noriega's house. This later was proven to be flour but that story was not retracted or corrected. Despite the dictators known involvement with drugs (encouraged by our own government), he did care about his people. Funds for education had been high on his list.

After finishing our classes, we were all assigned to various locations for the remainder of our time there. Our month long assignments varied from a church-run home for twenty-five girls, to a congregation in Cerro Viento (both in Panama City) to four other locations in rural areas away from the city.

My assignment saw me as supply to a church in La Chorrera, as well as a helper in Las Guabitas which was a marginal rural community west of Panama consisting of some sixty-nine persons. There was no place for me to stay there, so I lived in La Chorrera with an Episcopal Panamanian deacon studying to be a priest. Her son and daughter also lived with her.

This was an interesting experience in itself. The iron bars on the windows did not keep out the flying insects, nor the neighborhood cats that occasionally made their way into the little living room. One day when I was alone and had settled down to eat a piece of chicken, I had to get up for a moment to answer the phone. I returned just in time to see a cat disappearing through the window with my chicken in its mouth. Another cat also brought old fish heads in as offerings and placed them under my bed periodically.

But what really gave me a chuckle was the rooster that sat on the high shelf in the bathroom. He would squeeze in between the iron bars and perch out of the sun, viewing his inside and outside domain. Having him watch me shower always left me feeling a bit self-conscious.

Victoria's house was always open, not just to nature, but to any local who also wished to drop by. In the evening, after the sun had disappeared, we would sit on the porch, and her friend who wanted to practice English invariably arrived for "English class," along with others who would come to Victoria for counseling or advice. It was a kind of Grand Central Station actually.

I often walked about the neighborhood after dinner which somewhat amused the populace. They could not understand why this *americana* would want to walk in the heat. But I found this time of the evening quite cool by comparison with the rest of the day and loved to investigate the local fauna and flora. The only drawback were the many vicious, barking dogs in almost every yard who would put up a ferocious display, lunging at the fences, trying to attack as I passed by.

Padre Val was supposed to give me instructions and show me around before leaving on vacation. But when I arrived, he had already departed for Spain, leaving me with instructions on how to finish digging the well and a septic tank in Las Guabitas.

Since it was thought to be dangerous to walk into Guabitas alone, Bishop Ottley insisted a social worker drive me in each day, or whenever the road was passable. Often, after each rain, we would have to get out of the car, collect rocks and stones and place them in strategic spots so we could get across the dip in the road leading to the bridge. This muddy stream we crossed was the only place my little congregation had to do their laundry.

The day before I arrived at Guabitas, they had killed a snake in the open air church. My first day on the job, we killed two, one of them a poisonous coral. My first public service in La Chorrera, I launched simultaneously with the biggest cockroach I had ever seen making its way deliberately along the floor in front of the altar. That was my first Sunday on the job and I was expected to give a sermon and lead a service in Spanish, something until then I had never even done in English! How grateful I was for Victoria who helped me prepare.

A continuous refrain that ran through my head that summer was:

> *It's hot and it's muggy*
> *It's rainy and it's buggy*

This was especially true as I walked with the *campesinos* through the deep grass along the narrow trail that led to the Pacific side of the Isthmus of Panama. I went with them to dig for clams, and to fish, and to see what going to their beach was all about. As I brushed off the ticks and waded through the mud and water—above my knees in places—I could not help wonder what my more sedate friends would think *if they could only see me now*. But for someone who loves the outdoors, I could not have chosen a better assignment.

I saw huge termite nests hanging from the trees. One day I patiently followed an eel over the tidal mud flats until I was rewarded by his showing me how an eel burrows, then *backs* into its hole. And there were crabs, skittering endlessly over the sand, and the frigates and herons, overshadowed constantly by the circling vultures. And everywhere was the wonderful tropical profusion of vegetation—the hibiscus, croton, stands of bamboo and occasional poisonous manchineel. There were also bumble bees and dragon flies and butterflies and just plain flies too attracted by the garbage that seemed to be everywhere in the streets.

The *campesinos* were very protective, always explaining what they thought I should and should not do. One big NO was to stay away from the trails that led to the drop-off points frequented by drug runners. *Malos hombres,* I was told. Unknown to me, I went one day with the children who wanted me to see how they played in the *agua dulce*, not realizing it was on the edge of forbidden territory. The entire village was upset when we returned so we didn't try that again. But the children and I had a grand time. The *agua dulce* (sweet water) was actually fresh water which accumulated in a large field of grass, then flowed on towards the sea. One could not see it because the grass was four to five feet tall. But the children would run helter skelter, throw themselves into the grass, then land in the water and plane through it. At first, I was very reluctant to do this, wondering what kind of snakes and bugs might be living there, but after watching the kids for a bit, decided to give it a try. It was really fun, and, among other things, the best fresh water bath I'd experienced in some time.

The villagers showed me how they put their sugar cane through a primitive press and how they ground rice with the *pilon;* and the day we waded through mangroves to the beach, they showed me how they used the fishing nets. One day too, they rounded up the few cattle they owned, so they could show me how all the ticks and worms were removed. That was the day one of the women (her name was also Marta) brought me a dish of food to eat just then. Knowing how little they had and what a sacrifice it was for her to do this for me, I could not think of turning it down. So I sat on the wooden corral fence as the men squeezed the large worms out from under the cattle's skin, popping them into the air, while I ate and prayed I would not get sick. *Marta de la molina* (she lived on a hill) also insisted I drink punch with it, made from the sugar cane and local fruit. That was all right, except that the water from their local well was polluted and I feared how my stomach would react. Nevertheless, I drank it all, and the antibiotics I'd carried from Texas kicked in before I got sick.

It was encouraging to see how the church operated there. In Guabitas, they were empowering people to help themselves through the implementation of various projects. The *campesinos* had been taught how to make blocks by hand. Their ladies equivalent of our ECW (Episcopal Church Women) were the ones who did this so they could construct simple houses. They had also learned to plant fruit trees and various vegetables and were beginning to raise cattle and pigs. I later helped them get a pedal sewing machine so they could learn to make school uniforms for the children. There was no running water or electricity in Guabitas at that time and most of the adults were illiterate. But their long term goal was to develop a type of industry, such as marmalade, so they might earn some income. In the center of their community, an open-air church had been put together by the men, with the blocks made by the women.

When John Kater dropped me off, he forgot to give me the Spanish Bible lessons I was supposed to have to aid me with the children whom I was expected to teach, so it was difficult at first trying to figure out what to do. I finally fell back on the games I still remembered from my childhood days and tried to teach them those, along with some geography and various songs. The children in turn taught me their songs and games and I soon had a good rapport with them. Eventually I got to know many of the adults as well. Many were beautiful, simple, people, trying hard to survive. And yes, there were a few rogues as well.

Coming so close after the invasion, much of Panama was terribly depressed economically, and in many areas it was dangerous. I had hoped to visit Colon to see the church where my parents had been married sixty-seven years earlier, but finally had to give up that idea. The train across the isthmus had stopped taking passengers and I was warned not to go by bus. "As soon as you get off, someone will mug and rob you," I was warned. The unemployment rate in Colon then was over 52%, with a crime rate to match. I kept thinking I would get there, but by the end of my six weeks stay, after Kathy—my roommate—had been robbed in front of a church, after Thomas had just missed being shot accidentally in the foot by a security guard, after several others had been stoned while driving the Diocesan jeep, and after someone was shot one evening outside the Napoli Restaurant where our group was eating dinner, I decided to forget about going to Colon.

Later back in Panama City, Rev. Kater, in telling us of his confirmation class, said: "I have to stress to them that here, in this day and age, they must accept the reality that there is a strong possibility they might have to die for their faith."

Unfortunately, the church in many parts of Latin America has been mislabeled by some as "communist." For helping the poor, people are murdered. This is because economic lines have been drawn which put people into compartments. It was hard for me to understand how helping people build a church, or a little house, or teaching them to read, or sew, or grow things, or helping them understand the basic rules of sanitation could be threatening. But it has been to some. That's because it involves change. And change can be frightening. I never got to meet Padre Val, but I wrote him a long letter before returning to the States telling him all the things I had done with his two congregations. Later, he answered me with a lovely letter which included:

*Quiero decirla muchas cosas más. Pero quiero que sepa que su presencia solamente como "americana" ha sido valiosísima. Porque aquí hay una tendencia a pensar que el sacerdote que se dedica a este tipo de trabajo con los pobres es un "comunista." Ahora que usted estuvo aquí ya me absolvieron de esto. Ya no lo soy.*[45]

I believe the church is alive and well in Panama and what few church dollars they have, they spend wisely. There is a program in place to train catequistas which is helping with the shortage of trained priests. But it will be some time before the Diocese of Panama is completely independent of the North American part of the church .Wisely, they are phasing out slowly in order to try to make up for the lack of funding they will be receiving in the future. As one *campesino* put it: "We all need to carry our burdens, each of us, like the ants, in order to help us all go forward."

# PART V

# 28

# EXAMS

My final year of seminary sped by. I almost wished I could have gone an extra year, just to take all the elective classes I could not fit in to my schedule. There was so much offered, but so little time. Still, aside from classes, the seminary gave us a great many other choices on the side, a real smorgasbord of events, and exposed us to all they could that was going on in the religious world. The library was filled with more publications than we could ever read; nevertheless, we were encouraged to look at as many as possible. There were various types of services, tapes, outside lecturers, including a series wherein business people came in and spoke about the ethical issues they encountered on a daily basis. We also had a marvelous diversity of students to draw upon.

I recall going to dinner one evening with a group of Hispanic students. Each told about his respective country. I was surprised to learn that priests do not have civil rights in Mexico. The constitution forbids their wearing cassocks and they may not own property. They are now allowed to wear collars, but the government does not like the church, I guess mainly because the Roman Catholic Church supported Maximilian of Spain against the government under Juarez. Nevertheless, a high percentage of the Mexican population is Roman Catholic.

A Honduran student felt the Anglican church was run by foreign *gringos*. It was his feeling that a required liturgy class would not be too useful to him (as far as vestments were concerned) since he said he'd be lucky even to have a congregation, let alone one that could afford vestments. He was upset that the canon in his church could not yet speak Spanish and said at one Ash Wednesday service, an English-speaking person had thrown down his prayer book and walked out when the first song of the service had begun in Spanish. It was a day when there were more Spanish-speaking than English-speaking parishioners present. He believed the church first came to Honduras for the United Fruit Company, not because it cared about the indigenous population. As in Argentina and China, he said the Anglican Church in Honduras followed capitalism.

One from El Salvador said that due to politics, he'd had to leave because he feared for his life. He had finally been able to get his wife and four children out and in to the U.S. after first spending time in Canada.

Another student, a doctor from Argentina, said he was one of 300,000 Lutherans in the entire country. About 95% of the populace are Roman Catholic which was his original church, but he now preferred the Lutheran theology so could no longer identify intellectually with Rome. He reiterated what many of them said: the Roman Catholic Church identifies with power in the various Latin American countries. He'd had to leave because his life had been threatened after disagreeing with the military under Peron.

One memorable program for me was when the seminary brought Jaci Marashin to speak to us about church music being developed in Brazil. He is an Anglican priest who writes music and, at that time, taught at the University in Sao Paolo. Brazilian music is so fun and vibrant. If we had music like that in our U.S. church services, I think they would be filled to capacity. They use flutes, the maracas, cuicas, drums and guitars, and at the passing of the peace, circle around in a kind of dance, then move on to the next person, all in rhythm. Some of the music I heard that night was by Silvio Meincke, Armindo Trevisan and Flavio Irala.

Since we shared libraries and some professors with the Presbyterian Seminary near us, we also had an annual football game with the "Presbys." And since the average age of our seminarians exceeded theirs by some twenty years, we were always hopelessly beaten. They could out run every one of us. But it was fun, nevertheless. I still have the somewhat outrageous "Order for the Celebration of a Football Game" (also known as a Moveable Feast). The opening hymn, sung to the tune of *We Sing a Song of the Saints of God* went thus:

*We sing a song of the saints of football,*
  *Brave martyrs one and all.*
*Who run and throw and tackle low*
  *And know just what plays to call.*
*And one is a tackle and one is a guard*
  *And one is a quarterback who thinks hard*
*They are all of them martyrs and we can guess*
  *How sore they must all be now.*

*They love this game so dear, so dear,*
  *At least it would seem this way.*
*For year after year they gather their gear*
  *And jump right in to the fray*

*And one is a fullback and one is an end*
      *And one is a center on whom they depend,*
*And there's not any reason, no not the least,*
      *Why they shouldn't win this game.*

*The martyrs here on the field today*
      *Uphold a tradition brave.*
*In spite of bruises, breaks, strains and pains*
      *They know just how to behave.*
*Whether throwing or tackling or running fast,*
      *Screaming, crawling, or breathing their last,*
*They are all of them martyrs of football God bless,*
*We're glad it is they, not us.*

This was then followed by the Reading whereupon the crowd was asked to join in the antiphon:
*Football, football, rah, rah, rah! Onward team!"*
Then the entire crowd was asked to clap if we could, but to do so only in an "orderly and unenthusiastic manner."

The final blessing and closing hymn was done by the "Drum Bishop," and then we'd all sing:

*We are the Anglicans, we are P.E.*
*Neither high church, nor low church,*
*We are Protestant, Episcopal and free.*
*We're not Baptists, Pentecostals,*
*We're not Presbys, white with foam;*
*We are the Anglicans, just one step from Rome.*
*We are the Anglicans, <u>via media</u>, rah, rah.*

It was always a raucous game!
After being "killed" and "buried," this was the year we got "resurrected." Whereas during first semester, I'd felt as though I'd been hanging over a chasm, not certain if I might fall in, now I gradually began to feel my topsy-turvy world righting itself. At last, everything began falling in to place. And life suddenly became exciting and hopeful, reminding me of a saying from the *Talmud* : "We do not see things as they are. We see them as we are."
Once, on a quick trip to Miami, President Foote invited me to have lunch with him. It had something to do with the music recording studio at the University of Miami which would one day carry Austin's name. It's what had culmi-

nated eventually after my asking the Hipps if they would watch over Austin while I was away. Tad took me to the Faculty Club and as various other subjects came up, it seemed like a good time to talk with him about the young professor who had been denied tenure. I guess I still felt uneasy about what my role had been in this and it was important to me that this be put to bed. But so much water had gone under the bridge, Tad didn't even recall what I was referring to, so there was no point in pursuing it. I could not help smile to myself as I recalled that awful week before leaving Florida. I hadn't been aware then of other forces shaping my life. But it also reminded me there are times when God really does protect fools.

I also couldn't help wondering where I would be assigned first and what it would be like after I was ordained a deacon. And how would it actually feel like to be a priest? We all couldn't wait to get out of school, get our first jobs and begin putting into practice all the wonderful things we'd been learning. In many ways, much of it had been education by osmosis, although it doesn't always come across like that until one looks back, sometimes years later.

Towards the end of our final year, we were given specific assignments relating to services we would be expected to perform in any future parish. Practical down-to-earth things like conducting a wedding, or doing a funeral. Along with some of my older classmates, I hoped for a baptism too as thought it would be great to be able to baptize one of my own grandchildren someday.

Much of the first semester of our final year was spent wondering about the upcoming General Ordination Exams which were given after Christmas break. Other than administer exams, my seminary had little to do with them. It was the National General Board of Examining Chaplains who put the questions together. The Dean saw them as an insult to the preparation of students; Professor Sugeno told us he had agitated for years to do away with them; another referred to them as "hazing." Still, despite the expense to the church and the heartache to many, they continued. And some students, when they returned home, if they didn't do well, got "killed" and "buried" all over again by their own dioceses.

The exams were given in seven areas which included Bible, church history, Christian theology, ethics and moral theology, theory and practice of ministry, contemporary society and liturgy.

The General Board of Examining Chaplains in a statement to all GOE candidates said, among other things, that they viewed the exams as "diagnostic and remedial to help commissions on ministry prepare candidates for continuing education in diaconal and early priesthood years." In each part of the exam, candidates were reminded they were looking for theological substance.

I thought I was doing all right in seminary, so assumed I would not have any particular difficulty. There were so many things required of us that I viewed the exams as just one more hurdle along the rocky path to ordination. I'd been told by those who had been through the gauntlet ahead of me that the important thing was to "Trust in the process. As long as you've done your work, you'll be fine." I'd always done my work and participated in the seminary at all levels, so naively believed that. It wasn't until a few weeks before the exams, however, that I began to have really bad "vibes."

At first, I thought some students were overly nervous; of course, each of us had heard at least one horror story from previous students; so a kind of anxiety began to build that was palpable. In such a close knit community, it began to affect us all.

A major part of the exams, we were told, would be open book; there was no way to study for those, so I put my efforts into organizing my notes, hoping I would be able to find any needed materials. Although I knew I had learned much more in Panama than I could ever have gotten from book learning, I began to wish I had not gone. I told myself I should have stayed home and organized my notes better.

I also thought I had pretty well gotten over exam fears, so that didn't bother me at first. But as the first exam day approached, I began to have second thoughts.

Our first question—Set 1—was Thursday, January 3, at 9 a.m. I had to drive to school to pick it up. Students who lived any distance away were at a disadvantage here. It normally took me 25–30 minutes round trip, except during rush hour, which took longer. Most lived closer than I, though a few others lived farther. The seminary and examiners made no allowance for this.

We were told the first question would focus on history, liturgics and the theory and practice of ministry, that it would be open book and that we had eight hours to complete it. The question was long with three parts, and involved writing a 1500 word article about the catechumenate for a congregation. We were expected to include a description, with reference to cultural contexts, of the practice of the early church both before the Edict of Toleration (Apostolic Tradition of Hippolytus) and after the Edict of Toleration (Ambrose, Cyril, et al) and were to give reasons for the renewal of the catechumenate. After this, we were then to outline a program for the training and formation of catechumens and end with a sermon appropriate to the occasion based on the Gospels for the principal service on Pentecost, Year B. It was assumed we would baptize adults at Easter and infants at Pentecost.

My first read through the question left me overwhelmed. In seminary, we were used to having eight *days* sometimes to prepare a sermon. But only eight *hours*, along with everything else? Until then, I'd only written a few sermons in my life, and never under this kind of stress. And the Edict of Toleration? I'd read about it certainly, maybe two or three years previously, along with all the other thousands of pages of assigned reading. From my vantage point, it belonged in all that unintelligible stuff I'd been exposed to the first two semesters of school, when the rest of my life had been so out of whack. Fortunately, I had a reference book to help put things in proper perspective, but I was in such a panic over having to write the sermon that I did not do the first half of Set 1 well, misread part of it and left a section out. I'm the kind who writes a sermon, then re-writes it several more times, often ending with something very different from the original. I *always* let sermons sit for several days, then go back and correct or re-write them. I guess that's because, for me, sermons have always been like Jacob at Penuel—a struggle with God.

So this first question undid me. My seminary had not trained me for this type of exam. And I began to wonder: *Have I totally missed the point of what's been expected of us?* Still, I did the best I could, and considering the time constraints, thought I wrote a fairly decent sermon, then delivered my answer to the seminary by 5 p.m. as required. But I had to spend so much time writing the sermon that it never occurred to me I had misunderstood, and thus left out, one part of the question.

Though emotionally exhausted, I could not sleep that night. We had to be back at 9 the next morning to pick up Set 2. I read it before driving home which gave me an opportunity to organize my thoughts. We were given until noon to return these answers which focused on ethics, scripture and contemporary society. I took mine back, drove home for lunch, then returned to get Set 3 at 2 p.m. This involved scripture, history, theology and the theory and practice of ministry. We had until 5 p.m. for this one. I was worried about not having enough time to write the exam and on my way home, due to going 10 mph over the posted speed limit, was given a speeding ticket. This netted the State of Texas $50.00 and did not help my emotional or mental outlook. It was the first speeding ticket I'd ever received and lost me valuable time. I tried to explain to the officer that I was in the middle of exams. She was very nice, but I still got the ticket.

The weekend gave us a break. I tried to stop thinking about the exams, but couldn't. They weren't what I'd expected or studied for; so rather than relaxing, my anxiety level kept going up. Given time, I know now I could have easily sorted things out, but by then, I was on such a treadmill, I could not change direction. Panic more closely described it.

Set 4 the following Monday was a 9–5 question. It was open book focusing on theology, scripture, and church history. It primarily dealt with evangelism. I thought I'd done well.

Set 5 the next day was from 9–12. It said "In the light of your work yesterday, write a 500 word essay on your understanding of evangelism. Then, in an essay of about 1000 words addressed to your congregation, identify four components of an Anglican strategy for evangelism. For each of these components provide a specific proposal for the parish to act upon and indicate how each proposal both proclaims the Gospel and respects individual conscience and cultural integrity." I did the best I could.

Set 6 was all closed book and consisted of short answers and coffee hour questions. I was certain I'd done well on that.

As soon as exams were out of the way, many of us left on the last trip we'd be taking together. We went to England.

Due to the goings on in Iraq at the time, Heathrow airport was full of security guards; and the International Student's House where we stayed was a far cry from the London hotels of my previous business trips. But the accommodations were fine and we finally all settled in.[46]

It was chilly that January and seemed incongruous to me that the seminary would send its students to Panama in the summer and to London in the winter! But I look back with fondness the day a few of us got out of the cold dampness and settled in to a wonderful place that served hot tea and scones.

We adapted quickly to the underground transportation system, along with a Britrail pass. The rest of the time we walked. Our first church service—the First Sunday after Epiphany—was at St. Paul's Cathedral. The second at All Saints, Margaret Street, was a "high" Anglican Church that Dr. Green wanted us to experience. I was surprised when they began to sing the *Tantum Ergo*. Had not heard that since my days at St. Mary's forty-four years earlier. It transported me back into another time, another century almost, recalling when the sisters used to sing it at Benediction. What amazed me was that I still remembered some of it.[47]

We did a lot of the tourist things. Saw Andrew Lloyd Weber's *Aspects of Love* at the Prince of Wales Theatre, as well as *Racing Demon* at the Olivier. And there was Madame Tussaud's, Churchhill's War Rooms, the Tate and Turner museums, the Tower of London with its crown jewels, and the changing of the guard at Buckingham Palace. We also got to St. Martin-in-the-Fields at Trafalgar

Square where we heard Mozart's Mass in C Minor, and one afternoon I visited the zoo, where for the first time in my life was asked if I'd like the senior citizen discount!

There were also the pubs as well as *Restaurant Elizabeth*, the *Richoux, The Baker and Oven* and *Running Footman*.

We saw Parliament and Big Ben and walked past No.10 Downing Street. At Canterbury we saw where Beckett had been killed in the Cathedral, as well as William Temple's resting place. And we visited York Minster with its beautiful choir screens, St. Peter's Vauxhall and Lambeth Palace. The chapel here had the most beautiful frontal I had ever seen. It encompassed a white ball with rays spreading outward into colored tongues of fire. Above it read "Light the visible reminder of invisible light."

We also visited the Anglican Consultative Council's office (later the Anglican Secretariat) and met with Kenneth Leach whose just published book—*Spirituality and Pastoral Care*—many of us had read, then went on to King's College at Cambridge. After seeing the chapel, we toured Trinity and Clare colleges, then on to Scholar's Walk.

There were also Salisbury Cathedral, Stonehenge and Coventry. Coventry made the biggest impression upon me, especially the healing chapel with its crown and cross. We also had breakfast at Oxford with Ian MacQuarrie[48] and his wife and met Maurice Wiles who just happened along on the campus while there. Our last night ended with a dinner at Dr. Green's Landsdowne Club in Mayfair.

Going to England when we did was a wonderful opportunity and I believe the sense of euphoria many of us experienced after exams probably added to the trip. It was a very upbeat fourteen day interval; but it was sad in a way to see those beautiful cathedrals—monuments to God—almost empty. We were told a very small percentage of the British population attends church. I think one sees more tourists than locals in some of them. Many of the churches are in effect, museums, like St. Isaac's in Russia. Lovely dinosaurs of the past.

# 29

# DISAPPOINTMENT

The final months of seminary often left me feeling as if I were on the crest of a giant wave, upheld by the prayer generated in our little community. Aside from the trip to England, I recall very little of what happened between January term and spring break. Whereas the General Ordination Exams initially did not upset me (I was still trusting the "process") now, however, their outcome seemed more like Dionysius' rebuke of Damocles—the constant shadow that something disastrous might drop on me. I finally reconciled myself to accepting whatever the outcome would bring, however, and made plans to go to Snowbird for March break.

The father-in-law of one of my classmates happened to be in the University of Utah hospital. So his daughter, Sarah, came with us for a short time with her little boy in order to visit with him. Preceding them were Austin, Dr. Green and his wife, Bishop Schofield and Elaine, Doris (our friend and secretary) and Pat Meyer (another friend from Miami.) The first day was really fun and had all the earmarks of a really relaxing week. Until Sarah arrived, that is, from Texas, with the results of the ordination exams. I was so busy trying to be the hostess that I didn't zero in on what every one was discussing until Bishop Schofield took me aside and asked me to go out in the hall with him. That's when the wave I'd been riding hit the beach leaving me mired in the sand. That's when I found out I had not done well. This didn't come as a total surprise because I knew I had not been able to finish one of the questions. Still, I never expected to be failed.

"A lot of people have trouble with these. Some people just can't take exams," said the bishop. I was dumbfounded when he said: "You can come back to the Diocese and take them again. Write Canon Masterman and work out a schedule with him." He didn't even offer to discuss the questions with me.

*Take those awful exams again?* For a brief moment I was afraid I was going to be ill. Surely I had answered *some* of the questions properly. I *knew* I had gotten some of them right. What had gone wrong? How could I have done so badly?

Now I would have to return to my diocese and take seven exams with seven different examiners.

It was probably a blessing to be surrounded by guests that week. Trying to look after their needs kept my mind off the exam results. Not only that, a midnight call from Canada helped put things in proper perspective. I was in a deep sleep when the phone rang. A voice on a static-filled line said: "We're calling to tell you your family is all right."

"What? Who are you?" I asked.

"We want you to know your family is all right. There's been an accident. Please don't call us back. The lines are all in use."

"What kind of accident?" But they had hung up. I lay there all night wondering what could have happened. All I knew was that my daughter and son-in-law were heli-skiing in Canada.

The next morning I found out. Doris had seen the late news. An avalanche had occurred and I learned later Leslie and Ed had been at the bottom of a mountain, watched as the avalanche roared down towards them. It had stopped short of where they were, but the remaining members of the group had been buried under tons of snow. Leslie finally called. They'd spent all that day digging out their dead ski companions. I was so grateful my daughter and husband were safe that failing exams didn't seem very important just then.

But eventually, I had to go back to seminary.

At first, I tried to shake it all off. But later, as my friends learned of it, I began to feel beaten down, ashamed and confused. I couldn't tie in where I was sure I'd been in seminary with the results of the exams. I'd always prided myself on intellectual accomplishment. I know grades had mattered to me in my earlier school years. And although the faculty hadn't given us letter grades, I knew I had been conscientious in all my studies. I had only twice in three years been asked to rewrite a paper. Some of my efforts had yielded honors. I'd never been led to believe I was failing in anything. And I'd been so looking forward to graduation, to going home, and to beginning my ministry somewhere.

"After you're ordained, no one's going to care if you passed the GOE's," everyone said. "They aren't that important." Maybe not to those who'd been passed. But would those of us who'd been failed ever be ordained? We couldn't help wondering.

Bishop Charles called from Cambridge. He was still the Dean of the Episcopal Divinity School in Massachusetts where he'd gone after being the Bishop of Utah. I told him how sick and discouraged I felt.

"Marta," he said. "Don't beat yourself up over this. One of our students has a PhD in ethics. She was failed in ethics, would you believe?

After the GOE's, it had never once occurred to me I would be asked to take more exams. We had been told they were supposed to be diagnostic. If any problems turned up, I expected my Diocese to check where they thought I might be deficient, then make any needed suggestions to correct the situation. I tried to explain to the bishop that it would be pointless for me to re-take the GOE's. I knew intuitively the areas where I needed reinforcement. Re-taking exams was not going to help my ministry one bit. I knew I needed more experience in sermon writing, more ideas in devising good educational programs for congregations, and help in knowing where to go for good resource materials. Some of this all came together later in the semester during my Field Ed training at St. David's in Texas, as well as when our class went to the Dixie Dude Ranch for a weekend. But I wasn't given an opportunity to talk about any of this, nor did anyone seem to care. A committee was in charge of my life from that point on, which meant no one was in charge. My bishop followed the "process," no matter how inane. Even though the Dean told me flat out I was prepared for ordination, that he would write the bishop to that effect, I doubted he would get far. My bishop had been in the military and went by the book.

About all I could relate to then was Jeremiah's lament. "O Lord, thou hast deceived me, and I was deceived; thou art stronger than I, and thou hast prevailed. I have become a laughing stock all the day...." (Jeremiah 20:7) If this was God's idea of a joke, I failed to see the humor.

Then, some of the other 600 phrases we'd had to learn for a scripture exam began to surface: "The Lord disciplines him whom he loves, and chastises every son whom he receives. It is for discipline that you have to endure." (Heb. 12:3–7). And "... He disciplines us for our good, that we may share his holiness." (Heb. 12:10) I told God I couldn't endure more discipline if it entailed more exams.

The next one that surfaced was "I know, O Lord, that your judgments are gifts and that in faithfulness you have afflicted me." (Ps.119: 75) If this was God's idea of a gift, I told him He could have it back. *I did my best, God. You know I couldn't do any better that day. Not under the circumstances."* I didn't think God heard me.

"Consider it pure joy when you encounter trials of various kinds" (James 1:2). *What a crock.*

Finally, I tried to settle on Romans 8:28. "God causes all things (good and bad) to work for good to those who love Him.

Eventually I discovered two other classmates had been failed on every question and five others had failed some of them. Several were passed in everything and, though wishing I had been similarly blessed, I certainly rejoiced with them. One failed classmate told me he had talked with Dr. Sugeno who had been helpful to him. I guessed he was trying to get back some sense of self-esteem and decided I needed that too.

"I'm really depressed," I told my history professor.

We talked for a bit, then he looked over my exam, reading some of the questions and answers aloud. "So what's wrong with that?" he asked after reading something.

"I don't know."

"Neither do I?" he said, then looked over some others. "I don't think you failed scripture."

"I thought we'd be examined in some music," I told him. "What was the point of taking three years of music? There wasn't one question."

Dr. Sugeno looked at me, back to my exam, then back to me. "What I've always found helpful," he said slowly " is to remember to start from a framework on all these questions. Take as a given that a God of love presides over all the universe. It is this God that is behind creation, that is involved in everything, and will be with us until the eschaton. In the center of all this is God, revealed in Christ, his life, and teaching, with the Holy Spirit at work in the world. Put everything else into that framework, then be able to back it up. When you think of God as love, as our Creator, everything else flows from that."

I knew God was love. I'd known that long before I ever went to seminary. So what was he driving at?

He sat looking at me in a perplexed way, then after a long pause: "Perhaps you've been drowning ... and none of us recognized it."

By then I was totally confused. I had no idea what he meant by that. I guess to this day I don't. Certainly I knew I'd been swimming upstream for three years, but drowning? Never! In seminary we'd been assigned papers to write; many subjects we'd been allowed to choose for ourselves. I obviously had not chosen subjects which examiners considered important. I wondered if instead of writing on the Psychological Aspects of Pauline Theology, should I have written on the Theological Aspects of Paul's psyche? I was demoralized when I left his office. There was no point in returning. Part of me tried not to care, but the part of me that had invested all that time and money and energy in my education was devastated. The learning would never be wasted, but would I ever be ordained?

The seminary had a policy of serving lunch at Rather House several times a week. I liked to go to this because normally I had to eat alone. This was an opportunity for me to be with my community (other than in chapel or in class) in an informal, social environment. At that time, Bishop Gerry McAllister was the chaplain in residence. I didn't know him well, but liked him from a distance, and was always glad when he chose to sit at a table where I happened to be eating.

Shortly after my return from Utah, he came in one day and sat beside me. At that point, I was still hurting, so when he asked how I'd done on my exams, I told him. I knew he was on the Presiding Bishop's Commission on Evangelism, so asked if he might mind reading my answers to the questions that had related to that subject. He said he'd be happy to, so I made an appointment to see him.

"I don't understand what's wrong with this," I told him.

After reading the questions and my answers, he said: "I don't either. There's nothing wrong with your answer. It's fine. You passed this as far as I'm concerned."

*Tell that to my bishop,* I thought.

His reply didn't change my situation, but at least, on that question, I felt vindicated in a way. By then, I was convinced had I done better on the first question, maybe my readers would have been more lenient. But the fact I had omitted the question on the catechumenate had doomed me. Not only that, in one other place, I had forgotten to mention the *Book of Occasional Services.*

If I were going to have to re-take the exams, I was determined to do so as soon as I got back to Florida; the first week, if possible. I hoped I'd be passed and ordained a deacon along with another student graduating from another seminary. The bishop had indicated earlier he would not place me in a job until fall, so I'd promised my sister I would get back to Utah and spend time with her. I feared it might be her last summer. Since she loved to play golf, we'd planned on that together.

My sister, just like my mother at first, had had difficulty accepting my decision to attend seminary. Our early upbringing in Mormon dominated Utah belied any connections to formal, organized religion. Religion, everyone knew, created more problems than it solved. Now I was beginning to think they were right.

If I was confused upon my arrival at seminary, for different reasons now, I was confused as the time approached for me to return home. I felt that I had failed my professors as well as my exams. But as Bishop Schofield directed, I wrote Fr. Masterman and asked if he could set up the exam schedule for me. He didn't answer my letter until nearly time for me to return home, then only to say we would discuss things when I got back to Miami.

But graduation was wonderful. Kermit, Leslie and Austin all came. I hadn't dared hope they would all be there for fear of more disappointment. But they were, and it was very special. I invited Ceako and he came too. Even some of my old friends from Stanford who lived in the area showed up. It was such fun to introduce them to my classmates and one another. It was a great couple of days. In all the pictures taken at that time, we looked so happy! I don't think I'll ever see more joyous pictures of me or my classmates. We'd finally come through the tunnel, resurrected at last! Some of the students already had jobs, and one classmate (who had been failed in three of his GOE questions) had already been ordained by his bishop.

When it was all over and my family left, I packed up my car, shipped what wouldn't fit in, then headed alone across Texas for the long trip home. I drove almost four thousand miles before getting back to Miami which included going to the ordination of one of my classmates.

When I got into Florida, the last day on the road, I was intentional about stopping at Bethesda-by-the-Sea. The bishop had told me he might put me there for my diaconal training. After walking down the long gothic-looking arch towards the chapel and reading a few bulletin boards along the way, I walked into the chapel and sat in a pew towards the front. Just sitting there, thinking about the possibility of someday being a deacon at this church, gave me a wonderful sense of awe and humility. I was over-whelmed with the atmosphere, the setting, the stained glass and the altar. I couldn't believe what a gorgeous church this was. There was such a wonderful sense of the holy, I suddenly knew God's arms were around me just then, and unexpectedly found myself crying. I couldn't help it. Before leaving, I knelt, thanked God for my safe trip, then again took in the beauty of it all. Though this was a long way from home, I hoped my first assignment would be here.

The following Sunday, home at last, I went to church at St. Andrew's. The bulletin had a list of those in the congregation graduating from various schools. It was the custom always to have a reception at our church for any graduates, usually in early June. But my name was not included. I decided this surely had been an oversight because I knew my sponsoring church would not leave me out intentionally.

I'd heard them pray for "our seminarian, Marta", so when I came out, nicely reminded the rector that there was no need to pray for me as a seminarian any longer, since I had graduated. I thought this a tactful way to remind him I was now one of the graduates.

"You're still a seminarian," he snapped "until you've done your make-up work and are ordained."

I could hardly believe what I was hearing, he was so abrasive. I was totally caught off guard. "But I *have* graduated," I told him.

"Graduate seminarian then," he replied, impatiently brushing me aside.

His attitude left me so crushed that I forgot about going to the reception. The peace I'd found in church didn't last. Through my tears, I could scarcely see to drive home. Not being remembered as a graduate was a minor omission, but to be so callously treated left me confused. If I couldn't get support in my sponsoring parish, where could I go? I'd never been what one would consider close to the rector, but I'd always thought we'd been on good terms. And he'd written me several letters during my three years away.

Austin, in his endearing ways, tried to cheer me up. "Hang loose," he kept saying. "It isn't the end of the world. You don't even need a job."

"But that's not the point," I told him. "That's just not the point." He had no idea how disappointed I was.

But he kept kidding me along, putting notes in a plastic flower we kept for that purpose near the kitchen sink.

The following week, I was informed I had to go see the Commission on Ministry again. I recall walking in and looking at all the people seated around a table. Although I could no longer remember their names, I knew several and recognized them from previous conventions. But many were strangers to me. Some nodded and smiled. The rest were impassive. The chairman was a priest I recognized from the Florida Keys. He introduced the members of the commission, then looked through some papers before him before beginning.

"It's come to the attention of this committee that you will have to re-take the canonical exams ..." He paused, "but someone has quoted you to me as saying that you refuse to take any more tests."

I'd totally forgotten a comment made that I would *never* willingly take another exam and couldn't believe the person I'd spoken with had passed this on to the committee. I looked around, could tell by the body language and the expressions of some of them that there was not going to be any leniency. "I don't believe taking more exams is going to make any difference as to how I perform as a priest," I said.

Silence.

"The dean of my seminary has said I am qualified to be ordained."

Silence.

"Several of my professors suggested I give you some of the papers I wrote while I was in school … as an example of the kind of work I do." I dragged out some papers and passed them to the person sitting next to me. He looked over the titles, then passed them along down the table where they stopped with the chairman.

More silence.

"Will you or will you not take the exams?" It was the chairman again.

I realized as I sat looking around me, had I been on this committee prior to my seminary experience and been judging someone else in the hot seat where I now sat that I probably would have treated them the same way I was now being treated. I would not have known anything about the seminary experience, nor what nor how we'd been taught. I would have viewed any one who complained as being a poor sport, an obvious failure and clearly not one who could represent the church. There was such a gulf between the committee, my bishop and my seminary, such a lack of understanding, it was pointless to try to explain.

If I'd been more laid back then, I would have just shrugged it all off, gotten up and left them sitting there. But after three years? After all those hoops? I'd never been a quitter, so I could not bring myself just then to chuck it all.

But later that day, I regretted not informing them had they bothered to read the canons, they would have at least known the church (at least those who had written the exams) had broken the rules regarding content. If they were going to hold me accountable according to diocesan rules, then why weren't the rest (i.e. those who wrote the national exam questions) expected to conform also?

As I looked around the table, I knew I was too vulnerable to make a case before the committee. The silence continued and the body language didn't change. I finally agreed to re-take them.

When I got home, there was a letter from a priest I knew in the West who was on the board of trustees at California Divinity School of the Pacific. He'd seen the GOE questions. His comment: "Marta, those exams were terrible. Even God had seven days."

# 30

# FATHER MANGRUM

Intuitively I knew I had to continue with my prayer time. I wasn't sure just then God was listening to me, or I to Him; but I knew I had to be faithful. Trying to pray, even a little, had a calming effect upon me.

As soon as I could get an appointment, I went to see Father Masterman. The last time I'd had any personal dealings with him had been when Chris was killed. He'd written me a beautiful letter. Seeing him now brought back sad memories, but I tried to concentrate on why I was there.

"Here's a list of your examiners," he said. "Call them and set up your own appointments. They'll all have different schedules, so you can work that out with them."

I was tempted to remind him I'd written two months earlier for just that reason but that he hadn't done a thing about it. "I'll bet the Standing Committee and the Commission on Ministry haven't read my exams."

"It's the policy of this Diocese that if you fail any of the General Ordination Exams, you must be re-examined."

There he went. Talking about the *Policy*, which of course was part of the *Process*. I couldn't help feeling angry. "If the business world were run the way the church is, there'd be few successful businesses around," I told him.

He looked at me quietly, not quite sure how to take my comment. "The church is sometimes better at teaching crucifixion than it is resurrection," he replied.

I wanted to tell him I didn't want to hear about death and crucifixion. I wanted to be caught up in *life*; but told myself I'd better keep quiet.

"We don't have anyone who can examine you in pastoral theology, so I'll do that one. I'll get it to you as soon as I write the questions. You can return it by mail."[49]

By the end of the week, I'd been in contact with six of the seven examiners, then debated about calling the last one, but finally did. He was the one who had given Caroll and Lynn and me such a hard time at Biscayne College years earlier. He wasn't there, so I left a message with his secretary.

Theology was scheduled first and I learned Father Mangrum would be my examiner. As it turned out just then, he was my bright light in a sea of humiliation.

"Marta," he said. "I've read your exams. I wouldn't have failed you. I wish I knew who your readers were. You have to realize, some of these people they get don't know where you're coming from. Some readers are bricklayers, or businessmen, or car salesmen. They have no right passing on what you wrote. I've kept track of you, ever since that day in North Miami. Remember me? Who I am?"

"Just vaguely," I had to admit.

"Well, I'm fat and bald, and I remember the day you were treated so abominably at Biscayne College. And you went and sat out in the hall the day of that review. They treated all you women so badly. You were near tears. Don't you remember? I went out and tried to comfort you."

I recalled the day all right and the abominable treatment, but it was all a blur now.

"Tell you what. Come on up. How about Thursday? We'll meet half way in Del Ray Beach. You and I can talk."

"Is there anything I should particularly concentrate on?"

"Oh, we'll probably talk about Anglican theology and the creeds. You're going to do fine, Marta."

In the meantime, I tried to get re-settled after three years away, and wondered how I would ever get the mildew smell out of the guest quarters.

Austin kept trying to cheer me up. "Maybe you can use this in a sermon some day," he said, handing me a limerick he must have remembered from somewhere. Since he'd stopped drinking, all his efforts now were channeled into humor.

> *God's plan made a hopeful beginning*
> *But man spoiled his chances by sinning.*
> *We trust that the story*
> *Will end in God's glory—*
> *But at present the other side's winning!*

That night, before going to bed, I reminded myself God was in charge and that He would see me through this. But just then it was a Bishop in Oregon I admired. I didn't know his name, but wished he'd been my bishop. He'd called all his ordinands the night before GOE's, told them he intended to ordain all of them in June, regardless of how they did. Any deficiencies would be worked out.

What a totally different experience that would have been for me and my class-mates if we could have had that assurance.

The third examiner called while I was trying to fix lunch the next day. I'd for-gotten all about him, so when his raspy voice came through over the phone say-ing who it was, it took me a moment to respond. I'd put the past behind me and felt genuinely good towards him. I hoped he'd be the same towards me. "Father Masterman asked me to call to set up a time to discuss the GOE's," I said.

"How about next Tuesday. Come by and we'll talk." He told me where to park and hung up.

I knew he was still opposed to the ordination of women, then finally decided I'd just mentally put him back in a snow bank if necessary.

Later that week, Austin and I attended a wedding. A priest I'd known for a long time was there. "Hear you didn't come out so well on the GOE's," he said.

"You've got it right."

"You should know. I was failed in ethics. I understand you have the same examiner. When I had to see him about it, he just gave me two books to read."

"And?"

"I was supposed to take an exam, but he never even followed up. So I got ordained and nothing was ever said."

*Oh. I should be so lucky,* I thought.

By now, I could not help seeing my failure in exams as an indirect punishment for spending a summer in Panama. *Should have stayed home and pulled my notes together better,* I kept telling myself. I had naively thought my diocese would give me credit for going to a third world country, for knowing the language and par-ticipating in the seminary's summer program. In "heaven," in my heart, I knew I had done the right thing, but the Commission on Ministry and the Standing Committee weren't interested in any of that. I felt they were more focused on Diocesan "policy" than reaching out to the Hispanics in our community. There wasn't one *latino* on the commission. Just that morning, the *Miami Herald* had said the county now had 953,407 Hispanics, nearly half the county's population, at least according to the 1990 census.

My three years away from Miami had put me into a different world. But something wonderfully good had happened in those three years. Despite the crash landing, my educational experience had been positive. Austin had stopped drinking. We were communicating really well. That was so much more impor-tant than exams. But now, despite the euphoria in some areas, feelings of panic were beginning to hit me all over again.

Looking at my notes one last time, I felt overwhelmed. What would I be asked? I looked up some more names, then tried to remember again who the Donatists were. And would Father Mangrum want me to know all about the baptismal covenant or the monophysites?

That evening, two of my ex-classmates called. They must have guessed what a funk I was in. Besides Austin, my only other support were my seminary associates. But they were so far away. Later, my theology professor called. "You'll do well, Marta," he said.

The next morning Psalm 102 from the Propers really spoke to me. It began: *Lord, hear my prayer, and let my cry come before you; hide not your face from me in the day of my trouble.* I felt it had been written for me.

But after breakfast, by the time I got through the front gate, I could feel the tension beginning to build. It wasn't the prospects of seeing Father Mangrum that unnerved me. It was the association of having to drive to an exam. It was like being back in seminary. Only this time I meticulously followed the speed limit, remembering that day in Texas I'd been given a ticket. Now, I just let the speeding cars pass by on either side of me.

The stands of melaleuca along the canals brought aspen to mind. And Utah. And the West. That's where I would like to have been just then. The tall thin trees with their white bark made me think of the canyons in the Wasatch mountains.

I finally reached the cutoff to Del Ray Beach and by then had a lump in my throat the size of a baseball.

The moment I saw his face, I remembered Father Mangrum. I recalled how he had, in my opinion, been a thoughtful, seasoned priest. As it had the first time we met, his appearance still reminded me of "tough love."

"Good to see you again." He introduced me to Marjorie, his secretary. "She's the other rector here," he joked. The warmth of his welcome enveloped me. Ten minutes later into the conversation, I noticed the lump in my throat had disappeared.

"I've always called that *Bloody Exam Day*," he said, reminding me of the last time we had been together. "I'll never forget that guy getting up and saying it would be over his dead body that any women would be ordained in this diocese. He treated you women so rotten. But they all succeeded. And now you. I can't tell you how happy I am that you've come back. And don't you recall my telling you that things would change?"

I nodded.

"Heard about your son. Used to say a prayer for him, *and* you, every time I passed Andytown."

I hadn't thought of Andytown for a long time. It wasn't even on the Florida road maps anymore. It had just been a gasoline stop on Route 27 where Chris had gone to make a phone call. That was before the storm, before the helicopter crash, before he was killed. Now, like him, Andytown ceased to exist.

"So what's the bishop got in store for you, once all this is behind you?"

"If I'm ordained, he's indicated he might send me to the Palm Beach area."

"What do you mean *if?* You mean *when.*"

"*When* then."

"That's better."

"Father Mangrum. I know my exam probably should have been better organized, but ..."

He put up his hand. "I've read your exams. You know more than I do. But we may as well talk about a few things. I've learned from your answers. Never heard of this catechumenate service. I've never used it. And that date ... 664? Whitby. Always had that mixed up in my head. I had to look it up last night and you were correct."

He was shrewd, and very kind, and I had to admire the way he was going about this "exam." He would talk a bit, set the background, then throw in a question.

He asked me what theologian had favored Aristotle and where Plato fit into the scheme of things, what the meaning of *contra mundum* was, and what Chalcedon had been all about.

I couldn't recall much about Marcion when he asked, but when I mentioned Pelagius, he defined "pelagianism," looking very pleased that he remembered. I realized he was reminiscing about his own seminary days, so I just sat and listened and enjoyed him immensely.

Then he touched on English history, suggested I look up Joseph Butler when I hesitated. (I'd mixed him up with Samuel Butler.) He brought up the Eutychian heresy; I got in the Athanasian Creed. We discussed Barth and Bultmann, and the Caroline Divines, the via media and Lancelot Andrews. And of course, the Oxford Movement, Cranmer and Elizabeth l. He probed, and I could tell as we moved closer to the 20th century, he didn't respond much when I began to discuss what was going on with the Filioque Clause. And though he beamed when I mentioned Walter Bruggeman and Matthew Fox, he didn't seem anxious to discuss either. He seemed happiest when telling me about his experiences, the theologians he'd studied in seminary, and some of the good times in his ministry. I encouraged him all the way.

There were wonderful, often very insightful things Fr. Mangrum said. And some, humorous.

"If you ever have to baptize anybody in one of those eight foot deep baptismal pools, make sure you have an alb on with lead weights in the hem ... the kind the Baptists use." And he went on to tell me how he'd had to peel off his wet underwear once, fearful that an acolyte would open the door before he could change so he'd be exposed in the raw to his entire congregation.

We discussed James and Charles and the Evangelicals. Then he continued: "Our church does its best at keeping people out. One of our bishops in Florida right now has a two year moratorium on accepting any new ordinands."

"There aren't enough jobs." I told him about some of my classmates having difficulty being placed."

"If you had to sum it all up in a few sentences, what would you say about God?" he asked.

Dr. Sugeno's advice came to mind. "I'd say God is our Creator, and a given is that He's a God of love ... and.."

"I'll buy that. You've passed your exam," he said. "Of course, you'd passed it before you arrived. There was nothing wrong with what you wrote. I would have passed you in all seven areas. For me, it's been fun, being reminded of seminary. I loved it. Went in with some strange ideas. But they made an Old Testament Christian out of me." He looked over at me and smiled. "Now it's time for lunch. If you don't have any plans, let me take you to lunch."

"I'm thinking I should take you."

"No, I'm the examiner. We'll do it my way."

At lunch I learned he'd been a "hawk" during the Vietnam War, that he'd been elected mayor of Wellington once, that he'd shaken Prince Charles' hand and been kissed five times by Zsa Zsa Gabor. "All kinds of people go to that church in Wellington."

He talked at length about some of his travel experiences, his trip to Grenada and to the Holy Land.

I told him about my experiences in Panama.

Then he frowned. "I've never forgotten that debacle at Biscayne College. It's now St. Thomas University, you know."

I hadn't known.

"*Awful* day."

"I do recall one of us got sick."

"It's no wonder. He shook his head in disgust. "After that meeting, I was incensed at the way you all had been treated. And I told the rest of them. For that I was not asked to rejoin the committee the following year. They gave me a lame excuse for not being included."

I decided not to tell him that the priest who had been in charge that day was going to be my examiner in ethics. There was no point in injecting negative vibes into the *force*.

When Father Mangrum took me back to the church and dropped me off at my car, he got out and gave me a hug. "If anybody gives you a rough time over these exams, I want to know. Hear?" Then, as an after thought said, "You just might enjoy reading Victoria Pym and P.D. James one of these days.... when you have some time."

I hugged him back. Father Mangrum had been such a breath of fresh air. He knew who he was, what he believed, and he hadn't minded saying so. Not only that, he had *affirmed* me. I don't think he could possibly have known how much that time with him did for my morale that day. He left me feeling that people always came first with him. He was the kind of priest I hoped I could emulate.

I skipped the Saw Grass this time and went on to Pompano Plaza. The iced tea tasted good. But when I saw the large thunderheads building up for an afternoon storm, I got back in the car and hightailed it for home, all the while marveling how that dear priest had made my day.

And later that evening, something prompted me to look through an old prayer journal. Father Mangrum had been correct. He *had* come out and comforted me .He had taken my hand, when I was crying, with people milling around us in the hall at Biscayne College, and had said a beautiful prayer about guidance and knowing God's will. My journal went on to say:

*If anyone had told me fifteen years ago I'd someday sit in public with an Episcopal priest praying for me, I would have scoffed and said "Impossible;" but one should never use that word where God is concerned. He has a way of turning us inside out, like a pillow case, then dragging us along behind Him, even when we don't understand.*

# 31

# TRY AGAIN

My second examiner was young, intelligent and I thought really very nice. He gave me plenty of time to talk. "What were your reactions to the exams?" he asked.

I was open and honest. "This has all left me demoralized," I finally said.

He talked for almost an hour, going over the questions dealing with contemporary society. Then he verbally tore my exam answers to shreds pointing out all the things he thought I'd said wrong. He then came up with a stack of five books, some containing various articles he wanted me to review. "I won't give you any questions on these books," he said," but they'll get your intellectual juices flowing."

I couldn't believe what I was hearing. Did he expect me to read all five of the books? Did he have any concept of what he was laying on me? Didn't he think my intellectual juice were flowing now? But more to the point, I realized I was coming out of a totally different paradigm. Although we'd never had any specific classes in feminist studies in my seminary, I'd run across several books that discussed the feminine viewpoint on some issues. I began to wonder as I listened to his remarks if this might not be an example of that. It wasn't that I couldn't think. It's just that women thought differently about some issues.

"Here's a list of possible subjects I'll be expecting you to expound upon." He read over them. They included language, homosexuality, the Fort Worth Synod, the role of women, poverty, racism, abortion, global and local decisions and their effects. "I'll be looking for integrated thinking in scripture, as well as theological substance and pastoral sensitivity."

I knew I was supposed to be able to articulate on being the church in the world and knowing the mission of the church. But after being told to read five more books, I didn't hear much more after that. But as I'd heard him analyze my exam intellectually, I knew we were coming from such different directions that I could never think the way he did. He so overwhelmed me, I thought perhaps I should just quit then and there and save myself more grief. His vocabulary was so esoteric, I began to wonder if we were talking about the same subjects. What he was saying didn't have much to do with love or caring as far as I could make out which had always been my yardstick for what was important. I didn't know how I could ever come up with what he was expecting. Seminary had never been this bad. I finally decided he was trying to impress me with all his big words and learning. As if reading my thoughts, he said: "My wife accuses me of being an 'intellectual snob' at times." Then he laughed.

My heart went out to his wife.

"It's okay to use theological language when talking with theologians," he added, "but never use that kind of language on an exam. No big words," he said.

I wondered why we'd had to learn and use words such as soteriology and ontology and eschatology if they were never to be used. And why was he using so many now?

He walked me out to my car.

"I don't think the way you expect me to," I finally said. "As for abortion, it's more important to understand people than to take sides on whether they should or should not have one. The church should be involved in teaching about contraception, and sexuality and good values and sexual health and how to prevent STD's and AIDS and helping women decide whether to have babies at all, or how many."

"That's fine. Say all that theologically and I'll pass you," he said.

By then I wasn't sure I even knew what he meant by his statement. Did that mean I was supposed to talk theologically without using any theological terms?

He must have sensed my dismay. "You haven't failed. You've just not passed an exam. But you will, eventually. I'll send it to you in the mail."

The traffic going home was slow. At least I had a chance to look at the Miami skyline. And as I paused to take in the beautiful blue-green waters of Biscayne Bay, wondered if God could pass theology.

The gate was open when I got home. Austin was out. A message from him on our plastic flower said: "Hope you are having good luck." Underneath he had drawn a smiling face with a halo. To his note I added: "One passed and six to go."

Later that week in the mail I found the exam from the second examiner and also a letter from Bishop Schofield. In all the turmoil of the week, I'd forgotten I'd written to him.

*Thank you for your Ember Day letter,* it began. *I can fully understand and appreciate your feelings at this time but I believe in due process you will come out of this a much stronger person and that your ministry will be extremely affective.*

(Did he mean affective, or effective, I wondered?)

*I'm sorry about what happened with GOE's, but as Dom Helder Cámara says, 'put your ear to the ground and listen, hurried, worried footsteps, bitterness, rebellion. Hope hasn't yet begun. Listen again. Put out feelers. The Lord is here. He is far less likely to abandon us in hardship than in times of ease.'*

*God bless you as you take your examinations and I look forward to seeing you during the summer. Once again, congratulation on graduating from seminary with honors in some of your courses. Faithfully yours, Calvin O. Schofield.*

I was drawn to the first paragraph of the bishop's letter. Maybe he did mean "affective." To be an effective priest, I had to be "affective." I had to have heart, as it were, towards others. Just then, however, thinking about the second examiner, I was wishing my bishop would be more affective towards me.[50]

Affections were needed for the stable and dynamic aspects of character. They would deepen, if I acted them out, but they would disappear too, if I ignored them. They were the habits of the soul. Habits I'd been trying hard to establish and retain. As Jonathan Edwards, the Puritan theologian, had said: *True religion, in great part, consists in holy affections.* Jesus washed the feet of his disciples. In my servant ministry as deacon, I could learn to do that also. It was not just imitation, but *participation.*

I still hadn't had time to make out a schedule for the rest of the exams, but having one behind me helped my outlook. I wrote Father Mangrum a "thank you," remembered to look up "utilitarianism," tried to recall all the arguments for a theory of a just war, then settled down to read the questions for my contemporary society exam. When I saw it, and the instructions accompanying it, I felt betrayed. The second examiner had simulated the exact way the GOE's had been administered, even the time limits, the type of questions and the way they were set up. It left me feeling stranded on the outskirts of a nightmare.

◆      ◆      ◆

Father_____, the ethics examiner, was nice enough at first. But I began to feel uncomfortable the following week when he began to tell the story of a statue that students had kept in seminary where he had been a student. "It was a statue of a saint who started out as a monk who wanted to be a priest," he said, "but he could not pass his exams. The monk was such an embarrassment to the church they finally ordained him, then sent him away to a remote outpost so he would not get in anyone's way."

I wondered where all this was leading and hoped he was not equating me with the stupid monk. The good feelings I'd intentionally had for him were slowly wearing off.

He looked sternly at me over the top of his glasses. "But it turned out he was a good confessor and people from all around flocked to visit him. Over the years, he made a great impact on people's lives." He then began shuffling the papers in front of him.

"I've read the section of your exam that relates to ethics and moral theology. How do you feel about this? Any comment?"

"I did the best I could with the time allowed," then added, "they always gave us time to reflect when we wrote papers in seminary. I know I don't do well under the circumstances that were forced on us during exams."

"There's another theory, of course."

"What's that?"

"There's a possibility you didn't want to pass this test. Did it ever occur to you that maybe you don't want to be ordained?"

The atmosphere in the room began to change and I felt the hair go up on the back of my neck. "I don't think so," I finally said.

"Sometimes things come out in unusual ways." He glared at me. "What kind of ethics background did you have in seminary?"

I told him.

He began to discuss various teachers and ethicists. He opposed Carter Heyward. "Was Cooper your teacher?"

"No. He'd resigned when I arrived. They hadn't hired a new person. We had an interim, a Catholic theologian actually, but who favored the Episcopal Church."

"What were your texts?"

I told him.

"You should read Kirk and Stevyk."

*Dear Lord. No!*

"I've been teaching a class in ethics." Then he suggested how I should approach his questions. I felt like Alice at the Mad Hatter's Tea Party. He talked about inclusive language and sexuality and other Anglican theologians he thought I should know. "As for the rest of your exam, the oral part with me, the canons require two examiners, so I'll have to get someone."

Something clicked. "Where does it say that in the canons?"

He picked out the canons from his bookshelf but couldn't find what he'd referred to.

*You won't find it there.*

"I can't seem to find it. I'll check it later," he finally said.

He proffered a sheet he wanted me to review, then decided to give me a copy of the final exam he'd given his ethics class. "Look it over and call me back. We'll go from there. I'm leaving the end of July."

"I'll be back in touch," I said.

The alarm went off too early the next day. When I turned on the light in the bathroom, the first thing I saw was a large cockroach sitting on my toothbrush. I hoped that wasn't an indication of the kind of day it was going to be.

As I drove out of the garage, I had to wonder why I was leaving it all to face traffic on a freeway. The previous examiner's remarks had gotten to me. Maybe I didn't really want to be a priest. Maybe I should stop now and give it all up. Then I reflected on how my prayer life had taken me to seminary and this is where it had landed me.

An hour and a half out of Miami, I finally arrived at the turnoff to the fourth examiner's office. Stopping at a convenience store, I asked for directions. The lady wasn't much help, but she let me use the facilities, so I bought some juice and a donut. As I stood eating and sipping through the straw, I noticed a cockroach on the floor. My first impulse was to step on it; but when I looked further, I saw five more running around on the tiles. *Part of God's creation*, I reminded myself. I could have snuffed them out, but didn't. I guess I identified too much with them. Probably from thinking about all that bloody English history—the beheadings and burnings at the stake—that gave me some compassion just then.

When I finally found the church, the secretary ushered me into the office of the priest who would be my history examiner. After a few niceties, he said: "We'll have three sessions."

*Three* sessions? My heart sank. It was going to be a long summer.

"Let's start with Jesus and continue through the apostolic ministry up to Chalcedon in 451."

Nestorius and the Monophysites came to mind. And then all I could think about was Professor Will Spong's remark once that it was more important to know who *we* were, than to know who Theodore of Mopsuestia was.

The priest spoke about the upcoming convention, about the problems he saw with the inclusive language resolution to be presented. "We need to affirm the

Trinity too, not throw it out or change it." He then gave me a list of books to read, none of which I possessed.

"You'll find out very soon, if you don't know already, that there's a lot of rejection in the ministry. Just because you wear a collar, you'll find people expect the impossible. And when you don't measure up, they'll reject you and criticize you and you'll really understand what it means to 'take up your cross.' I know this is painful for you, but you might look at this as training for what it's going to be like in the future."

*Good gosh, he sounds just like Father Masterman. All the emphasis on crucifixion.*

"You can try to look at this as a relaxing summer, as an interlude to review and grow."

*Relaxing?* Did he have any idea what the rest of my life was like just then? I kept thinking of my sister, dying in Utah. And noticed after he began discussing the type of questions I might get, I could feel a lump forming in my throat. By the time he got to Jesus and St. Paul, how they differed, I could hardly swallow.

I stopped at the Diocesan bookstore in Miami on the way home and winced when I saw the price of all the books he expected me to buy. Seventy dollars worth! Didn't he think my seminary had given us enough to read? I easily had $5,000 worth of books at home just as up-to-date as the ones he was recommending. I finally bought one.

The Marriott seemed like a good place for lunch. The blue water and boats on the bay helped me relax. After a bit, I found myself asking for God's help and guidance.

I spent the rest of the week writing the pastoral theology exam as well as doing most of the ethics test. I thought the questions were all fair.

With the rector and the assistant away, the following Sunday the deacon was in charge of the service at St. Andrew's. She said a Deacon's mass and gave a good sermon on the prophets. It all left me wistful. She was doing all the things I had been doing at my Field Ed church at St. David's before coming home. Now I was being treated as if I'd never even been to seminary.

One of my classmates from Texas called after I got home. Like me, she'd had a bad experience, only her bishop had reviewed her answers personally and asked her to write him a paper on just one subject he felt she might improve upon.

"Marta, I recall a man in our diocese who was failed a few years ago. He was told to re-take the exams. The next thing I heard, he'd left. I could not understand why he would not re-do the exams. It didn't make sense. Later, I heard he'd surfaced in another diocese in Texas and gotten ordained a year later. I couldn't imagine anyone's leaving after being so close to their goal. After three whole years, just to walk off! It didn't make any sense. But it makes plenty of sense to me *now*. I really understand."

That afternoon I tried to start studying for the canonical in church history. I tried to read Gonzalez' book on the history of Christianity, but couldn't get past the first three chapters. It was too demoralizing. It just made me think of my first semester at seminary, how lost and depressed I'd been. So I walked around the house, tried to remind myself of the things that made me happy, then remembered to spread more crystals on the guest area rug. At least the mildew smell had abated.

My guests from South America arrived Monday morning on their way to convention. I picked them up at the airport and got them settled. We had a good visit, and when the Bishop saw what I was reading and why, told me about his canonical exams.

"I was asked what the difference was between the continental reformation and the English reformation," he said. "Do you know how to answer that?"

"I'd say one was religious and one was political."

"The continental was from the bottom up; the English was from the top down," he told me.

"Oh," I said, resisting an urge to tell him that's what I'd said, only in a different way, but I mentally filed his comment away in case my examiner would see things his way. It was becoming clear to me that people all saw things his or her own way, just as I did.

On the way to the airport the next morning, he said: "Under any other circumstances, I'd be calling you 'Mrs. Weeks,' but since you are a postulant, I call you 'Marta.'"

"I'm glad you do, Bishop," I told him. "Only I'm not a postulant. I'm a candidate."

"Ah, perdón."

Austin was still trying to be upbeat and helpful. "You know what an insomniac, a dyslexic and an agnostic have in common, don't you?"

I couldn't imagine.

"They wake up in the middle of the night wondering if there's a dog!"

For the third time, I called the priest who was supposed to examine me in liturgy. He'd promised to send me questions in the mail. Over a month had gone by and still he had not responded. So I finished up ethics and concentrated on history. The examiner had told me he expected me to know a lot about Christian thought. St. Ambrose, St. Augustine, Origen, Tertullian and Clement came to mind. I doubted anyone would be asking me any burning questions about them once I was ordained. And if they did and I could not recall, I knew where to look them up. This all seemed so pointless.

I dropped off the ethics answers, then went home briefly before returning to the Gables to see Bishop Richards. It wasn't until he began discussing discursive prayer and the possibility of reading something like the *Cloud of Unknowing* that I began to cry. I didn't want to, but the tears kept coming. The thought of having to read another book just then, on top of the twelve that had been thrown at me, was too much.

He backed off immediately, looking rather perplexed, and I cried even harder.

"I'm so tired of jumping through hoops. I can't believe the way the church treats people." I just saw discursive prayer as another assignment. It all came tumbling out. "I've tried and tried, but I don't know how to fit in. I'm not sure I want to be an Episcopalian any longer."

"Where would you go?"

"What difference does it make? I just want to be *me*, Bishop Richards. Everyone keeps trying to put me into their little box, only I can't fit the way they want me to." I sobbed and sobbed. "I could be a good free-lance priest. If I could just be *me*," I said again.

The bishop got up and handed me a box of Kleenex.

"What kind of relationship do you have with your rector?" he asked.

"It stinks!"

Bishop Richards winced.

I didn't tell him how difficult the rector could be and how he obviously didn't like women. I just told him how discouraging I found the "process."

He gently asked: "Where would you like to be right now?"

That was easy. "In Utah, playing golf with my sister."

"Surely you can work out an accommodation with the bishop."

Bishop Richards just didn't understand. I knew I would never be ordained if I didn't stay here and re-do the exams. How could I possibly remember every nitpicking detail if I didn't get it all behind me now? At least everything was still fresh in my mind. I finally reached a point where I didn't care and got up to leave.

"Please don't go," said the bishop. "Where will you go?"

I didn't answer him. I didn't know, and I was too miserable to care.

"Please. Why don't you come back next week. I want a chance to think about things. I can talk to the bishop."

"I can't be prayerful anymore," I told him. "The church is making me cynical, and distrustful, and mean-spirited. That's not me, Bishop. I don't want to be like that. I don't want to be mean." I tried to blow my nose, then remembered one of the questions that had been on the GOE's. "Do you know what one of the questions was on the short answer part of our exams?"

He looked at me quizzically.

They asked: "In what book of the Bible does the word 'immediately' appear 42 times?"

I don't recall much more of what was said, except when I finally left, I told him: "I think I prefer to make money, Bishop, and give it away." And I walked out. Later, I had to ask myself: "If I had only a short time to live, would I be doing what I'm doing? Would I be worrying about Arianism, or Marcion or the Investiture Controversy?" When I answered "Good God, no," I was finally able to put a different perspective on it all. I was really able to get past Jeremiah's Lament (Jer.20:7) into thinking more in terms of faith. "A faith that gives substance to our hopes, and makes us certain of realities we do not see." (Heb.11)

# 32

# AT LAST

On July 31, the examiner for Scripture called. Mike Cassell said he had returned from his vacation early and would schedule me for August. "Know all the main characters in the Bible," he said, then mentioned "Abiathar, Sarah, John Mark, Demas, Abigail, John of Patmos."

"Have you read my exams?" I asked.

"No, but I don't think most Episcopalians know anything about the Bible." He rattled off a lot of other things he expected me to know. "I'm just doing what the committee asked me to do."

There was that word again: *committee*. Was anyone in charge, I wondered?

The liturgy questions finally arrived, so I got them out of the way, then concentrated on Scripture.

When I had first spoken with Mike, I'd gotten the distinct impression he was young and possibly a little overweight. He had a boyish voice almost on the phone and I guess it was his statement that he was going to get married and go to England on his honeymoon that led me to believe he was a very young priest. So it was a surprise when I drove up to St. Joseph's Church in Boynton Beach to discover when he walked in and shook my hand that he was tall, tanned, slightly balding, thin, and probably closer to fifty than the twenty-five or thirty I had envisioned.

I'd given myself time to look around first and was pleasantly surprised to find such a large compound. It included lots of land, a school, and lovely church. The inside reminded me of "high church." There were Stations of the Cross, stained glass windows everywhere, a pamphlet rack, and a prayer place with a statue to our Lady of Walsingham. The beautifully needle-pointed kneelers with Biblical quotations reminded me of why I was there. "Come into my office. Bill should be here in a minute."

Bill Hamilton arrived on time. He was a priest from Lake Worth, pleasant and a bit overweight. I felt as though it had been his spirit I'd mixed up with Mike's.

The quiz began. I got a few, then missed a few. I'd always been so intent on knowing all the books of the Apocrypha and what each one was about that I hadn't realized it was the bridge between the Old and New Testament. I mixed up King Herod and Herod Antipas and King Herod Agrippa for a minute.

Mike mentioned Quirinius. "He lived at a different time than Herod. The Bible is wrong on that point. Fundamentalists have trouble with that one. Let's face it. The Bible is not always factual," said Mike.

"Adam?" continued Hamilton.

"Mankind," I said.

"Our bishop says it wasn't the apple that caused all the problems in Eden. It was the *pair* on the ground," said Bill.

I sat there like a wooden Indian visualizing a *pear* on the ground, wondering how that tied in to the exam, and thinking about the bishop and a conversation I'd had with him the previous evening.

"*Pair,*" he repeated. "The couple."

"Oh." I smiled. "Thanks." Bill Hamilton was trying hard to put me at ease. He and Mike were a delight compared with some of the others.

"What nationality was Abraham?" It was Cassell's question. I wasn't sure.

"Arabic?"

"Which country?"

I'd been so geared to the scripture questions expected that all I could think of for a moment were the maps in the back of my Bible, those covering pre-modern times. They had not included contemporary geography, so for a moment, I could not shift my orientation. I finally said "I think Iran," then tried mentally to impose a picture of a contemporary map on the ancient ones I'd been studying. I knew I'd had to memorize so many trivial things that I was beginning to lose the whole picture.

"Abraham would have been an Iraqi," he corrected. "Pretty mind-boggling when you think about all that's going on in the world now, how nobody gets along over there."

A scene from a WW2 movie flashed through my mind. It was of a fighter plane going down. I wondered if Rev. Cassell was going to shoot me down.

They continued with questions covering Samuel and Kings. Hamilton broke in. "And Jesus descended from David. David was good and bad. Very human. But in our brokenness, God accepts us, forgives us."

I had to think a minute about where Artaxerxes fit in. But mostly, I got their questions. I kept waiting for them to get harder, but they never did. I was sure I'd be asked about Phygelia and Hermogenes, or Onesiphoris, or Epaphroditus and Onesimus. But I wasn't.

After about an hour and a half, Cassell and Hamilton agreed I was pretty well informed on Bible content. "You've passed fine," said Mike. "I'll let you know about your written work in a few days." I didn't tell him I'd considered bringing him the test my seminary had given us just to see if he could pass it. That test had consisted of six hundred questions. I'd gotten all but six.

Worn out but hopeful, I finished taking the last canonical in history the next day. By then, I was beginning to feel I'd been swimming against the tide far too long. I about sank when the examiner said "You've passed." Then he added "I think you might like to read Pritchard's book on the Episcopal Church in America." I agreed and floated upwards, then dashed home to finish packing. Austin and I were to be in Denver the next day.

The afternoon mail contained a letter from the second examiner, the young man who had impressed me so favorably at first. When I reached the paragraph that said "*I must inform you I am unable to pass you on the basis of your essay,*" my euphoria fell into a million pieces. I knew I had written a good exam. I couldn't believe his letter. It reminded me of what the navy had done to one of its recruits in training. The young man had kept telling his drill instructor he could not swim as they expected him to. So the instructor kept throwing him back into the water to teach him. The recruit eventually had a heart attack and drowned. "*Well,*" I told myself, "*I'm not going to drown!*" But I kept thinking about a cat I'd once seen playing with a little mouse it had caught. I had been about five years old at the time. The mouse had been bleeding and could not get away. And the cat kept knocking it back and forth between its paws. I couldn't believe he hadn't passed me!

I went to my desk and took out a sheet of paper. "*Dear Father_____,*" I wrote. "*You are not only an intellectual snob as your wife so rightly says, but you are also a horse's ass!*" I knew I wouldn't mail it, but it made me feel better.

It was then I knew I could no longer be part of this "process." As far as I was concerned, it was dysfunctional. By participating, I was showing I accepted it. I had been called to be faithful to God, not this idiotic nightmare. I think it was my guardian angel who came to my rescue, because after reading over the examiner's evaluations of what I had written, I felt prodded to write a letter I definitely planned to mail:

> *Dear Father_____,*
> *Regarding your letter of August 13, I would like to make*

*several comments on the exam that you gave.*
*You may recall that you told me to review five different*
*sources for this exam. However, you clearly specified that*
*there were not going to be any questions on what you*
*recommended I read, that this was only to "start the juices*
*flowing." So when you said in your review that I did not*
*mention baptism, of course I didn't. It was my understanding*
*it was not to be included. I looked over the Book of Occasional*
*Services as well as the two articles in Merriman's book. I also*
*bought The Catechumenal Process which you recommended*
*(and incidentally, which I think is a fine book to have for*
*reference). The other two books I did not have nor was I able*
*to get.*
*Still, it was with total confusion that I read over*
*Question 1 on the exam. It made very little sense to me. It*
*was about "ecclesial models" and I frankly didn't have the*
*foggiest idea what that was all about. The four books you*
*mentioned in the first paragraph of the question did not*
*mean much either. The only one I had heard of was Richard*
*Niebuhr's Christ and Culture, but I'd never read it nor was it ever*
*assigned to be read in seminary. It was optional in one class I took that had*
*A 75 book bibliography. The only Niebuhr we read was The Children*
*Of Light and the Children of Darkness, (but that was Reinhold)*
*and that didn't have anything to do with ecclesial models. I had to surmise*
*from*
*your question what I thought you might mean, which doesn't say*
*a whole lot for the clarity of your question. Considering that, I think I did a*
*very*
*good job of answering it and I'll stand by my answer.*
*Re. No. 2, if you had read my exam, you would know that I*
*included the information on the 69$^{th}$ General Convention's resolution on*
*abortion. (Set 3,p. 4). There was no point repeating that, especially since you*
*limited the time I was allowed to write this.*
I added a few other comments, then ended with: *As for many*
*of your other comments, you are certainly entitled to your*
*opinion. But so am I. It's interesting to see where you are*
*coming from. And I appreciate your evaluation of my exam.*

I sent a copy of my letter to Father Masterman.

When we got to Denver, I called one of my classmates who had landed a job as an assistant there. It was fun catching up with her life since our graduations in May.

"I was so naïve," she confided, when we got on the subject of the church. "Seminary was so genderless. Now that I'm out, I didn't expect to be so disliked by male priests."

"Some can be pretty obnoxious," I agreed. "But there are a lot of nice ones too. When a male candidate in our diocese was failed in ethics, he was asked to read two books. His examiner never even asked him one question. I had the same examiner. He made me write six essay questions and do a case study on substance abuse."

"That's not fair."

"I don't really care anymore. I refuse to take another exam. If three years of seminary didn't do it, more exams aren't going to help. The bottom line is that I have to be responsible to God, not an impersonal process that stomps all over you."

I was reminded of the Spaniards when they imposed their religion and culture on the native inhabitants of South America. It was called the *tabula rasa.*[51] This was the missionary method that ignored the significance of the language, rites, customs and culture of an indigenous people in an attempt to evangelize them. The Spaniards superimposed their beliefs without trying to understand the people they were conquering. Rather than truly converting them to Christianity, they merely imposed their own layer of religion on the culture. I hoped I would not end up like the Indians, but I knew nothing would ever "take" if I couldn't be myself. I could no longer fit into the diocesan box, whatever it was. But I *knew* I could be a good priest. I just hoped it would always be on God's terms, in response to all the blessings and love that had come my way in life. I didn't know it then, but it was out of the oscillating structure of my being a Non-Mormon/ Episcopalian that some of my ministry would develop. It would entail many associations with people totally turned off with organized religion, yet genuinely seeking a spiritual foundation in their lives.

After Denver, Austin and I went on to Salt Lake City and I accepted the possibility that the bishop might never ordain me. But I knew I would never go back and take another test from that priest, or anyone else. I had no idea how Bishop Schofield or Fr. Masterman might react to my letter. But on my return, there was a letter from the Diocese congratulating me on passing all of my exams. I don't know what transpired between Fr. Masterman and the second examiner. I never asked. I just know, in time, I finally made it.[52]

I've given too much space here to the subject of exams. Priests certainly should be informed and well-educated. But seminary students should be helped, not hindered, in their endeavors. Much heartache could be avoided if the various dioceses affirmed their seminarians throughout their entire seminary experience.

Most students who are failed—and quite a few are—say very little about their experience, probably because it's so humiliating and degrading. I'm sure they try to forget as soon as possible. But fledgling deacons need affirmation, not bashing. The Bishop of Oregon, who affirmed his group, knew how to make the system work. If diocesan bishops require aspirants go to seminary, certainly they should not let three days of exams supersede three years of schooling and training.

In his autobiography—*One Man's Journey, In Search of Freedom*—Obert C. Tanner wrote: "Entrenched powers, whether in authority roles, accepted ideologies, or institutional structures, are common and necessary to every structure, yet these powers often work against our finding the best solutions to our problems, the best answers to our questions.... ."

I used to wonder why those in charge in my Diocese never sat down with me and told me why my answers were unacceptable. They just slapped me with seven more exams to take. But the good news for me is that I'll never have to be in that position again. And I am immensely grateful to have been at seminary during the interval of a difficult time in my marriage. ETSS reinforced my beliefs that ministry should be in the realm of the practical as well as the theoretical. And of course, the *theological!*

It seemed appropriate I be ordained a deacon November 30, St. Andrew's Day, the saint's name of the church that sponsored me. Later, the name "Andrew" would be an even more poignant reminder to me of those times in my life, when a devastating hurricane carrying the same name, destroyed much of South Florida and the area all about us where we lived. That storm cut a swath thirty miles wide and wiped out 350,000 homes.

In closing this section, I include the following excerpts from a letter written by Dr. Sugeno which was sent to me some time after graduation.

◆    ◆    ◆

## The Episcopal Theological Seminary of the Southwest
✝
## January 31, 1991

The purpose of the General Ordination Examinations (GOE) continues to remain unclear despite years of effort at clarification. Presumably they were intended as a diagnostic instrument to be utilized by bishops in devising an on-the-job training program for newly ordained clergy following graduation from seminary. In fact they have, for the most part, served as qualifying examinations to determine whether the examinee should be ordained or not and after that determination has been made the examinations serve no further purpose.

It is clear that the GOE's were intended to replace the diocesan administered canonical examinations. The canonical examinations lacked standards, they were unevenly, if not arbitrarily administered. The GOE's in contrast, have established universal standards, been thoughtfully composed and carefully administered.

Pre-ordination examinations were instituted at a time when ordinands read for orders under the bishop's supervision. At the time no seminary existed for the education of prospective clergy. General Convention set forth a recommended reading list for those reading for orders but the education and examination of ordinands was the responsibility of the bishop and diocesan authorities. The establishment of seminaries shifted the primary responsibility of theological education to the seminaries which reported to the bishops and standing committees on the progress being made by their students in preparing for ordination. Canonical examinations were not eliminated but their importance diminished. In some instances they were but pro-forma ceremonies.

GOE's have shifted the focus of responsibility to an impersonal instrument, administered and evaluated by people unknown to the examinees and not answerable to them or to the diocesan authorities. Students see the GOE's as the last and in a sense the most important hurdle to surmount in their ordination career. In the long and difficult road toward ordination that a candidate must traverse, the GOE has come to represent a priestly formational system that is marked by a series of tests and hurdles involving scores of people, anyone of whom can blow the fatal whistle to stop the progress toward ordination. It is ironic that a church that prides itself on being pastoral has devised a system so impersonal and anxiety breeding. The GOE's epitomize that system.

The examination favors people who have agile minds and who have facility with the <u>written</u> word as the mode of expression. It does not examine people's ability with the spoken word or people's ability to reflect and meditate over a long period of time. It does not show one's ability to relate to people nor to carry out the primary functions of a priest—to preach, teach and to lead in worship.

In the past bishops committed themselves to particular prospects for the ministry from the outset of their seminary career. Seminary and bishops shared the pastoral responsibility for preparing ordinands. One went through seminary as a candidate for ordination rather than one preparing to be tested for qualification for ordination. Bishops and commissions do not intend it but the ordinands interpret it as the last and major obstacle in the obstacle ridden path to ordination. And horror stories of bad experiences with GOE's abound, adding to the anxiety of those preparing for the ordination.

From a seminary faculty point of view the GOE's get in the way of seminary education. Student preoccupation with the GOE's saps energies and attention away from classroom work. That is particularly true of the senior year of seminarians as the examinations are administered in the middle of the academic year. Pre-GOE anxiety and post-GOE anxiety and exhaustion cheat the students of a year of concentrated work in seminary courses.

An evaluation of the impact of GOE's on the quality of priestly training has yet to be made. So far as I know the GOE's have not raised standards in priestly formation in any discernible way and in so far as GOE's have contributed to the anxiety and the hazards of the ordination process they have served as obstacles to effective priestly formation.

Surely we can do better than we have in preparing people for the ordained ministry.

Respectfully submitted
(signed)
The Rev. Dr. Frank E. Sugeno
Professor of Church History[53]

# PART VI

# 33
# ORDINATION TO THE DIACONATE

My diaconal ordination was a joyous time. Even my old Spanish teacher—Sister Anna Teresa—from high school days came. She was a sister of the Holy Cross, so when I asked if she'd be my presenter and witness, she got permission from her BishopPatrick Ziemanthe Roman Catholic Auxiliary Bishop in charge of the Santa Barbara District where she lived. I recalled sisters usually traveled in pairs (like Mormon missionaries!) so invited her to bring someone else. She came with her own sister—Charlotte Marie—also a nun in the Holy Cross Order.

Frank Corbishley was the Master of Ceremonies and Bishop Richards read the Preface to the Ordination Rites. He gave an explanation first telling the congregation that in order to place in context what would be taking place that morning that they were to listen carefully to the reading. He said: "The preface is a kind of history lesson which helps us understand where the action we take today comes from in the long and apostolic history in the church's life."

The Preface mentions the different ministries of bishops, priests and deacons and part of what he read was: *persons who are chosen and recognized by the Church as being called by God to the ordained ministry are admitted to these sacred orders by solemn prayer and the laying on of episcopal hands. It has been, and is, the intention and purpose of this Church to maintain and continue these three orders; and for this purpose these services of ordination and consecration are appointed. No persons are allowed to exercise the offices of bishop, priest, or deacon in this Church unless they are so ordained, or have already received such ordination with the laying on of hands by bishops who are themselves duly qualified to confer Holy Orders. It is also recognized and affirmed that the threefold ministry is not the exclusive property of this portion of Christ's catholic Church, but is a gift from God for the nurture of his people and the proclamation of his Gospel everywhere. Accordingly, the manner of ordaining in this*

*Church is to be such as has been, and is, most generally recognized by Christian people as suitable for the conferring of the sacred orders of bishop, priest, and deacon.*[54]

Austin agreed to be a presenter, along with Sister, the rector and our senior warden, then Dick Spoerl. I had been afraid Austin might not agree to be there, but he actually seemed to enjoy himself, even though he later told me he'd been rather uncomfortable.

Jim Daniel (a family friend) came from Connecticut; and classmate—Tony Pompa—came all the way from Pennsylvania to be the litanist. Doris Hodges and Sandy Cummings were lectors, Jan Clarke helped with the chalice, and Caroll Mallin (who by now was an ordained vocational deacon) read the Gospel. Kermit and Leslie were oblation bearers; and the choir, under Ed Sagi's direction, outdid themselves learning several songs I wanted.

Bishop Schofield preached and reminded us that our Lord had come to serve and that all orders were first diaconal orders. He said that bishops, priests and deacons were to help all baptized persons in commissioning them to go out into the world to help them make Christ known to others by word and example.

"What is Marta getting herself into in this world today?" he asked. Then he went on to recall that just as the world had changed forever after the dropping of the atomic bomb in 1945, the two serious things in our lives now were the fatal AIDS virus and the whole question of our existence on the planet due to the greenhouse effect. He thought these two problems were raising the serious issues of life and of our own mortality. He mentioned how everything we did as Americans could affect others beyond us and specifically said, "They tell me in the Caribbean that when America sneezes, we catch pneumonia."

He also said that just as Saint Andrew had been called many years ago, I was now attesting to the same thing. When he asked me to stand for the "Charge," he reminded me he had shared some of my disappointments and pain, but then went on to say that the most important gift I could bring to my ministry was the gift of myself and a sensitivity to human need. "You have seen life, shared in life in many arenas. You will be involved in many of those. You have an understanding of people in the market place. You have an understanding of who God is and how God works in your life."

I'd been so depressed at not being ordained on schedule with the other seminarian who had returned to the diocese, that I hadn't realized what a great trade-off it was since at my own ordination, I got to choose my own music. I wanted it to be peppy and meaningful to me; so it included Ian Mitchell's Folk Mass rendition at the Nicene Creed. (I'd been invited to play this once with a guitar group at the National Cathedral in Washington D.C.) And I also included *The Chris-*

*tian Life* by Linda Wilberger Egan and Dan Schutte's *Here I am Lord* based on the sixth verse of Isaiah.

My sister wasn't there. She couldn't understand why I had to be ordained twice. First deacon, then a priest. It made no sense to her. "I'll come to your *real* ordination," she told me, "*if* I'm still around." Mother didn't make it either. She was ninety-five by then and had long declared her traveling days were over.

The music I chose said a lot about where I was. I know I identified with the Communion song, *For the Mountains shall Depart,* by Hank Beebe.

> *For one small moment have I forsaken thee,*
> *But with great mercies will I gather thee*
> *For the mountains shall depart*
> *And the hills be removed*
> *But my kindness shall not depart from thee.*
>
> *For the Lord hath called thee as a woman*
> *Forsaken and grieved in spirit, and a wife*
> *In youth when thou wast refused saith thy God.*
>
> *For one small moment have I forsaken thee,*
> *But with great mercies will I gather thee*
> *For the mountains shall depart*
> *And the hills be removed*
> *But my kindness shall not depart from thee.*

Professor Green was there representing the seminary, as well as one of my classmates, Cristina Condit. She was the first student I had met after arriving in Texas. She had a PhD in nutrition and had been a missionary before going to seminary. The congregation from St. Andrew's was wonderfully supportive too. Sandy Miller was in charge of the reception; someone made a cake with my name on it, and lots of people gave me gifts or contributed to my discretionary fund. It was the beginning of a new life for me. For a few weeks, I was lifted into another dimension.

I know I was too excited and nervous, happy, yet apprehensive, to concentrate on the readings that day. It was not until later I could zero in on what had been read, some of which included Romans 10:8–18:

*The word is near you, on your lips and in your heart (that is, the word of faith which we preach); because, if you confess with your lips that Jesus is Lord and believe in your heart that God raised him from the dead, you will be saved. For man believes with his heart and so is justified, he confesses with his lips and so is saved.*

Some of St. Paul's epistles had given me trouble in seminary. I'd often viewed him as a theological thorn. Was this a coincidence that St. Paul be read at my ordination, that I be reminded to believe with my *heart*, not just my intellect?

At least the Gospel read affirmed where I was, despite my ongoing spiritual struggles. It was about Jesus' calling Simon Peter and Andrew as they cast their nets as He walked by the Sea of Galilee (Mt. 4:18–22). The magnificent stained glass wall at the back of the church with Jesus calling Andrew to follow was a beautiful depiction of the Gospel. It ended saying: "Immediately they left the boat and their father and followed him."

I knew that's what I wanted and was trying to do also.

# 34

# GETTING A JOB

Bishop Schofield would not ordain me a priest until I had a job, so of course I prayed one would open up. I had thought I might be invited to go to Bethesda, but it didn't happen, so I had to give up the possibility of going there. But shortly after that, the bishop told me there was a good chance of a place in another church closer and north of Miami. An assistant was needed and he said the rector would get in touch with me.

He soon called and made an appointment and I drove up to be interviewed. I was so excited. At last, maybe I would get to begin my formal ministry. It was a lovely church next to a waterway. The rector asked me a lot of questions, told me about his church's programs and congregation, then indicated during our conversation he wanted to hire me. He emphasized that I would be free to develop my own ministry and would have plenty of leeway in the way I wished to pursue it, then said he would get back to me. I left feeling I finally had a job and couldn't wait to tell Austin.

A few days later, the priest called back. "I'm going to be in Coral Gables next Tuesday," he said, then suggested we meet for lunch. On the appointed day, he arrived with his wife as well. "I want her to meet you," he said.

After ordering our meals and settling in to a convivial conversation, he asked if I would like to be the assistant. Even though it meant I would have to find an apartment and spend much of my time away from home, I said "yes." This job would give me some experience at last. By now, many of my classmates had already been placed in jobs. Furthermore, after all the trials of getting through the "process," I wanted to show them I was capable and really wanted to serve.

"Well, we really do want you to come." He sipped his iced tea, then smiled nicely. "We certainly need extra help, but there's just one thing." He paused a moment, then put down his napkin. "Our budget just can't afford to pay for an extra person at the moment, so what I suggest is that you donate $50,000 to the

Diocese. Then we'll have the Diocese pay you $25,000 for your salary for a year; the balance of $25,000 I'll use to hire a new secretary we need also."

It took me a minute to comprehend what he had said. Then I couldn't believe what I had heard. He wanted me to pay my own salary? After three years of graduate school? After all the pain, the "process," the three years away? I was expected to pay my own salary? Plus pay for his new secretary?

I knew I was much wealthier than the average seminary graduate; still, I felt strongly that I should be entitled to compensation; and that did not mean paying my own salary. Any monies received from the church would certainly go to my discretionary fund to help others, but I felt I should have the right to decide where those monies went. Not only that, if I weren't being paid something other than from my own bank account, who would take me seriously? Had the fact I'd been helping to support three different priests been known by this priest? I didn't think so. But if so, was he trying to cash in on it now?

I looked over at his wife who had said little during lunch, and was now looking down at her plate. Did he bring her so I would be less apt to make a scene, I wondered? I was terribly disappointed but tried hard not to let it show. Nevertheless, I could feel myself crumbling inside, all the while not wanting to believe what I had heard. He's taking advantage of me because he knows I want a job. This isn't fair[55]. Instead, I just said "I think perhaps I should discuss your proposition with the Bishop." His wife didn't say a word. Since I had previously offered to take him to lunch, I reached for the bill.

"Look," he said hurriedly. "I'll pay for my wife. I know you weren't expecting her."

"That's okay." If he was so strapped that he'd pull a stunt like this, I decided he needed help. I handed the bill and my credit card to the waiter and there was a long uncomfortable silence. Before this bombshell, I had planned to order more iced tea, but forget that. I kept wondering why this priest hadn't been honest with me. Why had he strung me along? Wasted my time! I'd had to drive so many unnecessary miles over the state of Florida since coming home. Now this? Part of me tried to blame it on the fact my readers had failed me and in my vulnerability, he was trying to take advantage of it. While another part of me was saying Talk about the glass ceiling. Wow! I'm being asked to pay just to be near some glass!

I should have told him I expected to be hired for my ability, not my bank account, but I didn't think of that until later. On further reflection, I decided he was the one who lost. If he'd just said: "Look, we can't afford to pay you very much, but let's go on faith. And if your being here doesn't generate better stew-

ardship or more parishioners, then we'll part company and no harm done."
Something like that. I would have knocked myself out for him and his congregation. I really wanted to be a parish priest. I really wanted a job. I expected him as
a potential employer to take me seriously.[56]

The bishop acted miffed when I told him the circumstances of the offer I had
received.

"You will not work at that church," he said, not under those conditions, then
added: "I can't predict, nor control, what some of my priests do, Marta."

I felt better Bishop Schofield had not put him up to it, but I still didn't have a
job. So I stopped trying to get my hopes up, and for a while, reverted back to
toughing it out alone.

My mother was more to the point. "How much do they pay you?" she asked.

"The church doesn't pay deacons anything," I told her. "Not unless they're
doing special programs."

"Surely you'll be paid once you're a priest."

"I think so, Mother."

"Well, let's hope so," she expostulated. "After all that schooling!"

The Bishop next told me he was going to put me temporarily at St. Andrew's.
He said it would give me some parish experience until a regular job opened up.
This was close to home and I should have been grateful; however, I could not
help wonder why the bishop would break his own rule (or perhaps it was Diocesan policy) about not putting clergy in their home churches. I finally decided he
was trying to do me a favor, but being an unpaid deacon there was the last thing I
wanted. The rector always seemed to be antagonistic towards women. It was not
a comfortable place to be a female deacon. There was a strange tension in the
congregation too which I had noted on my return from Texas, and though I tried
hard to pray for him, it was difficult. My inner psyche kept sending signals that
"tough love" was needed here. But he had a terrible temper which was one reason
I could not bring myself to confront him. Rather than listen to my inner prompt-
ings, I tried to stay out of his way as much as possible.

Some time after this, the bishop called and said there were three openings in
the Diocese: a church some distance north of Miami; two small churches in the
Florida Keys which would involve being a circuit rider, and an inner city job as
chaplain at Jackson Memorial Hospital in downtown Miami.

Although I'd been trained to be a parish priest and wanted just that, the first
and second jobs now both involved moving. By then, nearly nine months out of
seminary, I had settled comfortably back into my home in Miami. Austin and I
were having a wonderful time together, and the thoughts of moving again now,

no matter how attractive the job, no longer held its appeal. But I also knew, it would mean I would probably never get to be a parish priest. After praying some about it, I finally told the bishop I'd go to the hospital.

# 35

# RETREAT

The Diocese sponsored a clergy retreat at the Duncan Center in February of 1992. Other than Field Ed in seminary, I'd still had little formal opportunity to be a practicing deacon; nevertheless, I was trying hard to keep my spiritual life in order so signed up to attend. My job at Jackson Memorial Hospital was scheduled to begin in March and I wanted to be as professional in my new job as I possibly could be. Two priests—Victor and Winnie Bolle—invited me to go to Del Ray Beach with them. Winnie had been the chaplain at Jackson ahead of me and also the first woman to be ordained in the Diocese, so I readily accepted going with them. I knew Winnie would be able to answer any questions I might have. I'd also been reading a book called *Peace is Every Step*[57] wherein it encouraged one to practice the "art of mindfulness." It was about living in the present, something I went determined to do!

At the Duncan Center, I woke up early the first day and took a long walk on the adjoining golf course. The Norfolk and Florida pine were spectacular black silhouettes against the pale pink sky of the dawn. Behind me was the full moon, so big it didn't seem real, as if it had been hung there by Disney. The golf course had a low mist which I was reluctant at first to walk in to, but as I approached, the fog kept disappearing. I viewed this as analogous to the life I was then leading. It was hard to see far, my future was so uncertain. As I got closer, however, things began to clear a little. There were begonias and impatiens planted near some of the tee boxes, and the tracks appearing behind me in the dew made it look as if I'd been walking in snow. But it was hard for me to think about God. The more I concentrated on why I was there, the more it all seemed to elude me. At least I tried to remember to breathe deeply which in turn helped me remember I was *trying* to practice the art of mindfulness. And that helped.

But the retreat did not move along as I had anticipated. The evening before, the retreat master had begun by introducing himself, then telling us of his background, education and experience. He spoke of silence, how people often think of silence as the absence of God, which of course is incorrect. Silence should be full and positive, full of God's peace and presence. Not only were we encouraged to slow down outwardly on this silent retreat, but inwardly too, so we could hear God speaking to us in the silence. "Do nothing," he told us, reminiscent too of what Bishop Richards had once told me. "But don't just rest and relax. For your retreat to be successful, you should go home *changed.*"

After my walk and breakfast, I went to his morning meditation which he began with the Baptismal Covenant asking if we truly believed in a god as the creator of our lives, and not just intellectually, but *existentially.*[58] "Everyone needs a long, autobiographical and honest account of their lives," he said. "God is always right here and right now, so we need to accept and acknowledge our lives right now." He quoted Jeremiah 18:1–6, the allegory of the potter, about how God molds his people.

I had come determined to practice the art of mindfulness, and that's exactly what he was saying. But other parts of Jeremiah were in my past. That's because I was still associating the prophet with all those miserable exams. The retreat master was really saying that God was trying to rework us into another vessel "as it seemed good to the potter to do" (Jer.18:4), and this was the time to let God do this, but I didn't want to listen to that. I couldn't face any more remodeling just then. He went on: "In order to find God, we all need to tell our stories and examine them. And that's where we'll find Him. God is in all of our lives. We can't hide anything from Him. When we pray for others, that's often very easy; then we won't have to look at ourselves. Most of us become priests so we can be respectable, or become someone. It's a way of escape for some." So he told us to "relate only to your own stories on this retreat and interact with God."

Some of my spiritual diary shows how I related to my own story.

*At Morning Prayer this morning, Fr Brusso got into it so fast, I got lost. I know nine months out of seminary has left me floundering trying to get back up to steam and into the momentum I used to have at school. And being immersed with all these priests is stressful. These priests do things so automatically. I'm used to having people tell you what page the service starts on. All these guys have it memorized. I couldn't find the Magnificat immediately. When I finally did, they were already finished and into the Psalm, and the Lord's Prayer, or some other reading.*

*Fr. M has lost a lot of weight in his dieting. When I looked at him, I could discern death. Am I projecting my own on to him, or is it his I see? This doesn't frighten me, but I'm puzzled by it. I know someday I must embrace death as a friend. I guess I'm trying to learn to do that now.*

*Walked with L. after lunch. He broke our silence for a few minutes. He told me the bishop will probably be getting flak over my placement at St. Andrew's because it's against diocesan policy, but since my main employment will be at JMH, and I won't be getting paid at St. Andrew's, he'll get away with it. He also told me the scuttlebutt about was that the bishop is granting me favors! I nearly fell over when he told me that. As if I asked him to put me at St. Andrew's! Favors? Good Lord! But L. was helpful. Told me where he sends people relating to social concerns, like abused women, food banks and alcoholics.*

*There have been moments on this retreat when I have felt almost crushed physically by the tension. But I feel a sense of peace when I'm around Fr. Mangrum or Winnie Bolle.*

*I must be more intentional with my money. How many years do I have left to get rid of it? How shall I go about it? And where am I going to put it or re-direct it?*

*I sat watching a man on the golf course today with a six or seven year old little boy, showing him how to play golf. The child did nothing but swipe at the ball and dig up divots and turf all over the place, but one could tell, he was trying hard and having fun. I was really happy for that man and that little boy. Maybe it was his grandson. I don't know. I could tell there was a lot of caring present. I wish I could have spent more time with my Dad.*

The second meditation after dinner was about owning our lives, including our failures. The priest said that "to know thyself is the foundation of humility" and that "feeling shitty about ourselves is not the same as being humble. Real guilt and repentance set us free whereas neurotic guilt does not." We were told to accept the reality of our unfaithfulness and to celebrate the Paschal mystery, both the crucifixion and the resurrection within us. He also said to "Consider humility on a practical level and give up being judgmental. Jesus was often asked whom to blame. Jesus only condemned those who passed judgment. The Son of God died on the Cross so we might be free, not guilty. The sum of all reality is not perfection, but love."

*I woke up at 4 a.m. It seemed darker on my walk this morning. More clouds. And the moon was hidden. There was such a flat feeling in a way. No ups and no downs though I'm feeling really discouraged on this retreat. I feel like I've been absorbing all kinds of "down" vibes. I'm beginning to question if there really is a God of love, because I'm finding it difficult to recapture any of the joy I've always known. Half way through my walk this morning, I remembered to breathe deeply and smile. That helped! In general, I've decided a bunch of male clergy are a pretty depressing group to retreat around. Maybe that's because they're all decompressing.*

*The sky was very different today. Pretty, but different. But I heard more birds, and saw a few more traps on the course I hadn't noticed yesterday. And I walked past the 18th tee today. Got about two miles in.*

At one point, the retreat master mentioned that he viewed becoming a priest a "cannibalistic process, like a mother (the church) eating its young." It could be that bad, he thought. And later, he said some people were "brutalized in the 'process.'"

I had to wonder what kind of experiences he might have had to say that. At the same time I wished he hadn't said anything, I guess because I was trying so hard to escape it all.

Later, he said whether we were called to become a bishop, priest or deacon, that this should be the locus of our sanctification, not just a list of duties. Beyond helping people, he said we were called to sanctify the world. "We all have a call to holiness. And we are called to share the divine life. We must claim that holiness for ourselves. God loves us as we are. But we must ask 'Where are our wounds?'"

Those statements gave me trouble too. My diary said:

*I have trouble with that. I can't see anything great about wounds. I want mine to heal. And I don't want to keep picking at the scabs to see if they have.*

By Wednesday, however, I was beginning to fit in a little better. He talked about God never being absent to us, though we could often be absent to Him. "Our fears, fantasies and drivenness keep us from God. Introspection, prayer and self-offering are what are important." He asked us to ask ourselves: "Am I a priest out of love? Or am I a priest so I can be worthy? So I can be something I think I'm expected to be? How am I keeping God at arms length? What are my false Gods?"

*I left later for my walk this morning. The moon was not as full. But it was lighter than yesterday. Not only were there less clouds, but I could see the moon. I walked much faster. One can go faster in the light than when it's murky. There was fog in the lower pockets along the course and today I heard tree frogs for the first time. And a train whistle. How that reminded me of the Great Salt Lake Valley.*

*Another of the retreat master's early meditation was on the Eucharist. He said in our Baptismal Covenant, we have been given a life which has as its center that which has already conquered death. The mystery of the Holy Eucharist is that God is taken into Himself and as we eat this, we too are taken into the life of God. We see God's love for us. The model God holds for us. Brokenness is what drives it. We become what we receive. The wafer is more than a pill to make us feel good. We are formed more in Christ's image. We can dare to hope. Don't pretend life is other than it is. Embrace the love of God. Embrace hope. Allow our wounds to become glorious.*

I understood that intellectually, but it was going to take me a long time to understand it existentially. I didn't want to see glory in wounds.

The final day of retreat, I was deacon at the mass and Jan Clarke assisted. I felt so much tension before going to the altar, I was almost numb. Once I got into things, however, I began to relax a bit. But I sensed so much stress. I knew my seminary training was trying hard to get to the surface, but it had lain dormant for so long after nine months, I began to wonder if I'd ever remember anything once I had a job.

The retreat master later said: "Most priests are trying hard to be someone, to be approved of. They're afraid they might not measure up." That was me all over and I wasn't even a priest yet!

*I was scared to death this morning I'd make a mistake when I was helping at the altar, especially with all those male clergy out there. But I've learned it's nice to be around female clergy. They're more gentle, more nurturing, I think. Men are afraid of their feminine sides, I've decided. Then again, I've learned this week I need more heart and compassion.*

I don't know that I went home changed. That would take a later retreat; more time for something like that. For sure though, I knew I hadn't relaxed or rested much.

# 36

# SERMON

In March, I finally began my job at Jackson Memorial Hospital in Miami and Bishop Schofield set the date for my ordination to the priesthood. I had always associated May with a wonderful sense of spirituality and had hoped to be ordained that month, but the bishop's schedule was full, so I had to settle for June 5th. By then I was also helping out at St. Andrew's on Sundays. In late May, since the rector had to be out of town, he told me I would be responsible to preach at both services. So the Gospel that May 24th in 1992 was from John 14:23–29. It was the Sixth Sunday of Easter and dealt with Jesus' promise to send the Holy Spirit to his disciples. It was also my birthday.

I knew I would soon have to stand up and be counted and reply to the bishop's questions that he asks of all ordinands. If I were going to represent the church as a priest, then I knew I had to be up front as to where I was in my journey, that it was imperative I be honest with the congregation. Interpreting the "needs, concerns and hopes of the world" as a deacon was one thing, but standing up and responding "yes" to all I thought would be expected of me as a priest, I viewed as awesome. I knew I still had unanswered questions, that there were still many bumpy spots in my spiritual life that needed ironing. There were times too when I knew I messed up or wasn't very clear about where God was in all this. Part of me was so excited I could hardly wait, but part of me too was scared to death. Just as seminary had changed me, I knew becoming a priest would involve even more change. In my mind, the priesthood meant total surrender, something I well knew I hadn't begun to come to terms with. Like marriage too, it would be a lifelong commitment.

I really struggled over that sermon. It finally began:

*God willing and the people consenting, I shall be ordained a priest soon in this church. This is my last opportunity to preach before that day. So I want to take this moment now to thank all of you who were part of the great pool of prayer that kept me* afloat while I was away. My classmates who belonged to Dioceses close by in Texas had many opportunities to go back to their home parishes and keep in touch, but this was not possible for those of us who were at greater distances. Since some of you don't know me at all, and some, only just a little, for those of you who might be present at my ordination in two weeks, I thought it would be in order to take time today to tell you a little about seminary so you will know where I am coming from, so you will know more of what you will be consenting to.

(I went on to tell them about some of my seminary experiences, the trips, the assignments, and my early and on-going impressions of the church. Then I referred to the Holy Spirit which led me to the readings for the day.)

*"Where the Spirit is, there is the church."*

*The Gospel for today has Jesus promising to send the Paraclete into the lives of the disciples. He promises that His presence will still be with them, even though his bodily presence is gone. Jesus did not set out to establish a church. His followers did that. But it is still the same Holy Spirit of the first century that is with us today, which directs our lives and who teaches us all things. Certainly my journey to seminary was influenced by the Holy Spirit.*

*One question postulants and seminarians are continuously asked is what brought them to the point in their lives that made them want to apply for Holy Orders. Because my life was always in such a state of flux, my answers always kept changing, except for one statement that did not, that being that my prayer life is what led me there. I think one would call that the Holy Spirit. But I have to confess I never thought about the third person of the Trinity. If anyone had asked, I would probably have said maybe it had something to do with one's conscience, or my guardian angel, or an ethereal kind of Tinkerbell, flitting about like a giddy butterfly, that went around with a wand touching people. Or maybe it more resembled a blue bird from the Tales of Uncle Remus which would give one a special "Zippity Doo Da" kind of feeling. I had a very checker board theology before trudging off to Texas.*

*Essentially, "the Holy Spirit is the one we consult concerning God. The Holy Spirit is God with us, here and now."[59] Maybe I wasn't too far off. But it is not some remote philosophical theory, nor an unknown mysterious power, nor a Tinker Bell or a Blue Bird. Rather, "the Holy Spirit is God present in the world." (Synthesis) The Holy Spirit teaches us all things revealing to us that Jesus, who was crucified, was God's way of relating to the world. This Spirit will teach us all things by pointing us to Jesus as the Savior. Essentially, it is a relationship of love. Jesus is clearly telling the disciples that the Father loves them already, but it is in the keeping of his words that they will come to know that love, not just as something intellectual, but as an intimate, per-*

*sonal experience. Jesus promises that he will stay with them forever and that this divine presence will be seen as Paraclete—or from the Greek "parakletos," meaning "one called alongside to help."*

*And we must remember that the Gospel of John was written in a time at the end of the first century when life was very hostile for the little community of faithful Christians. There were persecutions going on; they needed assurance. So John, writing around 95 A.D., stressed the importance of Jesus' presence being with them again.*

*For those of you who do not know, I should probably tell you that I am a bit of an anomaly in my family. No one quite understands how I fell into the clutches of the church. When I went off to seminary, some asked why I was going off to join a dying profession. After all, reasonable, thinking people didn't really believe all that sort of stuff. Poor Marta, Poor Mother, Old Marta, Aunt Marta, Cousin Marta, Weird Marta ... becoming a priest? One of my delightful nephews recently asked when he could call me "Aunt Father Marta." People do wonder about me.*

*Occasionally, doing my rounds at the hospital, I have to wonder a bit too. One day last week, the first patient I visited had been stabbed in the stomach, the second had been shot in the head during a robbery, the third had been pushed off a bridge. When I get depressed in oncology or the AIDS ward, to keep up my spirits, I find myself humming the tune: "What the World Needs Now is Love Sweet Love." And so it goes. On days like that, and they're mostly like that, it's not always easy to talk to people about a God that loves us, about a God that is with them. Why do you want to believe that? I can hear an inner voice asking. And an inner voice replying "Why not?" That's often all that's left for some of my patients to hang on to. And when someone asks "Why me?" I don't just say "Why not you?" I try in the best way I can to help them experience God's presence in their lives. I don't always succeed, but I try to be there for them. And there really are times when the Holy Spirit does break into people's lives in rather remarkable ways. It's nothing I do to bring it about. But believe me, it happens.*

*A letter that turned up on my desk Friday, from a patient whom I visited for several months, said: "Thank you for your visits of calm assurance of hope and faith in a higher power of healing which we both shared, which helped me through many a painful day."*

*It's for people like her, as well as those who have no faith at all, that I find my job such a reward and a challenge.*

*What some people do not understand is that one of those legs of the stool that we Anglicans sit on is called Reason, and that's what keeps me in the faith. But many people find it hard to be reasonable. They would rather close their eyes to changes and cling to a literal interpretation that defies reason and drives would-be seekers away.*

*And there are some who would rather look at the Scripture part or Tradition part of our heritage and point out what's wrong, rather than what's right with it. It's much easier to point a finger at all the religious types in the world who can't get along, and be against the Jim Joneses of our day, than it is to jump into the fray and be __for__ something.*

*Of course there are mistakes in the Bible; of course some of the statements of the early faith have been intellectually undermined by the Enlightenment. But some choose to stop here, rather than try to understand what it is all about. They do not understand that the Bible is not a record of an objectively establishable history but that it expresses particular experiences of God which are often projected back on to the history of the religious community. This is true of the Gospels too and so we must see the narratives about Jesus as partly an expression of the living religious experiences of early Christian communities, as they reflected on the life of Jesus and their new experience of life in the Spirit.*

*"Religion, in its symbols and rituals, its narratives and practices, opens up paths to transcendence and transformation which purely scientific thinking leaves unexplored. Whereas science is a matter of tentative hypotheses, religion is a matter of being grasped by an overpowering ideal." And in the Christian faith, the disclosure of this ideal is in the person and life of Jesus. In a sense, Christianity __is__ dying, but it is also being continuously resurrected, because as we move through history, just as in seminary, who and what we are, and how we relate to God and history, changes.*

*Keith Ward, in his book called __A Vision to Pursue,__ talks about the vision beyond the crisis in Christianity. He sees that we have now begun to live in the Third Stage of religious thought and practice. After the First Stage of local and limited religions came the Second Stage, bringing the great scriptural traditions, with their holy texts which claimed final and universal truth. But the rise of the historical consciousness and the findings of science have brought a crisis for those traditions, and beyond the crisis, the Third Stage is on its way, transcending the second as the second transcended the first.*

*When the Bishop asks me if I will be loyal to the doctrine, discipline, and worship of Christ as this church has received them and I respond that "I solemnly declare that I do believe the Holy Scriptures of the Old and New Testaments to be the Word of God, and to contain all things necessary to salvation," this means to me, where I am in my spiritual journey, that:*

*I believe when Scripture and reason do not agree, that it is time to take another look at Scripture, and delve deeper into the faith.*

*I also believe that tradition is great, as long as we do not worship it.*

*And I believe the Holy Spirit still leads us in 1992, just as it led the early disciples.*

*I have to tell you that I don't always understand why I am, where I am, at this juncture in my life. But it has to do with faith. Since I was not there when Jesus promised to be with his disciples, I can only have faith in their faith, but this I can do because I have seen the evidence of it in my own, as well as other people's lives.*

*If you come to my ordination, when the Bishop asks if it is your will that I be ordained a priest, and if you will uphold me in this ministry, I want you to know that I can only trust that God knows what He is about. Sometimes there are days, when I feel as though I were back in the tunnel when I first began seminary. But I know now that this is only a reminder to me that God is not through with me yet. I am still learning and growing and changing. Like all of you, I am still on the way.*

*And when the Bishop sings the "Veni Creator Spiritus" or "Come Holy Spirit," I pray it <u>will</u> come and that it will guide all of us as we move along on our spiritual pilgrimages.*

*With your help, and with God's help, I can only tell you that <u>God willing and the people consenting</u>, I shall do my best to be a faithful priest.*

And I meant it.

# 37

# PRIESTHOOD

June 5th turned out to be the Feast of St. Boniface. Since I knew nothing about this saint, I determined I should at least study up on his attributes and try to find something I might have in common with his life. The first thing that I learned was that he'd been called *Winfred* before being named Boniface by Pope Gregory. So that was a nice place to start because his name reminded me that my mother had told me once she had considered naming me *Winifred* because my Dad was named *Frederick*. I didn't get this name, however, because in Argentina where I was born, the law then required that all children have a Spanish name. But at least the saint's earlier name helped ground me in something familiar to which I could relate.

I also discovered Boniface had been a missionary to Frisia (the Netherlands) in 716 and later devoted himself to reforming and planting churches, as well as organizing monasteries and dioceses in Europe. In 722 the Pope ordained him a bishop and ten years later made him an archbishop. In 753 he resigned his see to spend his last years again as a missionary in Frisia. But sadly, on June 5, 754, he ended up being murdered by a band of pagans while awaiting a group of converts for confirmation.[60] I didn't like the way his final day ended at all and hoped that would never be my lot!

Ordination weekend was a wonderful time for me, but I know it was difficult for my sister, Shirley, who had to travel all the way from Utah. By then, despite the ongoing spread of the cancer, she'd outlived by two years the predictions of time remaining to her.

Austin was my presenter, along with my sister, as well as Jack and Jane Mullins (old friends from California), Nancy Harrison (my former Beloit College roommate dating back forty-five years) and Winnie Bolle. Winnie had been the first woman to be ordained in our Diocese and had also been the chaplain at Jackson before me.

On this occasion, Bishop Schofield celebrated the Eucharist, Frank Corbishley was the Bishop's chaplain and Leslie Gregory, a seminary classmate with a lovely voice, sang the litany. My theology professor, Dr. William Green, preached. I doubt I would have remembered anything he said had he not sent the sermon later to me.

I had invited President Tad Foote from the University of Miami to be a lector and he graciously accepted, as did my nephew, Kirk, who came from the Virgin Islands. Pat Meyer read the Psalm and Jan Clarke the Gospel. Leslie and Kermit were once again oblationers with Ed Sagi in charge of music. Bill Shepard sang and there were trombone and trumpets! Ushers included Barbara Kacer, Drew Daniluk, John Adams and Graham Black. The crucifers, torch bearers and servers were represented by the Llewelyn, Crawford, Higgs and Garwood children. Sue Ellen Greenwell and Julie Hill were on the altar guild and Doris Hodges took care of the guest book.

The flowers were in memory of Christopher, my Dad, my brother-in-law, Aunt Alice and Uncle Harold Mays and Austin's parents who, though all long gone, I wanted to be there in spirit. My mother, as before, did not come, but I was later really touched when a home Communion set arrived inscribed from both her and my long departed father, something I'm sure the Episcopalian gentleman (Jim Daniel) in Connecticut who helped her with mail encouraged her to do.

There was so much going on due to house guests, the ordination and a catered dinner party the next evening—not to mention the celebration of my first Eucharist the following Sunday morning—that only a few things stand out now that I can recall.

A heavy June downpour accompanied by an electrical storm and much thunder began late on Friday afternoon culminating with a bolt of lightening hitting the church. Austin found this peculiarly fascinating. "Boy, God's making a statement!" he said. Just what God's statement might be we weren't sure, but it did knock out the power to the church which upset the rector and did not help his disposition. Although the lights were back in place for the 7:30 service, some of the dimmer switches would not stay on by themselves, so Father Elsner's wife, Alice, who was present, stood throughout the entire ceremony with her hand shoved against a socket on the electric panel. Whenever she tired and had to change position, the lights would dim way down, then come back up once her other hand was back in place. Some told me later they thought this had been done for effect! I was on such a spiritual high I hardly noticed, but later was informed of Alice's selfless contribution to my ordination.

Something that tickled me was what I was told transpired when an old school friend, wishing to give me something practical, had inquired as to what a newly ordained priest might need.

"Why don't you try oil stock," was the reply.

"Oil stock?" repeated my friend.

"Yes."

Jaqui later told me she thought about Exxon, Texaco, or British Petroleum but thought that an unusual type of gift for a new priest. "You mean like one share?" she'd finally asked.

The person trying to be helpful didn't have a clue as to what she was saying. "What do you mean? Oil stock doesn't come in shares," they replied.

"It does so," said Jaqui.

"Oil stock comes in little bottles!"

After more confusing conversation, my friend was finally led to understand that "oil stock" was for baptisms and blessing the ill.

Too, I was pleasantly surprised and pleased Bishop Charles was present.

Also, Austin by now was getting his stride. As usual, if it had anything to do with the church, he was either incorrigible or down right irreverent. Once his drinking days were over, Austin took my aspirations to become ordained seriously; nevertheless, he refused to be serious when the subject came up with others. When asked once what it was like being married to a priest, he said: "Well, she's been promoted from sex goddess to high priestess," or "I love screwing the church." On another occasion, he said: "The only way to keep women priests in line is to send them to the ladies' room."

That evening of my ordination, he purposely wore his damascene tie clip with a grinning devil on it. "The other side has to be represented," he insisted. And when someone asked if I had preached yet, he said: "Yes, she gives brassiere sermons." When they'd look at him questioningly, he'd say: "You know. Uplifting."

What I have read and re-read many times from Dr. Green's sermon at my ordination were these words:

"... *Jesus is the model shepherd because he knows his sheep by name. The intimate relation between shepherd and sheep is depicted earlier ... the sheep hear his voice as he calls by name those that belong to him and leads them out ... he walks in front of them; and the sheep follow him because they recognize his voice. It is said that Jesus' knowledge of his sheep is analogous to the Father's knowledge of the Son and the Son's knowledge of the Father.*

*... Emerging from this image are two perceptions of priesthood that continue to inform our understanding of the pastoral ministry. One is functional, based on what the model shepherd does. The other is characteristic, based on who he is.*

*As the model shepherd does various things to provide for his sheep, so priests perform different functions in caring for those committed to their charge. Some of the basic ones are specified in the Examination which in this service follows the Creed: proclamation and instruction, healing and reconciliation, confession and absolution, and above all, stewardship of the Divine Mysteries. These are only a few of the tasks associated with priests. In all of them they participate in the priesthood of Christ, the model shepherd.*

*But priesthood is more than the discharge of priestly functions. In fact, priesthood is misunderstood and seriously distorted when the primary emphasis is on function and the leadership role. The church is in grave danger when, as Kenneth Leech has said, 'the symbol of priesthood is no longer the altar or even the pulpit but the desk' and 'when the office becomes something you sit in rather than something you say.' (Leech, K.: Spirituality and Pastoral Care. P. 128)*

*... As the words and actions of the model shepherd express his person, so the pastoral actions of a priest reflect her/his identity. What a priest is is far more important than what he or she does. Beyond being a celebrant of sacraments, the priest herself/ himself is sacramental. What is unique to priesthood, what underlies and finds expression in the several ministerial functions is traditionally designated by the word "character". This refers to the permanent relation between the priest and the spiritual gift of ministry in the church. It is this "character" or "identity," sealed at ordination, that is more essential to the reality of priesthood than any mere exercise of pastoral duties. This sense of priestly being, internalized and integrated with one's humanity, establishes vocational integrity and gives direction to one's continuing formation. This does not mean, of course, that priests are superior to lay persons, that they are necessarily more devout or intelligent or understanding. The difference is not moral or intellectual, but sacramental. A priest becomes what Austin Farrer has called a "walking sacrament."*

*These two perceptions of priesthood, based on the model shepherd, are not competitive but complementary. Being and doing are closely related. Through the exercise of priestly functions, priestly character develops and deepens while priestly character underlies and unites priestly functions.*

I was asked to stand for the "charge."

*My dear Marta. When, in a few moments, apostolic hands are laid upon your head, God will have sealed your vocation. The Holy Spirit will, through his continuing apostolic witness, grant you a share in the shepherding of Christ's flock, to the end that you, too, may attest to the Lord's presence in the breaking of bread.*

*You bring to this ministry many gifts and diverse interests: a restless, inquiring mind; a keen sense of justice and fair play; a genuine compassion for the oppressed and outcast; a strong commitment to fiscal and ecological responsibility; and a history of generous support of educational, cultural and ecclesiastical institutions. In a world where everyone seems to have a price and nothing has value, you stand out as a person of integrity and dedication. These gifts are not for everyone, and they will be the greatest burden as well as the greatest joy of your priesthood.*

*Permit me to share with you this wise counsel which the late Archbishop Michael Ramsey gave to persons about to be ordained. 'Remember your inheritance, the Catholic Church of all ages, the country of the saints. Claim this as your own country, and go on living in it. At the same time, be concerned about the tremendous issues of the world we live in: poverty, affluence, pollution, race, war, violence, revolution. It is not that you will know the solution to these matters, or will make them the stock in trade of your preaching. It is rather that by your concern you will be sensitive to God's concern. Through our concern about the world in which God is present in judgment and mercy we learn to be in touch with the true God when we meet God in Church and in the sacraments.' (Ramsey A.M.: Christian Priest Today, pp. 87, 24)*

*Marta, I anticipate for you a ministry that is frustrating yet fulfilling, hazardous yet secure, effective yet lonely, enriching yet demanding, prophetic yet compassionate.*

*Given who you are and the standards you are likely to set for yourself; given also the growing understanding and support of your family; and finally but most important, given the powerful yet silent working of the Divine Spirit in your spirit, you cannot fail, for your 'sufficiency is from God who has qualified you to be a minister of the new covenant.' God bless you. Go in peace. Amen."*

At 8 a.m., on the Sunday after my ordination, I celebrated my first Eucharist. It was Whitsunday, June 7, 1992. My sister promised to come. I can still picture her in the back of the church, "close to the exit" she later informed me in case she had to throw up. I wasn't sure if this was due to a new medication she was on or whether she was talking about my having been embraced by the church! I never knew how to take some of her comments. But I think she viewed me somewhat as a traitor to our childhood, just as she had viewed our mother as "selling out" when she decided to get baptized in her nineties. This seemed a little curious to me, since I knew Shirley had once joined the Mormon church after much proselytizing from a Mormon roommate in college, then left the Mormons and become baptized a Roman Catholic. But she made it clear this was only because she liked the priest who occasionally dropped by to have a drink with her. When the priest died unexpectedly, she dropped that church as well.

Leslie Gregory, my classmate from Texas, gave me a framed inscription as listed in the "Common of the Saints" in the Book of Common Prayer. It was from Acts 20:24b and said: "If only I may finish the race and complete the task the Lord has given me."

I wasn't sure what tasks the Lord would be sending my way, but could only pray he would give me the strength, ability, courage and wisdom to complete them.

# PART VII

# 38

# FIRST JOB

After ordination, my ministry was launched and Bishop Schofield told me after mid-August, there would be no further need for continuing weekends at St. Andrew's. This was a real relief because I had a full plate at the hospital and the rector did not like me around anyway. On more than one occasion, whenever I'd asked a perfectly sensible question, he'd snapped "What's the matter? Didn't they teach you anything in seminary?" He made it very clear that his seminary in New York City was THE seminary of the church, implying of course that all others attended were inferior. I tried to pray for him but that didn't work, and I couldn't fit him into a mental snow bank as I had with the former priest who had given me such a bad time, so I finally fantasized his being part of my invisible congregation, filled with people who I felt needed prayer.

I likened this to John Macquarrie's statement in *The Concept of Peace* that "where people are praying for peace, the cause of peace is being strengthened by their very act of prayer, for they are themselves becoming immersed in the spirit of peace." Eventually I began to see him in need of God's love. Then I began to feel sorry for him, and eventually didn't feel the need to pray for him at all. Of course, I'd really been in need of praying for a widening horizon within myself, but didn't recognize it. In retrospect, I know now I should have confronted him on certain issues, even though it probably would have involved a knock-down-drag-out shouting match to resolve things to clear the air. But I didn't. At that point in time, I thought confrontation was something to be avoided.

Five months into my job at the hospital, I also began to understand what burnout entailed. One of my clinical pastoral education instructors had once told us that an ideal load for a chaplain was a ratio of one to thirty-five patients. There were a thousand or more listed on the green sheets printed out each morning at the hospital. From this list, I tried to determine which patients to visit, and by the end of the day returned home pretty exhausted.

More often than not I found myself the go-between where some nurses and patients were concerned. This was because the nurses were incredibly overworked at times and some patients could be pretty abusive when talking to them. In some instances, I could recall the nurses would retaliate by giving them their medications last. Or by ignoring other requests altogether. One amputee I visited had been so verbally abusive to the nurses that they mostly refused to answer his call button. He was a nicotine addict among other things and had insisted on smoking. Of course, you are not allowed to smoke in a hospital room, but he'd been getting cigarettes smuggled in until they caught him and took them all away. When I showed up, I told him: "I don't mind if you smoke."

"Well go tell those fu—nurses that," he said. "They don't give a fu—damn about anybody."

"We'll have to go about it the right way. There's a right way and a wrong way, you know." He stopped his litany of swear words." I'll get you a wheel chair. If your doctor doesn't object, then I'll take you downstairs. You'll be able to smoke outside on the hospital grounds." This eventually gave him an opportunity to meet and talk with other patients who had also lost limbs. He couldn't wait for me to show up each day and almost overnight, his personality changed . Before he was moved to a rehab area, I heard him apologizing to the nurses. I don't mention this to push smoking or berate nurses, just to point out that chaplains are needed in busy hospitals.

Not long after I began working, I was called to visit a woman recovering from surgery. After a short conversation and a prayer, I was totally blown away when she began telling me about her "out-of-body" experiences. Until then, I'd discussed my experience in high school with very few people, mainly because I had never truly understood it. I was afraid I'd be thought of as "crazy". This lady really lit up my life. She'd had more than one experience and was very matter-of-fact about it all.

I never really knew what to expect when I went into a room. One time I was cruising the halls and noticed a man in a bed in large room. There was no equipment around the bed and the clipboard on the outside of the room only said "Unknown male."

I went in and checked on him and he appeared to be a little "spacey." His eyes were partly open, but I got the impression he might be on drugs of some kind because he couldn't focus too well. "I'm a hospital chaplain," I finally said to him. "Would you like me to say a prayer for you?" He nodded, so I reached down and put my hand over his, closed my eyes and began to pray aloud. As I was about half way through the prayer, with his other hand, he abruptly reached out and threw off the sheet. I looked up to discover he was chained to the bed. Not only that, he was stark naked and had a full erection. My first reaction was to think *What if a nurse or a doctor walks in and sees this? They'll think I had something to do with it!* And of course, I guess I had. After all, I'd been holding the man's hand and been speaking in a soft feminine voice. But never had I expected this. I had the presence of mind to reach down and cover him up again, then hi tail it out of there as fast as possible. It was a long time before I could even bring myself to return to that floor. When I told Austin later about it, he said "Gosh Marta, the poor guy probably thought he was getting his prayers answered."

Eventually, the hospital sent me to San Diego to attend a Hospice Conference. While I was gone, Austin decided to go to Utah. While we were both away, Hurricane Andrew headed for South Florida. It struck on August 24, 1992. That particular day in my California conference, there were discussions being held as to how to interpret dying patient's dreams. During our breaks, I would hurry up and down on the elevator, between my hotel room and the lecture hall, tracking the storm's progress.

After several days, we were both finally able to get in touch with some of our neighbors who advised us to stay away until water and electricity were restored. Eventually I joined Austin in Utah, then returned home on my own when I had to be back at work.

It was eerie coming alone down Old Cutler Road, the night of a full moon, having to go through military check points and seeing the moon's reflecting light on Biscayne Bay. The water had always been hidden behind foliage, now totally gone. With trees strewn everywhere, our own yard looked like a giant wood pile. Never could I have even gotten to the front door had it not been for the kindness of a friend (John Seykora) who had spent considerable time with a chain saw clearing a path into our property. At least the house was still standing (unlike some others around us) though it took a full year before there was any semblance of normality back into our lives. We were extremely fortunate in that even though our home had been in the north wall of the Hurricane's "eye", and the person we'd commissioned to put up our hurricane shutters had not materialized, the fact we'd had the architect design our home to withstand 150 mph winds saved it. Only one window was broken, and that from a flying missile. The rest had been protected due to the overhangs installed in keeping with its design as a solar home. Since then, I've never been able to read Psalm 29:8, however, without thinking of that storm. ("The voice of the Lord makes the oak trees writhe and strips the forests bare.")

Many of the staff at Jackson were burned out, trying to carry on their jobs when they had lost everything. Our own hurricane clean up, while trying to deal with contractors and repair people, coupled with my work, left us more than exhausted. And often, there were days at work when there never seemed to be enough time to decompress between emergency situations. The following I found in a prayer journal entry:

> ... *there's a lot of post traumatic stress syndrome and not just in the patients. The staff are really tired. I know I am struggling to keep in touch with my prayer life. It's been so difficult of late; but I know harmony comes from within me when I can reach out to touch Christ in others ... if I can keep these thoughts alive by committing them to paper, perhaps this will help ... I need to integrate my inner life with the outer life I see, but much of it has been so depressing of late ... I know I'm a bit down ... I need to meet it head on and turn it back into something positive.*

On one occasion, I recall locking myself into a conference room and turning off my beeper, just so I could have a few moments to pull myself together. One of our supervisors too, who had little understanding of a chaplain's role, had begun to emphasize quantity over quality, which should never be the determining factor in chaplaincy work.

And due to my hospice training, I began paying more attention to dreams, and not just those of the patients, but my own as well. For years, I had admired the writings of Carl Jung, and knew that to ignore a dream was the same as ignoring a love letter to oneself, or from God. So there were two recurring themes in particular to which I paid attention. Both dealt with the same subject, though in different settings.

In the first, I was in a large building, like a railroad station, and there were many people around, but I could not understand them. I was trying to tell them something only they did not understand me either. I was not afraid, but felt terribly frustrated because I could not communicate. Finally, there was a line of women, and they told me I was in Moscow, that I would have to learn how to speak Russian. But I didn't think that would do me a bit of good. What surprised me was they told me this in English. Then I would wake up.

In the second dream, I was standing at the foot of a large mountain watching the rocks come down. There had been an earthquake apparently. I was not afraid because the rocks were at some distance and I knew they would not hit me, but as I walked along, suddenly I saw a very small child crawling along the ground towards a large grate over a culvert which had water underneath it. I thought:

*That child might slip through the grate and be drowned. I should help it.* So I hurried towards the grate, and by the time I got to it, the child had fallen through, but it had a string and ribbons tied around it and I was able to pull it back out by means of these. However, I could not get the child up through the grate and knew I had to hold on to it or it would get away from me. Then I saw a large group of people standing further up the hill. They were watching the earthquake and I began to call: *Help! Help!* I was calling as loudly as I could but knew they would not hear me because no sound seemed to be coming from my mouth, even though I knew I was shouting. Then the baby was up through the grate, only the ribbons and string were caught and I could not get them loose. At that point, someone finally came over to me and asked what was wrong. I told them I had to get the child free, and they said "Why don't you just cut the strings?" And I said *I don't have a knife,* then woke up.

The dream left me with a sense of suffocation, danger and frustration but especially a need for change. But a sense of relief also that I had been able to hold on to the child.

Certainly this symbolized a lack of communication in my life. It also indicated the child part of me that needed restoration and saving. The fact that the child was going towards the water had real significance for me too. I still remembered that wonderful experience I'd had before the "big change" years previously. I saw it as part of my trying to get back to it, away from all the confusion and frustration in my life just then.

In retrospect, I believe several experiences the previous week had also contributed to my being unsettled. The first had occurred late one afternoon just as it was time to go home. The nurses were changing shifts as I was visiting a patient on the top floor of one of the buildings. He was in a great deal of pain and told me he couldn't take much more. He wasn't in the burn unit, but he told me he'd been burned in an accident. He was clearly in bad shape and I asked him if he'd been given any sedatives or pain killers. "They won't give me any more," he said. "They tell me I can't have any more."

"Surely they can do something to help," I said. "Let me see if I can find you a nurse or a doctor."

"No one listens," he moaned.

Chaplains are carefully taught as to their relationships with patients. We're not even allowed to give a patient a drink of water if they ask us for it. Anything patients request goes through their caretakers first.

I went out into the hall and could not find anyone. There were no nurses on duty and those who had been on duty had left for the day. I couldn't find a doctor either. The floor was deserted. I was already late catching Metro Rail but felt I could not leave this patient until someone attended to him. He was clearly (to me anyway) in a great deal of pain. About twenty minutes later I found a nurse at the far end of the corridor at a nurse's station and asked if she'd come and see the patient. "That's not my area," she said.

"This man's really in pain," I said. "Can't you do something to help him?"

"Someone will attend to him shortly," she promised.

I went back and sat with him for another fifteen minutes, hoping someone would come. But no one did. Finally, due to being expected at home for something Austin and I had planned, I had to leave. But not before praying with the patient and assuring him someone would soon be there to see him. Reluctantly, I finally left.

That night, I kept waking up and thinking about him. The next morning, I knew he'd be my first visit. On the way into the hospital there was a crowd and a lot of commotion going on around one of the buildings, but I paid no attention since I was so intent on going back to my patient. When I got to his floor and went to his room, I was surprised to see he was no longer in the bed. "Where did they move him?" I asked.

"He jumped out the window," I was informed. "He just committed suicide," which explained all the commotion I'd just passed by.

That experience left me devastated. Though I'd done nothing wrong, I berated myself for weeks for not calling a night nurse and asking someone to check on him. Or for not going earlier to work that day. It might have made a difference. I still feel sad whenever I think of him. But then, I'm also reminded to say a prayer for all those who are in pain or suffering now with the firm conviction that God is always the One in charge, even though we may not see Him in the picture.

There was so much going on at Jackson, it was hard to take it all in. I developed a great deal of respect for the doctors and nurses though, especially those in the Emergency unit or the Ryder Trauma Center. And I found it interesting whenever I had an opportunity to speak with the other chaplains. One older Catholic priest had befriended me my first week on the job and helped teach me to find my way around the hospital. He was really a nice, elderly gentleman. But I had to laugh when told by one of his patients that he had told them not come to my service because "Episcopalians worship Henry the Eighth."

Another time I stayed with a woman whose husband was dying of liver failure. She would stand out in the hall when the nurses had to be with him for various procedures. One day she said "When I married 'J', I had no idea I would be marrying three men. The first was the one I thought I'd married. The second was the alcoholic and the third was the recovering alcoholic." I've never forgotten her, I guess because what she said hit so close to home.

I also spent time in the orthopedic ward. It seemed as though half the men in some of those units were there due to football injuries suffered years earlier. A few were helpless cripples who might never walk again. If it wasn't their backs, it was their knees or their hips. You name it. I've never thought of football as a glorious sport. Even though it helps some students get scholarships, it's a violent sport that can destroy lives.

I loved my job at Jackson, but after a year there, knew it was time to move on. Also, though I'd been trained to be a parish priest, and had thought all along that's what I would be, I knew then I should be a "free lance" priest. That's where my creativity was; that's where I felt God was calling me. But there was no job description in the church for this. I had brought the subject up more than once, but no one had really listened or taken me seriously. This was no doubt because the average person getting out of seminary didn't lead the kind of life I was leading. Even before accepting the hospital job, I'd had to make arrangements for a short unpaid leave in order to attend a business meeting in Australia. I loved being a chaplain, but there was little to no flexibility in the job, no time to do other things I knew I should be doing. I also think being with dying and sick people all the time had begun to overwhelm me. I knew I was all the people I was dreaming about and that they were different aspects of who I was. Certainly I didn't want to lose the child in me. I wanted to keep my spirituality intact. I wanted to get out of danger, save myself before I got lost. Most of all, I knew I had to break free from the stifling circumstances in which I often found myself and find a way to cut the strings, to follow where the Spirit was leading. Also, I wanted to baptize living, not dying children, and to date, I hadn't even had the opportunity to baptize my own grandchildren, something I was looking forward to doing.

So after a year at JMH, I knew it was time to move on. Bishop Schofield agreed to let me be a "priest-at-large." He was probably relieved too. It would mean one less priest he would have to place in another job, of which there seemed to be a major scarcity just then. It also meant the Diocese would no longer have to pay my "package" which was minimal at best.

# 39

# PRIEST-AT-LARGE

Many assumed "priest-at-large" meant "supply priest," but that's not what it meant to me, not in the conventional understanding of the term. So I found myself struggling to define my ministry to others in the context of what I had asked to be my job description. Those who pressed further for more specificity I told there was a possibility of a short term job in Salt Lake City, partly so I could be near my sister who was dying of cancer, all of which was true. Still, it was not really defining my ministry. I was merely defining how I was fitting myself in to life situations over which I had little control. I also knew I had to get out of a framework of reacting so I could begin to get into one of pro-acting. Being with dying people had been a constant reminder of my own mortality and (though I had a proper will in place in the event of sudden death), I still knew I needed to make more decisions which I had been keeping at arms length for far too long as to what to do with accumulated monies.

That's what I'd been praying over when I took a trip in April of 1993, a few months after beginning these reflections. The reason for the trip to a large extent was the culmination of many of those back burner things that had been simmering while I'd been away at seminary. It was time to put closure on some of them. It was also time, with God's help, to begin defining my future goals with more clarity. That's when I said to Austin: "I'm going to give away a million dollars this week." And he said: "Have fun." And I did.

The Dean of Stanford's School of Humanities and Sciences had invited me to visit the campus if ever I got back to California. I support and believe in higher education and have a nostalgic attachment for my alma mater, even though I look back on some of my Stanford memories as being sad. That's because my father died when I was there. (A geologist who worked for him who had attended Stanford told me when I was thirteen years old that it was a good school and that I would like it. So I had decided early that's where I'd go someday if I could.)

I recall walking up the hill above Junipero Serra drive, then over to Stanford's Humanities Center. Just as I arrived, I spotted President Gerhard Casper in a dark suit, perspiring, looking as if he'd run all the way across campus. He shook my hand, sat himself down and said breathlessly "I want to thank you for your support of the University. I am coming to South Florida to see the alumni. I understand there is a club there, that you got it started." He mentioned several gifts they had received.

It was fairly obvious, the way he blurted everything out, that he'd probably been primed by the man accompanying him as they'd hurried across campus, that he'd had to state it all immediately lest he forget and leave something out.

I felt sorry that this giant of an intellect had been forced out of a meeting no doubt to come and thank me for previous gifts. But University presidents have to do these kinds of things now. It's part of their jobs. "Yes, there's a club there," I told him. "It's still active."

When he'd caught his breath, he began to talk about his "awful morning." He was obviously very unsettled, angry and hurt. A typical day in the life of college president, I decided.

He continued: "The *Daily*[61] think they can criticize me, but that I don't have a right to criticize *them*. I commented to a group that I had been reading some of Rabelais, and now they are saying I am rabelaisian. Would the students at the University of Miami know all about Rabelais?"

I was totally taken aback. At the time, I could not even recall who Rabelais was![62] But by his account, the *Stanford Daily* apparently had been vociferous in saying rather than read Rabelais, the president should be inspecting bathrooms on campus!

We talked briefly about other things, then later, when he bid "goodbye," I recall saying to him: "Set your priorities, President Casper. Be pro-active, not re-active." I knew I was seeing in him some of my own unsolved problems.

Later, I could not believe my own audacity of taking the liberty to give advice to the president of Stanford University. But flying east the following day, I began to tally up where the remainder of the million dollars would go. A quarter of a million had just gone to increase an endowment at Stanford; at least a quarter million (and later more) would go to fund a chair for the Episcopal Divinity School in Massachusetts. And the rest? I hadn't quite made up my mind at that point. But I did know that from then on, I was certainly going to be more pro-active with money.

Looking at the clouds below as the plane approached the airport in Boston, I realized I had always associated priests with poverty, chastity and obedience, this absorbed from my days in Catholic boarding school. But times had changed. I was a priest now and could hardly fit the definition of poverty; with three children and forty-four years of marriage, I could not exactly fit the description of chastity either. And as for obedience? Well, I would write the Bishop periodically about what I was doing in the church. I was sure, as long as I did not rock his diocesan boat, that neither he nor the suffragan would pay any attention to me at all. In that, I was correct.

After spending a few days in Cambridge with Bishop Charles (Dean of the Episcopal Divinity School) and his wife, Elvira, I went on to see my mother in Connecticut. But not before I told the Dean I planned to establish a chair in his name. This resulted in something I had not at all anticipated. Once he got over the surprise, he then told me he could not accept this until he told me something about himself, then proceeded to take me to see the chapel on campus. In front of the icon of Jonathan Daniels,[63] he said: "I consider this gift a real honor and a wonderful bequest to this school, but you must know that I am gay and you might want to change your mind about the gift ... now that I've told you." He then added he planned to "come out" in due time, but that he wanted me to know before that.

Unfortunately, some church people are in to gay bashing, so I guess I should not have been surprised at his sensitivity on the subject. I also realized this put him in a difficult situation. He wanted to help his institution certainly, but he had to be true to himself as well. I admired this in Bishop Charles, but it made no difference to me. "It's no big deal.... .I have wonderful gay friends," I told him. "Why would I want to change my mind?"

He looked surprised, then grateful. It was clear he had not expected this response. Shortly thereafter, Bishop Charles did "come out" to the entire church at the Bishop's meetings in Panama City. And the chair in pastoral theology was set up in his name. Sadly, but I guess predictably, he and Elvira got divorced. Now I visit them separately. They are both beautiful people.

One of my reasons for going to New York City was to attend a dinner/fund-raiser sponsored by the Teleios Foundation headed by James McReynolds. He had been our interpreter and leader when some of my class had gone to Russia during seminary. This was to be held at Madeline L'engle's New York apartment. Since I had read some of her books and had already supported some of the Russian programs, I thought it might be fun to attend.

I debated whether to wear a collar. There were to be Russian Orthodox priests present and one of the stumbling blocks in Anglo-Russian Orthodox relations is the ordination of women. I wanted to enjoy the evening. Most especially, I did not want to make any one uncomfortable. But after thinking further, decided this demanded I wear a collar. I wanted them to realize *ordained* women were helping their cause.

Madeline L'engle and her daughter first did some readings from Madeline's book of poetry while we drank wine or ginger ale. And later, her novels and stories were read from, before dinner was served. It was probably the closest thing to a soiree I had ever attended.

There were some nuns present, two or three male priests, a Russian seminarian, a professor, as well as a sizable group of women who all seemed to be devotees of Madeline. As I watched her, the real belle of the evening, holding court with her many admirers, I kept being reminded of Canon West and the evening spent in his apartment with seminary classmates prior to our Russian trip. It was like déjà vu, but with a different caste of characters. Even the dog in her living room reminded me of one of the many unruly dogs that had been in the Canon's apartment some years earlier. When I felt compelled to mention this to a woman sitting next to me, she said: "But that is the Canon's dog ... that's Tino. Madeline took him in after Canon West died."

Another reason for being in New York was to see "815"[64]. I'd heard or read about it long before attending seminary, so called ahead and made arrangements for someone to show me about.

Walking down Second Avenue, I recall the wonderful feeling of freedom and exuberance that enveloped me, and the peculiar discovery that I was free from the turmoil and anxiety that had always punctuated previous visits to this city.

The first time I could recall being there was in the 1930's with my mother on the way to Venezuela, how I had recoiled from the tall buildings, the noisy streets and the unrelenting traffic that seemed to swallow my soul. Even then, I was concentrating on survival, because I could think of nothing worse than getting lost in this awful place, far from any recognizable spot or person who would know me. I held my mother's hand so tightly, she had to pry it off, and except for moments when I had to sleep, kept her always in sight.

There had been subsequent visits to New York when I was in high school, meeting up with children of other ESSO employees, taking the Grace Line ship to La Guaira for summer break. Also, during our first year of marriage, Austin and I had driven all the way to Scarsdale and back to Colorado during a two-week vacation. Although his father took us to see some wonderful musicals at Radio City Music Hall, the city had struck me still as dangerous and alien.

Later trips were to see accountants or attorneys for various business meetings which Austin detested and which consequently upset me as well. Even the theatre and dinners with people who saw us as clients, and the bank invitations to art exhibits, never gave me the peace I experienced walking down Second Avenue that early May morning.

The next to last time I had been there was with a business advisor and attorney, after Robert Holmes a'Court, the Australian financier, had raided Weeks Petroleum. I could not help recalling the mixed feelings I'd had at that luncheon in contrast to the way I was feeling now. By then, I knew Mr. Bond (who raided Mr. Holmes a'Court) had gone bankrupt and landed in jail for various financial peccadilloes. But by God's grace, prior to that, he re-paid the monies owed to us before the market crashed. And though we lost our interests in the company, we came out relatively unscathed. The last visit, as mentioned, had been on my way to Russia with seminary friends.

This was the first time in my life I had ever been in New York City alone, on my own, in charge of my own life; and hopefully, in response to God's nudging.

Several priests in Florida told me not to expect much when I said I was going to "815"; so it was a pleasant surprise to walk into the building and see pictures of Archbishop Carey, Edmond Browning and Archbishop Tutu. There was a chapel to the left and a reception desk in the middle in front of the elevators. I was informed by reception that the person who was to meet me had called in sick. I inquired about finding someone else, eventually was told to go to Advocacy, Witness and Justice on Floor 5 where someone would try to help me. A nice woman showed me about that floor and informed me that Brother Richard would meet me in fifteen minutes at the Resource Center on Floor 10.

Floor 10 turned out to be Contracts and Grants. They sent me to Floor 8 where the Resource Center loomed just off the elevator. It was locked, so I wandered about until someone came to my aid. Eventually, the door was opened and I found myself in the Sherrill Resource Center. Brother Richard, my guide, came in immediately after and proceeded to squire me about. We didn't go to Floor 9. "Communications," he informed me. "I doubt that would interest you … not much to see." So he took me to 7 where I saw the office of the Presiding Bishop. I asked to see the financial section where I knew several people's names with whom I had corresponded by mail, but they were not in.

My guide skipped the 6$^{th}$ floor. "Evangelism, not much there to see," he said. I thought at first I'd misheard. Then the GOE's came to mind, of the emphasis that had been placed on evangelism. If there was "not much there," no wonder we'd been flagellated with that question two days in a row. Maybe I should have gone up to see what Communications was all about. Maybe there was a connection! And that reminded me of the time in seminary I'd told Presiding Bishop

Browning instead of being assigned dull theology assignments, we'd probably all benefit more from readings by Garrison Keillor!

Then there was Ministry and Development after which I found myself meeting the Bishop of the Armed Forces. Bishop Kaiser warmly welcomed me when he heard I was from Florida (Bishop Schofield had at one time been head of that committee.) He took out time to explain to me what areas his job covered, then gave me a plastic covered Eucharist service booklet along with a Jerusalem medal and pamphlets for hospital use.

Brother Richard ended our tour on his floor where he worked on matters pertaining to General Convention. I think part of this included his ministry also because he showed me a box plus the little stove used to melt wax for Episcopal seals. He was responsible for getting these put on to the parchment scrolls signed with a ring by each bishop after he/she was consecrated. Brother Richard made copies of these for the archives apparently, then showed me Jane Dixon's which was still in the box. Several other recently consecrated bishop's scrolls were also there.

Brother Richard didn't show me the conference room, but when I left him, I went there on my own since I had seen Bob Libby's signature just ahead of mine on the register. I guessed he might still be there. Bob was a priest from Key Biscayne at a meeting for *Episcopal Life* and I had hoped to invite him for lunch. I did get to see him, but his day was all pre-planned, so I left, found a fruit stand, then headed back towards my hotel. Turning to leave, I heard a voice directed towards me. And there stood a previous rector, Alan Brown, from St. Andrew's, smiling, returning to work after several weeks out of the office. We chatted, then went our separate ways.

Continuing down 43rd Street to Lexington Avenue, I could not help think what a small world it was. In the church, as in the international oil business, one could not travel far without running into someone they knew, or had known, or that knew someone they did. It was like being part of a great luminescent web that entwined itself about the globe. And as you became part of it, you were drawn deeper into its mysterious, unfathomable center. It left me with a sense of confidence that in God's Big Plan, I was hopefully included. But what really amazed me, as I reflected further, was that fact that New York City didn't frighten me anymore.

On my flight back to Miami, I made a list of where the remaining million would be allocated, then energized by the trip, began to look forward to my future. The next million I determined would go in a very different direction.

# 40

# ST. JAMES, MIDVALE

Shortly after Easter, a letter arrived from the rector of St. James in Midvale, Utah, confirming a previous discussion we'd had on the phone. St. James was the church I normally attended when in Salt Lake City. "Would you like to be an interim for the summer of 1993," he asked, "so my associate and I can plan our vacations?" I wrote back that I certainly would.

When I got to Utah, I discovered St. James had grown to the point where they had moved from the previous church and now had a larger, modern building further south in the Salt Lake valley. With the support of the vestry and the congregation, they were trying hard to meet the needs in the community where they were planted. This at first involved an after school program for latch key kids with working moms which eventually grew in to day care. It was a great congregation. They went camping together, had golf tournaments, attended baseball games and supported an outreach program that not only gave food at the church to drop-ins, but also helped St. Vincent's soup kitchen on a regular basis feeding the homeless and/or hungry. They sponsored a group for people leaving the Mormon Church also, as well as the usual Bible study, book club, ladies' group and mid-week Communion. It was a young, rapidly growing church with a loving rector.

After being there a few weeks, I commented to him on what a good job I thought he was doing. He just shook his head, smiled, then said: "We never know, do we, when we get out of seminary how God plans to use us. We think we have an idea, but we don't, not really. I was failed in my exams. It was such a painful experience. The day we got our results was the darkest day in my life. I was at CDSP[65].... was supposed to have lunch with one of my professors. But I couldn't face him.... or anyone else. I was so depressed. I couldn't even call him to cancel our appointment. I just walked up into the Berkeley Hills, found a place, looked at the ocean, sat alone, and cried. Later, my bishop wouldn't even read my exams or discuss them with me. I felt like such a pariah. I can't tell you how badly I felt after all that effort." Then he smiled again. "If only someone could have told me that day that I'd someday be rector of this beautiful church...."

I know he knew of my experience. I'm not sure why, but I couldn't talk to him about my failure just then. I guess I was still trying to get some distance from it. But I think he just wanted me to know it was okay. I learned a lot from him that summer about being a Christian.

He gave me a great deal of flexibility in my schedule. The tensions stored up from my job at Jackson Memorial Hospital, not to mention the hurricane recovery, all began to subside. I had an opportunity to spend time with my sister and worked hard in my large vegetable garden begun for the soup kitchen. I could not have asked for better weather to grow the produce. I had a love affair with that garden. Unfortunately, so did some of the creatures that came to visit. The raccoons loved corn as much as I did. When it ripened, they usually helped themselves to several ears at a time. My sister warned me to really watch out for them because they'd been known to destroy an entire patch overnight if given a chance. Either they weren't that hungry when they found my patch, or the nun's prayers kept them at bay, or the little gismos I'd installed in the field scared them off because I lost very little to the raccoons. The quail and occasional pheasants and deer didn't do too much damage either as I usually got to the garden early enough to scare them off.

But it was the gophers that were my nemesis. Gophers are very smart. The gismos mentioned were battery powered beepers that gave out a piercing sound (to a gopher anyway) to keep them at bay. But they quickly figured out that if they burrowed under and immediately close to these mechanisms, the sounds went out over them and they seemed to be able to live with that.

One day I was weeding the pea patch and couldn't believe what I saw. Five feet ahead of me, an entire pea plant about 18 inches high (covered with fresh green pea pods) was slowly disappearing into the ground. The gophers had dug holes and were living underneath my sound systems, then reaching up and pulling down their dinner. After all the work I'd done, that really made me mad! They had an enormous underground network and were literally thumbing their little noses at me. But I had an extensive accumulation of old hoses which I was able to attach together and shove down the holes. I then turned the water on full force. After a long wait, and picturing the water going to China, I finally began to see gophers slowly beginning to surface, crawling out of the various tunnels. Close to one spot where I'd put the hose into the ground, several feet away from me, appeared the most bedraggled-looking gopher I had ever seen, pulling himself upright after spilling out of the hole. His whiskers were askew, his fur was soaked and mud on his head was dribbling into one of his eyes. About all he could do was sit up and blink at me. Normally, I would have hit him with the shovel, but he looked so forlorn and unkempt, I didn't have the heart. Instead, I gave him a lecture.

"You and your cronies get out of my garden. You've got one day to take yourself and your little buddies out of here," I told him. "And don't you DARE come back." He sniffed, blinked three or four more times, scurried through the plants to the edge of the garden and disappeared into the hill. I removed all the battery-powered implants spread throughout the property and furiously marched into the house. The next day, the gophers were all gone and I never saw them again. I wondered if they had understood my lecture, or if the water had scared them sufficiently, or if the gismos had attracted them and once they were gone they didn't find it a challenge any longer to be there. Whatever, the garden produced a ton and a half of vegetables that summer which I dutifully delivered to St. Vincent's. And there were times when I was weeding, or turning in the ditch water, or just resting under one of the apple trees, I tried to picture my long-gone grandfather, or my guardian angel, or maybe even God, sitting nearby, chuckling in the breeze.

I read once that a job can change people, that they grow into it somehow whether they plan it that way or not. I know now that being a priest is certainly like that. I was not at all the same person at the end of the summer. Things I went to Utah thinking were important weren't a bit important by the time I left. At the hospital, I had sometimes found myself listening to people because I knew I was supposed to, only at times wished they would get finished so I could go on to other things. Now, I was discovering I was listening because I really wanted to. Because I could see persons, often hurting persons, precious in God's eyes. After telling people for a year at Jackson that God loved them, I was beginning to really believe it myself. And not just intellectually.

It was so gradual, I'm not sure when it happened. But I know having a caring, discerning spiritual director was a major component in all this. That, and being part of St. James. The congregation obviously reflected their rector and associate rector who were compassionate, loving people. I learned just by being there, and at times felt overwhelmed with the gift of God's grace. And perhaps the nun's prayers had something to do with it too. The Carmelite sisters promised to pray for my garden. And since we shared an irrigation ditch, they also let me use their irrigation turns in exchange for fresh vegetables that summer. So the weather, the garden, the sense of joy and freedom I found were an added plus to the challenge and fun of truly being involved in a parish.

That was also the summer I hated to turn on the television set. Along with the terrible problems in Rwanda and Bosnia, immigrants were again flooding South Florida. There was a desperate situation in Haiti and it seemed as if there was nothing but violence in the news, as if the whole world were going mad. Not only that, my sister's cancer was spreading. I couldn't wait to get out in my vegetable garden, just to watch the miracle of what all those little seeds I'd planted were growing in to. I'd sit under the old apple tree my great grandfather had planted, watch the spring that my grandfather (who had been a water witch) had discovered with a forked willow stick, and watch the water bubble up, then flow into the north spring. In that peace and quiet, I would be forever reminded of Buenos Aires and my first experience of what I can only call God.

In September, after things began winding down at St. James and much of the produce had found its way either to St. Vincent's soup kitchen, the nuns, or Crossroads Urban Outreach, I flew to Texas for the dedication of a building.

Being back at my seminary after two years away was like being in a time warp. Certainly I had changed. I was no longer a student anymore either. On arrival, I was included in a dinner at Rather House. After a discussion on the ramifications of Rite 2 versus Rite 1 with the difference in tempo and rhythm dissected (the conclusion being it was "much better to do one for six months, than jumping back and forth," according to the Dean), the conversation proceeded with some very good dinner stories.

But being there was reminiscent in a way of my first time at seminary—alone, with Austin at home. At that time, I'd left him home drinking. Now, he was home. *And I'm the one drinking* I told myself. At least I was that evening. And yes, the dinner wine was excellent!

A tape was shown afterwards in the living room. It included my systematic theology professor talking about training students to think and talk theologically. *Goodness,* I thought, *this is just like being back in class.*

At least the panic wasn't in the pit of my stomach any longer, although I had the distinct sense of not belonging. I felt like an alien who had just dropped in from another planet. I saw a lot of things differently now. It was such a good feeling not being a student, immersed in papers and assignments, not having to worry anymore about exams. But I suddenly had the feeling too that it was okay if I saw things the way I did and that I was on an equal footing at last with everyone else. Somehow in the past two years, I'd become my own person. I'd found my own identity; or at least more of it.

But all these people, thanking me for the new center on campus. It was all so incongruous. The dean had approached me for a gift my first week at school. I had agreed to help out, but never expected a building to carry my name. I'd suggested earlier, when asked, that it have the name of one of the faculty, someone tied in to the seminary in a meaningful way, but the Dean wouldn't hear of that.

As I watched the tape, some students in it were referring to "the beautiful city of Austin, Texas." Austin *is* a lovely city, but all I could think about just then was the crushing humidity since I'd gotten off the plane. After the dry, cool air of the Wasatch Mountains, it was as bad as being in Miami with no air conditioning.

The next day, Bishop McAllister was part of the service, procession and dedication of the building. I couldn't help wonder if he remembered the afternoon we'd sat and discussed my exam question pertaining to evangelism! As we processed from the chapel to the Weeks Center, I could not help reflect also on the many times in seminary I had taken similar walks on this same path from chapel, only then I'd been submerged in all the tensions that had gone with seminary life. These, happily, all seemed to have disappeared. For the most part now, I was floating over it all. But surveying all the people about me, I still wasn't sure I fit. Still, there were many of the same professors. And there were the trustee's wives, dressed nicely, some with very attractive jewelry. I should have related to them. But seeing them looking so nice only reminded me that it had been all I could do just to fit in a manicure to get rid of the garden dirt under my fingernails. I tried to picture some of the women picking corn or digging potatoes, but couldn't. Well, maybe Helen, the bishop's wife. *And* her husband. Jerry was nice. They were both okay. They were <u>all</u> okay, I decided. I was being judgmental. *Knock it off. You've been in the weeds and hot sun too long.*

It was really an interesting interval, and the next day, I returned to Utah.

The end of September, I awakened to the smell of wet aspen leaves. It was raining but the view was breathtaking. The hills were red from turning leaves and the yellow aspen were interspersed with the dark green of the pines. A low bank of clouds hung below the peaks half way up the mountain. I could not see if there was snow on top, but the temperature was falling. Snow would come soon. It was time to leave for home, except Utah was home too. But it was time to bed down the tractor, pack up the accumulated files and clothes and say goodbye to the blue jays. Still, it was going to be difficult to return to Florida. Maybe it was because I'd gotten in touch with my spiritual roots, my real roots, in Utah and was afraid I might lose them again.

The night before leaving, I put on my warm jacket from Antarctic days and walked around the Snowbird complex. By now there had been two days of snow with temperatures in the 30's.

There's something quiet and peaceful about fresh snow falling, and I loved watching the fog and clouds move up the canyon. I'd been enveloped in fog much of the day, and spent one last time curled up with a good book and cup of tea in front of a beckoning fire.

By morning, the car doors were frozen shut. It took considerable energy to get them open and get my car to the valley. I dropped by to say goodbye to my sister.

"Mother will kill me if I die before she does," Shirley said. Behind her remark, I know, was the fact that our mother had said often when we were growing up that we should take care of our bodies. It was our duty because "God only gives us one."

But Shirley, I think in rebellion against the prevailing culture of the Salt Lake valley, learned to love alcohol (until a doctor told her to stop drinking, which she had) and also cigarettes, which she still puffed on incessantly. Whether her habits brought on the cancer, I do not know; certainly they could not have helped. "You break the news to Mother," she insisted before I left. "I won't tell her I'm dying. But she needs to know before it happens."

I didn't know how I would ever break this sad news to our mother, but reluctantly agreed.

# 41

# SHIRLEY'S DEATH AND BACK TO MIAMI

It was in January of 1994 when I was called to return to Utah. I had been with my sister and her family over Christmas, but thinking she would live a bit longer, returned to Miami. Coincidentally, she died on January 30, the same week of the month, years earlier, that Christopher had died in the Everglades.

One of Shirley's children called and asked if I would please "do something" at the service they had planned, then emphasized "just as long as it isn't religious." I agreed, though wasn't quite sure what that meant, but finally decided my niece was trying to say "as long as it isn't sanctimonious and you don't sound like you're proselytizing." By the time I reached Utah, I'd managed to write some short comments relating to my sister, then ended with the audience's participation in reciting the 121st Psalm, something I felt my two nephews and niece could accept.

It was an upbeat funeral. Shirley's younger son—Kirk—welcomed everyone and I followed with the reflection and Psalm. Her children had hired an opera singer to sing, so *The Sun Whose Rays* from Gilbert and Sullivan's *Mikado* was impressive. Her older son—Richard—gave a very good eulogy followed by audience participation in singing *Climb Every Mountain*. This was followed by an invitation for those who wished, to reminisce about their friendship with my sister. Friends and relatives regaled us for over an hour with tales that gave credence to my sister's reputation. Even the veterinarian for her cats attended and told a humorous story.

One memorable escapade related was about the time she and a friend, dressed as nuns for a Halloween party, stopped by to drop something off at someone's house. It so happened the people had out-of-state guests that evening and were preparing to have dinner. The hosts did not bother to tell their friends that these were not real nuns but proceeded to ask Shirley and her friend if they'd care to join then for a cocktail. To the wide-eyed astonishment of the guests, my sister and her friend not only had a drink, but Shirley reached into the folds of her "habit" and drew out a packet of cigarettes and lighter and proceeded to have a smoke as well. The guests must have left Utah with a very skewed view of Catholic nuns from the west! Many other stories followed and the service closed with everyone's singing *I'll Be Seeing You.*

Though not traditionally "religious," it was an uplifting liturgy. The *Book of Common Prayer* clearly defines the liturgy for the dead as an Easter liturgy which finds all its meaning in the Resurrection. The liturgy, therefore, should be characterized by joy, and that defined my sister's service. Certainly there was grief, but it was an authentic celebration of Shirley's life, with no "churchy stuff." She would have approved, and on second thought, I suspect she planned most of the details herself.

The test of my allegiance to the family came when I was asked to "do what you want with all the flowers." Her children were busy evenly dividing up what she had left for them in the house and did not have time to be concerned over trappings from the funeral. I mention this only to cast light on something that had transpired just before her death.

A well-meaning friend, who had been instrumental in getting Shirley to make a large donation to the American Cancer Society for a building a few years earlier, visited and asked if she would be able now to endow this same building which carried her name. They were apparently in need of more operating funds. This was a few days before Shirley died. Given the circumstance and severity of her illness, and the short time remaining to her, my sister did not take kindly to this request. Her will was in order and she felt she had given the Cancer Society enough. So Shirley directed her children to please give her the prepared obituary which was to go to the newspaper upon her death. Instead of the phrase "in lieu of flowers, please send donations to the American Cancer Society in Salt Lake City," she changed it to read: "In lieu of donations, please send flowers."

So many flowers arrived at the house and the funeral home, we were inundated, almost buried ourselves in them. There were bouquets, large floral sprays, trees, plants, huge baskets of flowers—you name it. One magnificent display of red and white carnations in the shape of a "U" (from the University of Utah) stood almost six feet high. I counted ninety-five arrangements at one point, then stopped counting. I told her children they could not just let all these beautiful flowers wilt or die without sharing them with *someone, somewhere.* "Do whatever you want," they replied. So it fell to me to figure out what to do. I reserved a few plants for her closest friends to keep; the remaining I took to hospitals, churches, nursing homes, an orphanage, a convent, any place I could think of that might benefit from their beauty, until I about dropped from exhaustion. I just could not bear to see all those lovely flowers go to waste; but with each delivery vociferously told my sister (wherever her spirit was) that in a way, although I could not blame her change of mind, this was <u>not funny.</u> Then I could almost hear her chuckling, saying how she had gotten the last laugh on the charities that had so plagued her. Knowing my sister, it was probably a final finger gesture to the cancer that had made her last years so miserable. She felt the cures foisted upon her were much worse than the disease itself and that in 100 years, we would look back on the 1990's as the Dark Ages of cancer treatment.

Our first little grandson arrived a few weeks after Shirley's death. Austin and I had never expected to be grandparents, so Bryce was a happy dividend. Then the rector at St. James asked if I would like to return to Utah for another summer. Of course I said "yes."

In retrospect, I know that entire summer of 1994 was an interlude of healing for me. By then, the University of Miami (after five years of delays due to problems with the city of Coral Gables) finally completed and dedicated the recording studio in Austin's name. It was the possible building I'd discussed with the Dean before leaving for seminary six years earlier.

Returning to Utah, as part of my ministry I continued to work in my soup kitchen garden. It did well, no doubt because I had so much irrigation water and it turned out to be the hottest summer in Utah since they had begun record-keeping in the 1800's.

At that time, one of my sister's cats had run away from my niece's home (where he was taken after the funeral) and kept returning to my sister's vacant property. He could not understand why the cat door was sealed or why he could not get into the house. "Where is Shirley?" his "meow" seemed to ask. I'd see him sitting in the lower field watching, but never letting me get near. I couldn't help feel a certain sense of kinship with the cat. That place had always been his home. It was all he had ever known, and he couldn't adjust to any place else. That had been my early home too, and it still had meaning for me. Often, if I didn't go too close, the cat would let me stand in the field and talk to him, but he'd move away when I tried to edge closer. Sadly, shortly after that, he was struck and killed by a car.

Going back and forth between Salt Lake City and Miami has always been a study in contrasts to me. It isn't just the Rocky Mountains versus the flat terrain of Florida, or dry air versus sticky humidity, but the total atmosphere of the two. The population of the State of Utah is probably close to 70% Mormon. In my thirty years of living in Miami, I have only once spoken with someone claiming to be of the Latter Day Saints faith.

On my eventual return in the fall after another strenuous summer in the West, our house was dark due to the hurricane shutters. After the high, dry Wasatch Mountains, the humidity was so pervasive it left me feeling as though I were trying to breathe under water. Entering the house, I could not recall at first where the light switches were, then nearly set off the burglar alarm. I felt like a mole, or one of the gophers perhaps, left behind in a Utah garden.

There was mail everywhere, in the mail box, on the back stoop, "immediate" mail sorted out and marked, mail on the piano bench, on the piano and mail on the floor. There were a few unpaid bills, some "emergency" mail Doris, our secretary, had put in an obvious place, university mail, charitable "gimme's," catalogues, newspapers, and packages. Two weeks of reading, give or take, I decided. And that was after Doris had already sorted out and thrown away much of it. No wonder Austin liked to have me come home first and had opted to stay several more days in Utah!

Before I could bring myself even to look at the mail, however, I dug out a bathing suit and swam twenty laps in the pool. It was always the best way for me to make the transition home. It was still a shock to see the hammock. But the gardener had obviously worked hard at removing dead trees resulting from Hurricane Andrew. We hadn't yet begun replanting, though in some places the heliconia was now fifteen feet high. Also, the jatropha had doubled in size and papaya and shefalera were sprouting everywhere. Without a canopy to keep out the sun, remaining plants plus those seeded by the birds were going wild. Where once had been green hammock, I could now look up from swimming and see clear sky and the beginnings of a pink sunset. A cusp of a new moon was high over the house too and I was struck with the contrasts in my life once again. Whereas I had been in snow the previous morning, here I was now, swimming in Miami.

My daughter called the next morning at 9:00. "Mom!"

"Hello, Leslie."

"Wasn't sure you'd be up ... jet lag and all ..."

"I'm up."

"Want to go out on the little boat? Gloria's coming. Thought it would be fun to get some rays ... take Bryce with us too."

"Isn't this the weekend of the Columbus Day regatta?"

"That's why I want to go. Couldn't make it yesterday. Want to do some cruising ... just look at the boats?"

It didn't take me long to make up my mind.

"Be here at 10:00," she said.

I was, and we took off in Leslie's *Contender*.

There were boats everywhere. The serious sailors were on their way back from Elliot Key, but Leslie was looking for friends, the non-serious sailors who had gone over to party. By the time we hit the channel markers near Elliot Key, I was seeing topless women on a few of the boats. One long streamlined motorsailer cruised by with a girl sitting top deck. She was half nude and displaying the largest bare breasts I'd ever seen.

"Think that's all for real?"

"Mom ... that's gotta be a plastic job," said Leslie, then giggled.

*How could she be so certain?*

I could see Mt. Trashmore in the distance, then we were soon caught up in wall-to-wall boats. Leslie kept trying to contact her friends on a cellular phone, but the circuits were all jammed.

"Not exactly the weekend to get away from it all," I observed, wondering how we would ever get through the maze. We circled a bit, then dropped anchor for a swim and lunch. On the way home, Leslie finally spotted one of her friends. When we eventually pulled out to head for home, six men in a dinghy cruised by holding up a large sign saying: **Show Us Your Tits**. Leslie grabbed her camera and snapped a picture.

"... too bad we don't have a sign."

"Yep ..." laughed Leslie. "Like show us ..."

"Never mind."

Leslie giggled again.

I told myself I could have spent the morning at St. Andrew's, but was glad I hadn't. I was happy to be seeing the aftermath of the Columbus Day Regatta, glad to be with Leslie, and my little grandson. The fact I'd been in a snowstorm at Snowbird two days earlier was not lost on me either. Here I was now, in a bathing suit, getting too much sun on Biscayne Bay.

There were people on jet skis weaving in and out. A park boat was citing a group for not having enough life jackets. Two ultra lights flew by, followed by a plane towing an advertising banner. It was a zoo. I could recall other times out here fishing with Austin when we'd never seen even one boat. Another boat went by with two more topless women. I smiled at Leslie and she giggled again. Yes, I was back in Miami. There was no doubt about that. And what a contrast. After conservative, uptight Utah, this just as well might have been Sodom and Gomorrah.

One reason for returning when I did was to attend the Diocesan Convention being held the following week. I had especially come back in order to vote for the next suffragan Bishop. It was a disappointment to discover I could not. Even though I had been working full time, I had not been able to vote at the Diocesan convention in Utah either because I was not canonically resident there. Now, even though canonically resident in Florida, I was barred from voting because I did not have a "sacerdotal assignment." "No voice or vote," I was told.

I sat there in the cathedral the following week thinking of all the things I could be doing, not to mention the upwards of sixty pounds of tomatoes I hadn't been able to finish picking in the valley in order to get back in time. My first thought was: *I don't fit, God. I don't know how to fit. God, where do you want me?* Like the man without a country, I was beginning to feel like a priest without a diocese. In all fairness to Bishop Schofield, upon seeing my dismay, he told me he would give me an assignment so I could vote. But that's when a red flag went up inside of me. Did I want an assignment just so I could <u>vote</u>? Not on your life. In other years, in other times, I would have jumped right back into the middle of it all, but now, I felt strangely detached, and very comfortable with that feeling. It was as if God's hand were on my shoulder saying "Wait ... don't get involved in more right now." It was a different thing for me. But so real, I could not ignore it. But it was a good convention and I was glad to be there. It was the 25th anniversary celebration of the Diocese of SE Florida. Since I'd been a delegate at the 1969 convention (when this Diocese had been split off from the Diocese of Florida), I truly felt like a small part now in the history of this Diocese. That fall of 1994, a Lutheran minister gave a tremendously funny after-dinner program. And Cal (our diocesan bishop) and his wife, Elaine, gave each person attending the banquet an engraved silver cup commemorating the anniversary. Bea Covol (the Bishop's previous secretary) returned briefly from Oklahoma for the occasion; it was the year Max Salvador retired and Mike Cassell was invested as Dean of the deanery.

For me, that convention marked a turning point in my spiritual journey. I knew after the strenuous summer of gardening and being an interim at St. James, I needed time to recoup my spiritual batteries. But this was the first time in Florida I'd been able to hear the prompting of my inner life so forcefully and so clearly.

# 42

# WOMEN PRIESTS

People have sometimes asked if I've experienced much discrimination as a female priest. Other than the few obnoxious male priests in my own diocese, I've felt little antagonism personally against me. Still, the church, along with teaching in higher education, is one of the bastions where women are still fighting for equality. But aside from the priest who wanted me to pay my own salary (and that of a secretary as well), I guess because I don't have to have a job in the church for survival, I've been lucky in escaping much of the patriarchal dominance many of my sister priests have had to endure.

There are still pockets within the church, of course, where some bishops refuse to ordain women. And it's taken a long time for women in general to become full rectors and bishops. But considering the many years of heavy handed patriarchy in most churches, the Episcopal Church has come a long way. Not the leaders in the field by any means, still Anglican/Episcopalians are light years ahead of the Roman Catholics. The most exciting thing to happen recently was the election of Katharine Jefferts Schori in June, 2006. She is now the first presiding female bishop in the history of the American Church, invested and installed November 4, 2006. Only time will tell, but she appears to me to be a real jewel in the star-studded sky of our National Church. I recall seeing pink buttons worn by some after her election at convention. They said simply: "It's a girl!"

Among the larger mainline churches, the first ordained woman to arrive on the scene was from Oberlin College in 1854. Unitarians followed in the 1880's, then Methodists and Presbyterians in the 1950's. It took Episcopalians until 1976; it remains to be seen when the Roman Catholics will come on board. Due to such an entrenched hierarchy and the current papal attitude in Rome, it might take another century for them to change, though they might surprise us. There were a few times in my early ordained years when I had a few Episcopalians refuse to take communion from me. But that never bothered me. I viewed that as their loss.

Shortly after leaving seminary, when I had to go to Australia on a business trip, I was subjected to a certain amount of harassment when trying to obtain my visa. One of my documents showed I was a priest and I later discovered they feared I was coming to join a woman's faction advocating women's rights in their church. This was before women were being ordained there.

Another situation was when I was asked if I'd be interested in applying for membership in the Society of St. John of Jerusalem. This is a wonderful organization that helps support an ophthalmic hospital in the Holy Land. When my theology professor asked if I'd like to be nominated to the Order, I told him I had enough charities and declined; but then when he said: "No women priests have ever been invested, Marta. If you get in, you would be the first." Well, that was different. "In that case, by all means, put my name in," I said. I take it as a personal challenge to break down barriers in the church. There are lots of women in the Order, but I was the first woman priest to be accepted. It's been rather gender lonely in the vesting room before services, but now at least there are three of us that I know of. Dr. Green sponsored one other woman priest and I sponsored Bishop Carolyn Tanner Irish for membership. However, when we went together, she was in a different vesting area with other new member priests being inducted, the other woman did not come, so I was still the only female that year in the vesting area. By now, I hope they have taken in more women.

Also, once when I was a Deacon, the Bishop of Venezuela asked me to read the Gospel from the pulpit when I was visiting. That was at his church in Caracas. I didn't think anything about it and was happy to accommodate the bishop.

"Well, you may not be aware, Marta, but you are the first woman who has ever read the Gospel in this church," said Bishop Soto later. "You shook up a lot of people today."

I had noticed quite a few men and several women walk right past me on their way out of church without even saying "hello," but never associated it with my reading the Gospel. I assumed they were in a hurry, or since they didn't know me, didn't feel it necessary to stop. I'd gone along being friendly and outgoing to everyone and hadn't even known I was being snubbed!

The Roman Catholic theologian—Rosemary Radford Reuther—very much an advocate for women, came to lecture once at my seminary. She pointed out that even though the Christian cross symbolizes the center of our Christian faith, this very symbol is used to exclude women from ministry. She said the Roman church insists "women cannot image Christ." Her response to such nonsense is that most Roman Catholic priests do not look Jewish either! Since women are fully as human as men, both are two versions of full humanity, women representing Sophia (wisdom) at times and men, Logos (the Word). But Jesus' maleness was merely one of his particularities, not a universality, since the Christian symbol encompasses all.

She viewed society over the centuries as having been constructed for the ongoing perpetuation of the patriarchy that arose at the time of Abraham, and pointed out when there is an imbalance in the direction of patriarchy, spirituality becomes skewed. Patriarchy as an institution is fearful of losing itself in matriarchy, which results in the subordination of women. I would venture to say the Taliban of Afghanistan are a prime example of this.

In seminary, we were told to be especially sensitive when holding services in centers or institutions that encompassed abused women. It was important we not equate God with masculinity since so much of the distress experienced by these women was associated with, or related to, abusive fathers, husbands or boy friends. It personally troubles me that many churches still preach Biblical patriarchy which only perpetuates unfairness towards women. I once heard someone say: "If God is only viewed as male, then males will always tend to see males as God." But God incorporates male <u>and</u> female. As someone else has said: "God is beyond male and female; beyond-ness is the source of our being." It's easy to understand why so many women priests prefer to use the terms Creator, Sustainer and Redeemer in place of Father, Son and Holy Spirit.

In looking over a 2001 church supply catalogue published by CM Almy and Son, Inc, I realize they have come a long way since their earlier mailings for clergy clothing. Those twenty years ago barely had any choices for my gender. But one recent catalogue shows a woman in a sea-mist clergy blouse on the front cover. Even though fifty percent of the student body of many seminaries are women, Almy's 2001 catalogue had only seventeen pictures of women compared with fifty pictures of men. Nevertheless, considering they never used to carry anything for women at all, I think a ratio of three to one should be seen as real progress.

Some years ago, I wrote the following letter to a clergy catalogue company:

> *Dear Sirs:*
>
> *After ten years of frustration, I feel moved to write to you and go on record as saying that though you have quality merchandise and prompt service, I have yet to meet a woman clergy person who is satisfied with the colors offered them in clergy blouses.*
>
> *If God had restricted the colors in nature to black, charcoal, gray, navy blue and dark brown, it would be a drab world indeed. And drab is exactly what women's clergy shirts are.*

*Perhaps our male counterparts enjoy them, but please don't stereotype the rest of us by the other sex.*

*I enclose some colored samples for you that I find uplifting and exciting. We really need more joy in the church, not a daily menu of drab, and more drab. I dare say more color could help rejuvenate the church, move us towards something more resembling mission rather than maintenance.*

*Please re-think your catalogue, at least when it comes to choices for women.*

The following year, the catalogue included one different color. Now, many not only have a better assortment of colors, but some even sport *stripes* (would you believe,) for both men and women clergy![66]

# 43

# EXPANDING HORIZONS

Not having a steady job had its advantages. It meant I could determine my own schedule and accept invitations both within and away from my own diocese.

On one occasion, I was asked if I could replace a Roman Catholic priest engaged to do Easter services aboard the Nordic Empress. This was an 1800 passenger cruise ship going to the Bahamas and he had to cancel on the last minute. Since I was not attached to any congregation and always missed not being able to participate in services on Easter, this sounded like a wonderful opportunity. It didn't pay, but included Austin's and my passage plus all meals. My only concern I told them was that they understand some Roman Catholics might not appreciate having their priest replaced by an Episcopalian, a female one at that.

"Oh, that won't matter," the cruise line director said. Well, it didn't matter to him, but I wondered what he knew about religious denominational differences, especially when, on coming aboard, I was told to report to "entertainment."

Austin and I got little sleep Easter Eve due to our free accommodations being directly under the dance floor. It sounded to us as though everyone aboard was partying all night long and made me wonder if any would attend an early sunrise service the next morning.

On reporting in at about 5 a.m., I was sent to the top deck and told I could set up in the Royal Viking Lounge. "There's a table in the center," I was told. This could serve as an altar. The "lounge" was really a bar with purple neon lights shimmering all around. Appropriate for Easter, I decided.

Always on the flip side, Austin said he would go out on deck to trip any joggers going by, in order to let them know church would soon be starting.

I was pleasantly surprised when about twelve (not joggers) showed up. It was my first Easter service celebration as a priest. I also preached. Afterwards, several told me it was a first for them too, attending Mass with a woman priest in charge.

The second ten o'clock ecumenical service was held in the "Strike up the Band Lounge." This was really a theatre and they set up the altar/table on the stage. To get there, I had to make my way through the gambling casino past all the slot machines. Recalling discussions in seminary about the church's need to be "in the world," I decided my seminary would be proud.

When I saw how many people there were, I invited several to be chalice bearers, and although few actually drank from the chalice, about two hundred and fifty came to communion for the bread. Two Roman Catholics (traveling with their Eucharistic minister) weren't sure what to do. They finally asked me if I'd mind if their minister gave them the communion. I didn't mind at all, but found it curious since I had been the one to consecrate the elements. But they'd never seen a woman celebrate Mass and I guessed their comfort level was being severely tested.

Through the Order of St. John, I met Elsie and Ernie Hunt, the Dean of the American Cathedral in Paris. In the middle of a dance floor at one of the Order's functions at the Harvard Club in New York City, Ernie and I discovered that not only had we both gone to Stanford, but we'd both graduated from ETSS as well. He invited me to Paris to preach. I couldn't talk Austin into going with me but decided to go anyway, so flew over by myself. It was a wonderful experience and I spent some time being involved in the life of the cathedral.

The American Cathedral is a beautiful gothic structure, consecrated in 1886 after the unveiling of the Statue of Liberty. It has a wonderful assortment of liturgical services, some in French and Taiwanese as well as English, where it serves as an American center for its international parish. Their program of fellowship, education, stewardship and outreach invite everyone to partake of their vision of a community informed by the Kingdom of God. Bishop Jeffery Rowthorn, head of the Convocation of American Episcopal Churches in Europe had an office at the Cathedral when I was there. He has now retired and been replaced by Bishop Pierre Whalon. The current Dean now is Zachary Fleetwood.

Being in Paris helped me relate to the immigrants coming to Miami looking for work, unable to speak English. At least *my* duties did not require I speak French!

On another occasion I was invited to preach at the Episcopal Divinity School in Cambridge. From seminary days, I knew seminaries could be unforgiving places to preach. Invited preachers are listened to, not only by homiletics professors, but also by students who are encouraged to analyze everything heard, and not just for the hermeneutics, but for the art of delivery as well. So it was with some trepidation I accepted. But after looking over the scripture reading that would be used for that day, I really had to chuckle. It referred to miracles. And *what a miracle,* I decided, *to have been asked to preach at all!* Once I got going, it was really fun writing the sermon, and even more fun giving it.

Another interesting experience was the house blessing I was invited to do in England. My nephew, who lived in Wiltshire, decided to take some of his parent's ashes to be entombed in the chapel of the old historic mansion he had purchased several years earlier. He assumed he would always live there and thought my sister's spirit would rather enjoy being in England. He even arranged a lovely dinner party for the occasion. The house included its own chapel (with some of the previous owners buried in it), so after prayers for them as well as for my sister and her husband's newly entombed ashes, the entourage followed me about as I blessed the kitchen, the Great hall, the dining room, the Minstrel's Gallery above the Screen Passage and the Great Chamber. I suspect Kirk wanted to make sure any spirits would be put to rest because he shared with me that he thought the house might be haunted. Some years later, he sold the property and left me wondering how my sister's and brother-in-law's spirits might feel now with Kirk gone.

One weekend Austin and I drove up to Jupiter to see our daughter, Leslie, and her husband, Ed. By then they had two little sons. Leslie had never gotten involved in a church, but we had briefly discussed having the boys baptized. I think the older one had been attending an Episcopal day school or kindergarten at the time and I encouraged her to find a church she liked. As Austin and I sat in their breakfast area one morning with Ed, I mentioned it would be nice to get the grandchildren baptized. When I had brought it up once with my daughter, she had said "Sure, I'll ask my friends over. We can have a party and you could do it in the pool." Years earlier, I would have seen nothing wrong with this, but I was still pretty fresh out of seminary and felt there should be some relation to a church besides just having me the only one there to represent it. The prayer book implies a congregation of Christians being present. Church was not very high on anyone's list. Austin diplomatically said nothing.

When I had asked Austin before agreeing to marry him that any children we might have be brought up Christian, that was fine with him. But he didn't clarify to me at the time that his idea of this didn't involve *him*. It was okay if *I* wanted to bring them up as Christians. I didn't realize then how upsetting his British boarding school had been for him. So I was the one that had all the children baptized; I enrolled them in Sunday School and I took them to church with me. Austin occasionally went with a little prodding, but usually preferred to stay home or take pictures. Once the boys reached junior high school age, they decided they'd rather do other things on Sunday. Kermit preferred building and flying model airplanes, then later building two real planes; Chris, if not with Kermit, had his own interests. And Leslie thought Sunday School was *boring*. They all kept pointing out that "Daddy doesn't go to church, so why should we?"

I wasn't going to make a scene over this. There were too many other demands on my time. I knew the children had been exposed to good values and, if I were going to be honest, I hadn't been wild about Sunday School either when I'd been younger.

But that morning with Austin and Ed, when I mentioned baptizing the boys, I was totally taken aback when my son-in-law said he wasn't in favor of their being baptized at all. "I think the children should make up their own minds when they are older," he said. "It should be up to them if they want to be baptized."

I couldn't help think of my own experience. "Baptism might give them a little head start in the spiritual realm," I joked.

"I don't want them baptized into any church." His tone was not humorous. "They shouldn't have their names associated with *any* particular church."

"Baptism is sometimes considered a legal document. It's supposed to be recorded *somewhere*," I responded.

"Not in a church. They can decide when they're older. If you insist, don't expect me to attend." He got up in a huff and left the room.

I was so surprised at his outburst that I didn't know what to say. All I knew about his religious background was that he'd been brought up in a Mormon household and, like my brother-in-law, was a Jack Mormon. Ed's father had been a Mormon bishop but it hadn't rubbed off on Ed. Of his three brothers and sisters, I understood one was still a practicing Mormon. His parents, both of whom were now dead, had been lovely people.

When Ed marched out that morning, I confess to being hurt and disappointed, but decided then and there I would never have the family torn up over a baptism. Who was I to question Ed's attitude? I'd certainly had my issues over the years. I knew God loved my little grandsons, and Ed too, as well as the rest of us. That's what was important. My beliefs were mine, and unless asked, I was not going to impose them on anyone. I guess I was trying to balance Ed's contempt for churches in general and my desire not to be seen as ramming religion down anyone's throat. I've always believed one should teach through example; so I backed off.

Still, in some ways, I think I made a mistake that day. I think I should have jumped at Leslie's suggestion to have a swim party, or anything else for that matter. Some of her friends had baptized children and it would have been fun. But I couldn't bear to be viewed as a meddling mother-in-law. My own mother and Austin had had a wonderful friendship and I guess I'd somehow expected to have the same kind of relationship with my son-in-law. Thankfully, I'd been brought up outside the Mormon faith. I figured Ed had enough of his own religious baggage to deal with and certainly wasn't going to add to it.

A year or so later, one of Leslie's school friends, who had delivered twins, called and asked if I'd help baptize them since she attended the Episcopal church. I was so delighted to have that opportunity, I couldn't help see it just then as God filling up that hole in my life. I do pray, however, that someday my children and grandchildren will experience the joy of being part of a spirit led, Christian community.

In November of 1994, Pres. Foote asked me to rejoin the Board of Trustees at the University of Miami. He knew I loved being involved in academia, that I might be persuaded. Despite having plenty of church activities, I nevertheless missed some of my old university friends. I put him off for a while, then finally said "yes" and returned in April, 1995. The Board meeting that year was at the Registry Resort in Naples and Chuck Cobb asked me if I'd say a prayer. He also said "Would you mind including in it some of our trustees who are ill?"

I've never been very good at extemporaneous prayer. I need time to compose my thoughts, so for a moment it was sheer panic. My heart was pounding like crazy when I went up to the mike, but I gradually remembered my prayer time that morning, tried to sink in to a sense of God's presence and somehow managed to thank God for the beautiful day and the chance to be together in a community of scholars. Then I asked God's blessings on the administration, the faculty, the students and trustees of the University. And I prayed for the ill—Jim Batten, Pat Cesarano, Victor Clarke and Ed Pfister. I then ended by asking God to give us all wisdom in the decisions we would be making as the University moved into the next century. In some ways, that meeting was like going home. There were so many faces I still knew. Of course, the University had grown and changed, but basically, it was I who had done the changing.

Some time after, I made a quick trip to Utah. The waiting lounge in Orlando where I changed planes on my return was filled with sticky-fingered children in Mickey Mouse T-shirts accompanied by exhausted and exasperated parents. There was no way to escape the news blaring everywhere via all the television screens in the airport. It was difficult to concentrate on reading and whether one wished it or not, one could not help watching Kato discuss his role after the murder of OJ Simpson's wife.

I wasn't sure if it was the news, all the commotion in the airport, or my own inner turmoil, but knew it was time to see my spiritual director. I had so many mixed feelings, all having to do with Utah, Miami and my inability at times to pull those worlds together. I wanted to be more in touch with the Holy Spirit, but at that point in my journey, didn't think my prayers were giving me any answers. At times, I felt I should go back to being a non-Mormon again. Period. Out of the church. Or at least mentally anyway, so I could get back to my roots. Was this just a manifestation of my usual spiritual struggles that would eventually pass, or something else? Should I tell Bishop Richards about my struggles with money and about trying to be more pro-active? When I finally reached Miami, I called the Bishop who said he could see me the following week.

Before barely opening my mouth, I was surprised when he asked: "How do you pray?"

Prayer is such a private thing. I was taken back a bit. "You mean, right from the start?"

He nodded.

"Well," I told him, trying to collect my thoughts. "I first try to focus on the three pictures from that book you loaned me once I used during a retreat." I should have told him I took deep breaths, tried to relax first, all that, but forgot.

"What pictures are those?" he asked.

I described them.

"You visualize them?"

"Yes ... it helps me get settled inside."

He sat quietly.

"You want me to go on?" He nodded as he got up to retrieve the book I had mentioned. I thought some more. "I praise God. And I thank Him for all my blessings. Not blessings in general, but specific ones ... like my home, my husband, my family, the food we eat ... well, you know, it sometimes varies each day ..."

He nodded again.

"And I pray for people I'm involved with ... like my parishioners, when I'm out West.... especially when I'm going to call on someone, for example, I pray for them. That usually tells me if I should take them vegetables, or if I should zero in on any special needs they may have." I shut my eyes, then realized everything I was telling him related to <u>mental</u> activities. "Of course, I pray for my family ..." I couldn't seem to stop talking ..." and I pray for you," I added.

He sat impassively.

"When I pray, I don't mean I necessarily pray for anything specific either. Usually, I just try to hold people up, surround them with God's love." I thought of my sister's death and nearly said I wasn't sure prayer ever did anybody any good. That made me think of golf. "For example, I don't pray for my golf game, but focusing on prayer has improved it. I don't know why, but it has."

I should have told him about the desert fathers, and the prayer of the heart that Henri Nowen writes about in *The Way of the Heart* and how I was trying to progress beyond all this mental, cataphatic stuff and become more apaphatic, but I had trouble collecting my thoughts. I was scattered all over the place. There was often turbulence when I went to see Bishop Richards. This day was no exception.

I almost told him that finishing up the frozen food in my fridge in Utah had reminded me of my spiritual life. On ice, waiting to be thawed, waiting to be put to good use again. That's what trips to Utah sometimes did to me. That's because the taxes on my property there kept increasing and rent was low. The garden was getting harder to care for; the field was a tangle of weeds just then, and my single mother renter had let most of the lawn and raspberries die. But I could not part with the property. It was all I had left of my roots. That's why I could never consider selling it, despite the fact that my father was dead; my mother was 98 and no longer lived there; my sister was dead; most of the people connected to my early life likewise were gone. Yet, that piece of land held the key to my past as well as my future. I couldn't let it go. It told me who I'd been, who I was now, which in some strange way was telling me who I could become. I wanted to tell all that to my spiritual director, but wasn't sure he'd understand. I left without talking about what was really on my mind. But Bishop Richards, as always, asked the right questions. That night, in honest prayer, I set it all out before God. In time, I knew I would get some answers.

# 44

# STEWARDSHIP

Respecting, saving and spending money wisely was part of my upbringing. We didn't have a lot of material things and I never expected that someday I would be wealthy. Growing up, I never had more than two dresses at one time in my closet, or two pair of shoes (four if you counted my galoshes and cowboy boots). Until I was nine years old, when not in school in Utah, I mostly wore jeans or my sister's hand-me-downs. Most "things" I might have wanted were out of reach, so I tried not to let them interest me. My sister and I both knew our parents were sacrificing for us so we could attend college, so we never expected to have toys and mostly made our own fun. When I was sent away at age thirteen from Venezuela back to school in the United States, first to live with my aunt and uncle., then later to attend boarding school. I was meticulous about keeping track of my meager allowance and expenses and always reported monthly to my parents where my finances stood. When I went off to college, everything I owned fit into a small suitcase. And as I got older, I observed that life was not really made secure by things anyway, but by one's triumph over them.

I am always acutely reminded of this at least twice a year when our church has a rummage sale. Our wonderful parishioner, Gladys Kendrix, always exhorts us all to clean out our closets and garages and to bring our castoffs to the church. Normally, society judges us by what we give. But I believe when I truly think about it—especially at rummage sale time, as I wander through the house—that God judges me by what I have left and by what I am doing, or not doing, with it. I can talk myself out of throwing away clothes not worn for years with the thought they'll come back in style in several years and think how much I shall save! Or I will just *know* that if I give such and such away, that I'll probably need it the following week. (Even though it's been unused in the garage for 25 years.) It's so easy to get attached to "stuff." And I guess the reason it's so hard for me to part with it at times is because I had so little of it when I was a youngster.

But growing up, I never felt deprived. We had plenty of good food. Money was important certainly, but values were stressed, not bank accounts. Paying bills on time was extremely important. So was telling the truth, being helpful to others, along with the importance of getting an education. I always looked forward to the day I would be able to earn money and happily started a popcorn business in Maracaibo when someone gave me a popcorn popper. My father helped explain to me how I should set things up and I thought it was wonderful to be in business, even though I experienced a major loss on the books when my first big order of un-popped canned popcorn coming to South America on a freighter was sunk by a German sub. But having some money all my own that I had earned myself at age twelve was a great experience. It reminded me of the extra coins my mother had given me as a youngster when she could spare them. As a five or six year old in Utah, this had meant I could buy a stick of licorice or six caramels for a penny, or maybe a Milk-Nickel or Snicker bar. And I always looked forward to Saturday afternoon movies in the summer in Utah. This was before I had a bicycle, so my sister would ride with me on the handle bars all the way in to Holladay so we could see *Tarzan of the Apes* or some western shoot-em-up for fifteen cents.

The most exciting day in my childhood was the Christmas morning I got a bicycle. I had wanted a bike more than anything in the world. Santa Claus was not an option and I was sure Mother could not afford one. So I thought I'd died and gone to heaven when it materialized. That was in 1936, when I was six and a half years old. Since then, not too many things have drawn me or gotten me more excited than that shiny new blue Elgin bicycle. Nevertheless, I do enjoy the material aspects of life and would be less than honest if I said otherwise. I think God wants us to enjoy life. And I do. But I also know that being creative and figuring out ways to save or make money can be just as much fun as spending it sometimes.

One summer I learned this the hard way. It was when my sister was in her last year of college at the University of Utah and I was going into my last year of high school at St. Mary's when our mother came to the States to be with us, leaving our father for the summer in South America. Our parents hadn't seen us for some time, so the plan was for mother to rent an apartment and spend several months with us in the States. There seemed to be a big shortage of short term rentals that summer, however, and all she was finally able to get was a sorority house on the Utah campus for three months. It was the Chi Omega house which certainly had much more space than we needed. Just the dormitory alone had something like ten bunk beds in it. But Mother had no sooner arrived and settled in with us when she was notified that our father had taken ill and she felt she had to return to Venezuela, leaving Shirley and me to live in the house by ourselves. She left us each about $35.00 apiece for grocery money plus blank checks made out to the appropriate people which we could fill in every month to cover such things as electric, rent and milk bills. But my sister was not about to waste her money on food and went out posthaste to buy something she'd always wanted. In the meantime, I'd seen a gorgeous little white radio that I absolutely adored and wanted for my room the following year in school. Knowing for certain Shirley would talk me out of my money or expect me to use it for our food, I bought the radio and figured we could both worry about food later. Between us, we only had about $10.00 left in cash to get us through the entire summer. Fortunately our mother had been with us long enough to stock up on dry goods like rice and cereal, soap and bread, etc, so for a week or two we did very well. Shirley had a car, gas was cheap, and we had a few relatives in the valley, so there were invitations now and then for dinner out. Many that we knew had vegetable gardens too so we were able to pick fruit or berries or corn or dig potatoes and carrots on occasion. We also had plenty of eggs and milk and cottage cheese due to the blank checks mother had left, so things were fine until about mid-July when we ran out of gas *and* food money. I recall a discerning friend of my sister's invited herself for dinner one evening and brought a large steak with her. Meat had never tasted so good to us! By then, however, we had discovered we could get two cents per bottle if we took them back to the grocery stores, so we spent a lot of time going through alleys and garbage cans in order to acquire some cash. By the end of August, we were basically on a diet of fruit and all the eggs and milk and cottage cheese ordered through the milk man. We didn't dare tell anyone what we'd done because our parents would have been very upset with us if they'd found out how totally irresponsible we'd been; but that was a wonderful summer in so many ways and I had that radio through my last year of high school and four years of college to remind me of it. One other thing I recall is how we slept on all those different beds in the dormitory every week. That way, we only had to do the bedding laundry twice before moving out!

Early in our marriage, when Austin and I were struggling, trying to make ends meet and save towards our children's education, we used to play "What if." What if we had $10,000 to spend any way we wished, what would we spend it on? We'd talk about a possible trip, or some "thing" for the house, or a new car. It was fun to dream. It was our vision of heaven in a way. We'd always had enough to live on certainly, but after paying the mortgage and keeping the car in tune and keeping the kids in clothes and paying the insurance, there never seemed to be much of anything left for us. Nearly overnight, all that changed however, only then, when we became wealthy, there wasn't time to enjoy the money.

When we became wealthy, having money coming in and trying to invest it properly was almost a headache; later, trying to be good stewards in getting rid of it, created problems and headaches as well. Wealth, we discovered, can be a burden.

In some respects, we know our children were cheated because of the money. By this I mean they will never have the feeling of accomplishment that comes from paying off a mortgage, or having to wait and save up for things very much wanted. That's why we kept their allowances at a minimum and encouraged them to seek after school jobs. When else would they ever have to work?

When I was in seminary, there were times when I wondered if God might view me as Cyrus—an outsider—to help Him with some cause. I couldn't discern any particular cause, but I felt often that I was an outsider. In Isaiah, the Bible tells us "I will give you the treasures of darkness and the hoards in sacred places, that you may know that it is I—the Lord—the God of Israel, who call you by your name. I surname you, though you do not know me. I am the Lord, and there is no other." (Isaiah 45:3) Though oil as we think of it had not been found in Isaiah's time, I likened the 'treasures of darkness' to all that Bass Strait oil which was giving me additional income, and felt I had been given it for a reason. And that I was like Cyrus, this outsider, whom God might be leading by the hand for His purpose.[67]

At the beginning, some monies I really gave prayerfully, but as time progressed, some I know I gave to please others; at other times I gave to get people off our backs too because there were so many after us to donate towards their favorite causes. We found ourselves the recipients of an unusual number of requests and letters, then when we gave generously, they would continue to return for more. Soon, it got to be too much and we found ourselves constantly trying to extricate ourselves from the charities and well-meaning people who were invading and destroying our lives. Money can be liberating, but only when one can keep the burden of having plenty and the obligation to share it, in proper balance.

We often found ourselves included in functions that we could not have cared less about. Some of the functions were very nice, many were interesting, some elaborate and even fun, but the bottom line was that we knew we were there only because we were aiding someone's favorite fund raiser. We weren't invited because someone wanted to know us better, for who we really were. It was only so their particular charity would flourish. And at times, we could not help question the value of some of the charities. If that's what it took to help others, so be it, but I could not help look back to the days when we had been accustomed to getting together with friends just to enjoy one another's company, without someone's having an axe to grind. It pained me to see those days receding into the background. Austin was very direct at times. "Take my money but leave me alone," he often said.

Having a little extra money can be wonderful; having a lot can create unforeseen problems. Money can't just be ignored. First off it boosts one into a higher tax bracket with the Federal Government. Whereas Austin and I had always been able to do our own taxes, we soon found it to be an impossible task and had to go to a major accounting firm. Our joint tax return, once a page or two, progressively reached to over two hundred and seventy five pages. "Because of Schedule C," we were told, or "Because that particular depreciation form requires 4 pages." There's nothing simple about the U.S. Government. It bothers me to hear people demonize the wealthy. Until they've been in their shoes themselves and dealt with some of the problems wealth creates, they should keep quiet. I see injustices in our tax system, and the "Fleecing of America" every night on the news is one reason I feel this way. Why should congress be allowed to waste so much? Political battles over taxes and the federal budget are ideological wars over who will hold the purse strings of the taxpaying public.

We've had "friends" want to borrow from us as well with the sworn promise they will pay us back. We have signed notes. And we have learned the hard way this is not a good thing to do, nor were they truly "friends." Loaning money to people gives them amnesia. It's best to refuse and send them to a bank, or else give it outright with no strings attached if they are truly in need. When asked to support people or their causes, it's good to be gentle as a dove. But it's also imperative to be wise as a serpent. There are so many people out there trying to take away other people's money. At the same time, we also must be continually aware there are many needy, deserving people who are willing to work, but who sometimes can't find adequate employment.

At a Diocesan convention in Utah, one of our field trips involved a visit to the Urban Crossroads Outreach Center. A proud young woman told us how she and her husband had been trying hard to make it on their own without welfare aid. One of their children was not well and required periodic medical procedures which, fortunately, her husband's medical benefits from his job covered. However, his job only paid him $8.50 an hour so they could not meet all of the basic necessities such as rent, food, diapers, medicine and transportation. Higher paying jobs he could apply for did not have medical help, so he was forced to stay at the lower paying one. When she tried to get a job, she was told she could not earn more than $175 a month or their food stamps and other benefits would cease. Child care costs more than that, so there was no point in her trying to work to improve their situation since she could not make enough to cover what they would lose. I think people who are trying like that should be helped to help themselves. Not punished for trying.

I told my spiritual director once that Austin often told me to spend more money on myself, especially on material things since, other than books, I seldom bought stuff. Austin had always loved new cars, camera equipment, CD's, tapes and all kinds of gadgets. Maybe he was feeling a bit guilty and wanted me to join him in spending more. I really don't know. So I told Bishop Richards I had gone out and walked through stores and looked at all kinds of things and nothing had really interested me. But after a full day of window shopping, did finally come home with something I really needed and wanted.

"And what was that?" asked the Bishop.

"A phillips head screwdriver," I told him.

My spiritual director is a very professional person. I don't think ever in the years I have known him has he expressed surprise or shown much emotion at anything I have ever told him. But I recall this day that the corners of his mouth curved upwards and I could see he was suppressing a smile.

"We spend half of our lives accumulating stuff," I told him. "And the other half trying to get rid of it."

Bishop Richards nodded and continued with his professional look.

But that got me thinking. The second time I got serious about spending on myself, I found a dress I really liked. And got it. Then I saw an evening bag that matched. It killed me to pay eighty dollars for that bag, but I did. Still, I thought it was an awful extravagance.

The following summer, I bought a tractor. That was the best present I've ever given myself. It was such fun and such a marvelous help for the soup kitchen garden in Utah.

The fourth time, I really went all out. I joined Austin, who was fed up with the airlines telling him he could not smoke, and bought an interest in a private jet. Austin subsequently quit smoking a few months later. But traveling by private jet is a wonderful way to go. I've never regretted a penny spent on that.

Stewardship should be a way of life in response to the Gospel, but it should be motivated from something within.

On more than one occasion, I have heard people say they feel guilty for having so much when others are having such hard times. I do not think we should feel guilty or apologize for being fortunate. Grateful, yes; but not guilty.

Giving should always be a spiritual matter. To truly give, we need first to make ourselves right with God. The more we can be aware of God in our lives and name all the things for which we can be truly grateful and thankful, the more joyously we will want to share with others. My yardstick for giving has always been to give until it feels good. Not until it hurts. We are called to give according to our means. And this probably means different things to different people. But first, if Christians, it helps to give ourselves to Christ and to one another. In community, we are one body. This is what we were baptized in to. When we are committed to giving until it feels good, God supplies us the people and/or causes whose needs we can meet, and whose needs deserve to be met.

I've learned some people feel since you have contributed once to their cause, however, that they own you. They expect you to spend all your time being involved with their goals and projects. It's very easy to become smothered and inundated by well-meaning people and their causes. That's why one must look within, and not always be reacting to things from without.

At first, I began asking myself the question: *If I were to die this week, where would I want my money to go?*

I asked that question for some twenty years and gave money away accordingly. Then one day I began to ask: *What if I were to die next week? Would I live my life any differently?* (This mainly applied to my dealings with people, my relationships, and to keeping my spiritual house in order.)

But eventually, one day, it dawned on me I was perhaps asking myself the wrong questions. So I then began to ask: *What if I knew that suddenly, within a few weeks, I would have an enormously reduced income, so much so that I would not be able to afford more than the very basic necessities. How then would I spend and use my money NOW? Would the way I am living with my fortune be any different? What would I wish I could, or should have done with it?* I began to look at things in a new light. I didn't stop giving. But after twenty years, I began to give, pray, and spend differently. And my life took on an exciting urgency. When I tried to listen to the Holy Spirit more, giving and spending had more meaning and life got really fun.

I know I have been blessed with more than I can spend or could possibly want to spend on myself in this life time. Twenty years from now, if I'm still alive, I want to be able to say that I spent the first thirty years of my life getting an education and rearing a family. The second thirty years I want to say I spent increasing and taking care of and being a good steward of the funds entrusted to me, and that I did it in a manner consistent with sound stewardship and a prayer life consistent with my calling as a priest. The final years of my life, I hope I can say I spent it trying to follow God's will which included my wealth. At present, I believe this involves a conscious and conscientious outreach relating to money in ways God continues to make known to me. But I want it always to come from my prayer life which I try very hard to keep in order.

# 45

# FOLLOW THE SPIRIT

The summer of 1995 I discovered a marmot family living by Little Cottonwood Creek at Snowbird. I would often see the animals sunning themselves on a flat rock by the stream when I'd go for my morning walk. It was the year our income tax became impossible (at least for the unsophisticated) to understand, and I could only hope the accountants knew what they were doing. This was also the first time I'd flown to Utah in our new jet and Salt Lake City got the Olympic bid for the winter games of 2002. It was also the summer I was an interim at St. James, replacing Jim Tendick. Due to the rain and cool weather, my garden ministry did not produce as much as hoped for; then, to add insult to injury, property taxes went out of sight.

My Aunt Maude also died that year. After her funeral in Florida, I presided over a memorial service for her remaining family in Utah. I also worked for a bill relating to taxation on farmlands introduced into the Utah State Legislature sponsored by Senator Poulton. And continuing my pro-active stance on giving, marched in to the School of Earth Sciences at the University of Utah one day and asked them for their wish list. A lot of people marched after me throughout the summer too asking for money for their wish lists. Sixteen priests, including eight bishops, to be exact. That didn't include all the other requests that kept arriving continuously via our forwarded Florida mail. The Episcopal Bishop of Utah asked me to play golf, then proceeded to ask me for enough money to fund a health care plan for all his lay employees. Considering the mountain of money the Utah Diocese was sitting on after the sale of St. Mark's Hospital, and the number of employees he had put on the payroll, this annoyed me. I didn't even have health insurance as an employed priest in his diocese, so wasn't very helpful. But John Kater, from CDSP, who asked for help with his Panama Project, I did encourage.

I look back on that summer as the time I came to terms with my own mortality. Not that I hadn't accepted it intellectually; we all know we're going to die.

But I was able to internalize it emotionally and spiritually in a way I'd never approached death before. It was all so natural. It didn't matter anymore. When God wanted me, I'd be ready. Not that I wanted to die, but it was going to be okay when my time came. It was that simple.

What may have triggered all this was the day I picked two hundred and fifty large tomatoes from the soup kitchen garden and hauled them to my car for delivery. I'd then planned to trim the raspberry patch and pick the rest of the squash before quitting for the day. (This after six hours of work already in the garden prior to picking tomatoes.) Only I was tired and couldn't seem to do anymore. I've always been one to go full speed, work until I'm ready to drop, then work some more. Only this particular day, I couldn't. I'd run completely out of steam and realized to my amazement, _and_ annoyance, that I was getting old, or certainly old_-er._ I'd been playing quite a bit of golf that week too which probably served to wear me out, but the idea of slowing down had never occurred to me. So I finally had to admit perhaps I'd never get to climb the Matterhorn, much less hike the thirty mile trek to Machu Pichu I had planned, or ski as I'd always intended—at least until age 85. All of a sudden, I realized I was going to have to rearrange some of those things on the back burner, and maybe change some of my priorities.

I didn't mind too much, though it was a bummer of an idea. I'd just never given it any thought until that summer. That's when I decided for sure to get my affairs more in order and start saying "no" to more things that didn't interest me. And "yes" to those that did.

One thing I did pursue that summer was my "Rainbow Wafers" project that has yet to take off. Still, I made the effort. The idea first came to me in seminary when all of us gathered around the Communion rail. Many of my fellow students were black, or brown and I used to wonder how they felt being given white wafers all the time. Sometimes, of course, we used brown or white bread baked by various students, which really made more sense, but if we were being trained theologically to believe God created all of us, that we were all members of the body of Christ, equal in God's eyes, then why didn't the Eucharistic wafers symbolically depict this too? There is so much racism in the church, in society. Everywhere. And so much denial over it.

I used to fantasize about having black and brown and yellow wafers, telling a congregation they represented our brothers and sisters in Christ, then watch the reaction of the white people when given a color other than what they were accustomed to receiving. God's grace and presence is so evident at times at the Communion rail. It seemed to me that introducing "Rainbow Wafers" could bring up unspoken feelings that might lead to a better understanding of others. Maybe it was a silly idea. But if I didn't pursue it, I'd never know. Besides, I knew all about failure; it hadn't destroyed me. So I went to a patent attorney, then approached the sisters at the Carmelite Convent where I knew they made wafers for the Roman Catholic Diocese.

Predictably, they did not share my enthusiasm. In fact, I think Mother Superior was horrified that I would even think they would cooperate in such an endeavor. I was told they had to follow specific guidelines in making the wafers and there was no possibility of any digression from that. The Roman Catholic Church only did it one way. The correct way, I was left to infer.

After seeing the sisters work so hard to support themselves and watching their dwindling membership at the Convent over the years, I had hoped they would join forces with me in order to improve their income. My intentions had been so positive that I had not expected them to put such a damper on my idea. Certainly I had thought they would look into it and at least ask their Bishop. But they didn't. And it never occurred to me to ask him. At the time, I didn't know where else to go with it; so it got dropped. But someday, perhaps I shall resurrect it and see if someone else will embrace the idea. I must do some research and find out who else makes wafers. It would only involve putting some harmless food dye additive into the ingredients as far as I can guess. Perhaps at an older age, I'll start my own business.

I also learned that summer I no longer depended on my spiritual director. Not that I didn't want to continue to see him at times, but in a funny kind of way, felt like a bird, finally able to leave its nest because it knew how to fly. This is not to say I did not go back; I think it's important to have a director. But internally, I returned on a different footing.

Coincidentally, a few years later, Bishop Richards gave me a thoughtful, spiritual book written by an Episcopal priest, about a person foundering in dry religion who is learning to reset boundaries.[68] In some ways, it described me at that point in my journey, and I found it immensely helpful.

I don't know when, or how, it happened, but that summer was another of those happier interludes of my life. I never knew I could feel so happy or so fulfilled in a job. It all ended when Jim returned from his sabbatical. But by then, I had so many other projects underway, it didn't matter whether or not I stayed at St. James. I could have remained one more month. But the church was short of funds. And Jim was back and I didn't want them to feel they had to pay me. Neither did I feel I should work full time without some form of compensation.

Though I loved what I'd been doing, I happily moved on. It was time for more changes in my life.

By that fall, I retired. Not from a job. I didn't have one. Not from the priesthood; I would always be a priest. But from the rat race, and my ministry, real or imagined, of always trying to please everyone except God. I knew God hadn't forgotten about me. But he'd been trying hard to set me free and I just hadn't always been listening.

I finally started throwing more unsolicited mail in the garbage, unread. I really began to learn to say "no" better, especially when unsolicited phone calls came my way. I honestly prayed for people I felt really needed to be prayed for, and became even more pro-active in giving away money.

I also made an effort to attend our clergy conference in November. Rt. Rev. Roger White from Milwaukee was our leader. He predicted in the not-too-distant future that sixty percent of our existing congregations would cease to exist unless we better communicated the faith.

"We need a massive telling of the 'story' and an ability to articulate the vision and mission of the church," he said.

More importantly, I recall his saying we needed to ask God what He had called us to be. It was not our place to tell God what we were going to be. He stressed a need to be like Abraham and Sarah. To "go in faith and forget the past." I liked that. It spoke to me. Certainly I determined to try.

I never felt Miami was my home until I had lived there twenty-eight years. This was because of the bond that had always bound me to my sister and mother so tightly during our early years in Utah. But after Shirley died and the family home went to my nephew, my roots there began to fade. Since the house was rented, I could no longer visit, still, I could look over the fence from my own property in the valley and it was almost like being there. Before mother died, I visited her often in Connecticut, but she was no longer the mother who had reared me in Utah. Her second later marriage to Austin's father, her increasing years and different interests now had changed all that. She'd been only too happy to leave the West behind.

Still, I had been telling people for years that Miami was my home, but I had only been talking about a place—a _house_. Inwardly, spiritually, Utah had always been my real home. But suddenly, one day, I woke up and Miami became my real home, too. Utah and Florida finally came together spiritually for me in a way difficult to describe.

The summer of 1996, I stayed briefly at Snowbird. It was hot and dry in the city, and the smoky air was seeping into the valley from forest fires in Idaho. My reason for going had been to attend the consecration of the new Utah Bishop-Carolyn Tanner Irish; so I asked Bishop Richards and his wife, Holly, if they'd care to attend with me. I realize now it had been my symbolic way of trying to bring these worlds together. They declined, and I was initially disappointed, but in the end, it didn't matter. Just having made the effort of asking validated something within.

I kept remembering what Bishop White had said, i.e. that we should not be trying to tell God what we're going to be. We need to ask him what He wants us to be. It all boiled down to how I was going to spend the rest of my life. With that thought in mind, in a letter later written to my spiritual director, I told him that primarily in the years left to me, I hoped I could learn to please God.

When I'm out in my Utah garden, working with plants, I get that wonderful sense of hope and expectancy that sometimes used to sweep over me as a child when my mother would tell us "Your Daddy's coming home." There would be so much joy and anticipation waiting for his arrival. I know he'll never come home again; still there's that wonderful sense of expectancy. I don't know what to call it. But I can't help relate it to God. God's grace breaking over me and telling me things are going to be all right.

In her book called *Pilgrim at Tinker Creek,* Annie Dillard refers to an Egyptian desert hermit, Abba Moses, who said to one of his disciples: "Go and sit in your cell and your cell will teach you everything."

In a sense, I've been sitting in my cell as I've been writing this. I've been trying to learn. There's so much to learn, if only I can remember to listen. When I can listen to God, then I don't have to talk. Then I learn.

When my sister and I were growing up, Mother always expected us to help with the chores. To the extent that we could, this included gardening. Austin used to say he could not fathom why I would still get out and dig and plant in a garden. He looked back on his "helping to do yard work" days with relief they were all behind him.

"What would people think," he'd ask, "if they knew you flew out to Utah in a private jet, then spent your time plowing up weeds, trimming shrubs, or cleaning out ditches and hauling rocks?"

I guess I didn't care what people thought. Of course, I didn't spend _all_ my time doing that, but he just never understood.

But I do remember as a child, how helpless I used to feel when faced with all those burdocks and thistles. And there was all that work my mother had to do when my father had to be away. Now I have a tractor. Now I can plow the weeds under or scoop them up with the soil, or ride over and squash them all. I get such joy, such pleasure and such a feeling of accomplishment from that.

And the rocks! They're really fun. Mother used to pay us five cents a bucket for picking or digging up either rocks or dandelions. When we'd fill a bucket with dandelions, she'd sometimes tamp them down a bit so we'd have to dig up more before paying us for a full bucket. But she couldn't do that with rocks! So I usually collected them, even if I could barely drag the bucketful to the rock pile. We didn't do it very often, but when we did, it was tough work for two little girls and rocks seemed more important to me.

Now I can put rocks in the front end loader of the tractor and haul them to the rock pile. Every time I pull that lever and watch the loader dip, and see all those rocks tumbling out and crashing down all over the pile, some part deep down inside of me claps with uninhibited glee. My tractor takes me back to reliving those early years, and it all seems so _right._

I've never met the Rt. Rev. Furman Stough, but I read something once attributed to him that I've always liked. He said: *When we finally do come face to face with our Lord, I don't believe he will ask how many souls we saved, or if we were a priest, a bishop or dean of a cathedral. I believe he will have just one question for us: 'Were you born again*[69] *in your spirit and did you enjoy it?* When I am doing something, if I can't answer "yes" to that question, then I try to pray over or re-think what I am doing.

I know there are days when I want everything to remain the way it is, when I do not want to take on anything new, or have anything change. But then I know it's time to move along to a new cause, or to look at an old one in a new light. God continuously demands change from us. Yet, we should not want it otherwise. Prayer can lead us to new and deeper insights. It can take us on paths we've never thought of using. In the words of the Psalmist, He "leads me beside still waters," "revives my soul," "makes my darkness bright" and "my way secure."[70]

God is never through with any of us. If we believe He is, then we are not on the right path. And I believe, in the church's tradition certainly, that often, unknowingly, the liturgy forms us. It's nothing we have to think about consciously. Nevertheless, it happens. I have so often said "to you all hearts are open, all desires known, and from you no secrets are hid"[71] from the *Book of Common Prayer* without thinking of the meaning. Over time, after much repetition, however, those words have lodged in my subconscious and remained there. And gradually, the shadows and hurts, repressed feelings, fears and disappointments have surfaced. Sometimes they have come like an unexpected volcano, but more often it's been like a quiet orogeny gently changing the way I view life.

I know there have been times when I should have done things better. But I know too I did the best I could with the light available to me at the time. And I think that's all God expects. Eventually, new avenues open up too that lead towards a greater sense of who God is and what He expects of us.

The day after our Diocesan convention in Boca Raton, the week Hurricane Irene dumped sixteen inches of rain in some areas of Dade County, Rick Hamlin, then the rector at St. Andrew's, asked me to celebrate Mass at both services. Though not preaching, I had read over all the Propers for the day and been touched by the one from Isaiah referring to Cyrus. It was the same quote that had initially caught my eye in seminary when I had often wondered what in the world I was doing there. Hearing this read that day gave me a profound and wonderful sense of having come full circle.

I truly sensed God's presence at the altar. Rick took over the deacon's duties. And as I sat looking at the beautiful stained glass window that incorporates St. Andrew at the back of the church, the one where Jesus is saying "Follow Me," I felt lifted by the prayer coming from the congregation. Nothing else seemed to matter just then, except that I keep trying to follow that command. I didn't know then where the Spirit would lead, but felt confident, as I do now, that I could continue to respond.

# EPILOGUE

One reason for beginning this book grew out of a desire to place something in the archives of my seminary. That was so women in the future, who were in the "process" towards ordination, might have something to read in order to compare how things had changed over the years, hopefully for the better. However, recalling that I never spent much time in the archives, I decided that was probably a futile goal. No one would ever see or read it.

So, in a sense, this became a kind of memoir instead which I began by reaching for an angel's hand. It's taken me to places I'd never thought of writing about. Some subjects popped up out of nowhere while others I'd anticipated discussing, never took off at all.

I never intended to include my mother's description of her grandmother's death, but trying to understand the crushing atmosphere she lived through in that community helped me understand things about myself and how my early upbringing in the same community influenced my life. Formal religion, or the lack-thereof, was always an underlying part of my early childhood which continued to hound and shape and challenge me throughout my teens and college years. I was confused about religion *and* spirituality because the two didn't always fit together. It took me a long time to realize I had become a priest so I could better define myself at last as a person.

I can't close without mentioning Mary once more (aka "Gail" in the Prelude). She was my very first friend, aside from my sister, Shirley. Although I depicted them both in the beginning in rather unfriendly terms, Mary was a kind and loyal individual, a true friend. I knew very little about her background other than that her mother had gone off to do things in the theatre, leaving Mary behind. I never heard her speak of her father. Since Shirley and I saw so little of our father too, I think we assumed that was the normal way to grow up. But it must have been difficult for Mary, going to school and living with her grandmother in the city during the winter, then moving out to be with her aunt and uncle in the summer. To my knowledge, none of them were her real relatives, though I could be wrong here.

The last time I saw her, we went to lunch, then she insisted we go to a cemetery north of the city so she could show me where her ashes would someday be placed. She was in great spirits and laughed most of the day, when not chain-smoking, that is. I'd tried to persuade her more than once that this was not a good habit, but the addiction went so deep, I'm sure it replaced food at times in her life. The only reason I knew when she died was when a letter came to me from a distant relative of hers who had been called from Atlanta to settle her final effects. Mary had been found with an unfinished letter to me which she'd been writing apparently when she died. It included my address. At times I can still clearly hear her excited wild call of "Ah.... .ooooooooo ... ga. Ah.... .ooooooooo.... .ga." I never thought to ask what it meant to her, or where it came from. But I wish I had.

My cousin, Hal, married a lovely girl, a nurse, and they had two children. Unfortunately, Joy died back in the 1990's. But Hal, now in his 80's, is still going strong. Last summer he joined a group of us from the University of Miami attending the music festival in Salzburg honoring Mozart's 250th anniversary. It was a lot of fun and everyone enjoyed his presence.

Of course, this all started with an unwelcome baptism. I'm glad I escaped that first one. I'm equally glad I was baptized later under more salutary circumstances. That day with Bishop Watson, Austin's Dad, and Betty Walton made me feel something special had happened. I later had our first son baptized at St. Marks's (also by Bishop Watson), but it was years before I answered the tugging in my heart and returned for confirmation to put things more right within myself. I'm grateful God gave me the opportunity.

Baptism can be compared to a new birth. I know I sensed a formal grounding in my life after that. In some ways, it validated my spirituality. It also reminded me of the beautiful experience I'd had as a very young child which, in retrospect, was also a baptism, although not in the churchy sense. But I believe everyone who is born is, at some time, touched by God's grace. I think I only vaguely understood at the time that my baptism was a proclamation that I belonged to something important, to a family really, where we were all "members one of another." (Eph 4:25; Romans 12: 05)

I hope and pray someday my children will see fit to have my grandchildren baptized, or at best, give them exposure to the Christian faith, so they will be able to make meaningful choices as they age, based on a solid foundation. A theology of hope begins with the Holy Spirit which, of course, relates to baptism.

The University of Miami now has a new president in Donna Shalala. Thanks to Chuck Cobb, it was fun being on that search committee. And the potential shortage of fossil fuels that Lewis predicted back in the 1950's is finally being pushed to center stage. I can clearly hear him saying "It's about time." Solar energy is more in the news now too and biomass and ethanol and other forms of energy are finally coming into vogue. Global warming, whether man-made or due totally to climate change (or both), is already changing the world.

I often marvel I ended up in the Episcopal Church, or any church at all for that matter. But there's something really nice about Episcopalians. They can question, and it's okay. They can elect gay bishops and debate abortion and have "Evolution Sunday", and champion contraceptives and are able to see between the black and white sides of discussions and can usually see truth in both. They truly are the *via media*. They can disagree on all kinds of things, but that's okay too. I find that comforting. It's when I get around people who insist they have all the answers that I get *really* uncomfortable..

My last services in Florida before I "sort of" retired were at St. James in Hollywood. The priest asked if I could help out while he left for a required month of chaplaincy duty in the military. After saying "yes," I discovered it involved doing two services in English and one in Spanish every Sunday which was a challenge, but I loved being there. It was a long drive up, however, and after the last service, I knew it was time for a change. Austin's health was fast failing and I wanted to be there for him. He died in February of 2005 and I so miss his gentle companionship. He was a wonderful person in so many ways and we had a truly interesting fifty-three and one-half years of marriage. I wish there had been more.

Austin loved his camera and all that went with it. However, when the new digital photography appeared, he saw that as a sure sign it was time for him to move on. Like computer technology, he refused to embrace it. "Takes too much time," he'd say. Still, he could always find time to wait patiently for the sunlight to change so his camera would catch just the right reflection on a lake. And he could always find beauty in a gnarled root, or a piece of bark, or bugs feeding off a leaf. The outdoors was his chapel. And I believed him when he said God spoke to him through the sunset, the waves that crashed along a rocky coast or the animals and birds he photographed. Given his dim view of religion, I was grateful he supported my becoming a priest, but he was adamant there would be far fewer wars and more peace if we had more agnostics in the world. Time may prove him right on that one.

Last year my seminary invited me back to receive an honorary doctor of divinity degree. I felt God was in charge of this, decided to view it as a miracle, because that's what it was. Standing in St. Matthew's Episcopal Church in Austin, Texas as the bishop hooded me, I couldn't help think of the priest in Utah when he'd told me how he'd been flunked in his GOE's, then ended up being rector of that lovely church. If only I could have seen ahead back then to this day in Texas! But it didn't matter. I'm just grateful God likes to surprise us at times.

And just as God called Moses, Eli and Samuel, He calls us to get our attention. I never knew when I was five years old what a circuitous route my life would take before I understood that God expected something of me. It's still not always clear to me if I'm doing His will, although He does make it pretty clear at times when I'm not!

I just know it's been over thirty years since I began the Theological Education by Extension course in the Diocese of Southeast Florida. It's going on nineteen years now since I left Miami and drove off to seminary in Texas. I'm amazed at some of the things that have happened to me since I was ordained and some of the experiences in which I've been privileged to participate.

I started out in the TEE class with two other white women and two black men. At the time, all of them, except me, said they intended to be deacons only. But time changes things.

Lynn Ramshaw, after starting a wonderful outreach ministry to the homeless at St. Laurance Chapel in Pompano Beach, went on to General Seminary. She became an ordained priest and is now in Ohio. Caroll Mallin remained a deacon, got a degree in counseling and continued working on her own, as well as helping various churches within the diocese. She is now semi-retired, helping at a church in Virginia. Louis Duty had a prison ministry. When I was working at Jackson Memorial Hospital, I heard he was ill at the Veteran's Hospital which was just across the street and did go to see him. But it was a few days before his death and I doubt he recognized me. I was sorry I had not learned sooner of his illness. Cyril White eventually went to seminary and was ordained a priest in 1995. He was the rector at St. Kevin's in Opa Locka. At his invitation, I preached there once. Though retired now, I know he's helped out at St. Faith's Church near Cutler Ridge as well as the Venerable Bede at the University of Miami.

It's been amazing to me to see how reading the Bible and struggling with God's Word can draw people together. I sometimes feel I've been much closer to, more open with, and know more about, the people I've met through programs like TEE, Clinical Pastoral Education, Bible study or the seminary experience, than in any other relationships in my life, my own extended family included. God's love has a way of breaking down barriers, shedding light on each of us in ways that seldom happen in other circumstances. We become more vulnerable certainly, more open to risk and rejection. But in the long run, we find out who we are, and why we're who we are, and are thus able (hopefully) to become more of what God would have us be.

It's been fifteen years now since I was ordained a priest; sixteen as a deacon. I can only say it's been a wonderful journey for me. Not always easy, mind you; but very special in so many ways.

My formal, paid, ministry started with the chaplaincy at Jackson. When I left the hospital after a year, the elderly Roman Catholic priest there said: "You'll be bored to death in a parish setting ... after all the excitement here ... you've seen more in twelve months than you'll ever see in a parish in a lifetime."

As far as life and death situations, he was absolutely correct, but there were other types of things I wanted to experience also. I wanted to baptize healthy babies, not just dying ones. I wanted to counsel and marry young people, not bury them. So I left Jackson. And after that, it became a spiritual smorgasbord: St. John of Jerusalem, St. James in Utah, as well as St. James in Hollywood, Florida, the Cathedral in Paris and the house blessing in England. I also got to Venezuela, Cambridge, Panama, the Bahamas, ministry by mail (and later, e-mail) and all kinds of invitations within my Florida diocese. From having very few choices, I found myself with more choices than I could begin to accept. The diversity and contrast were amazing. I went from a little congregation of eight or ten at the hospital to blessing a football game once at Joe Robbie Stadium[72] where there were upwards of 35,000 in attendance.

I believe it was Stephen Covey who said "We are not human beings on a spiritual journey. We are spiritual beings on a human journey." However we wish to view it, the journey can be pretty amazing.

The last service I did at St. James in Utah, something unusual happened to me. I'd always seen that congregation as my second family, and when going back was asked if I'd care to preach or help out. I explained I was "on vacation," but when the new rector and deacon had to be gone at the same time, thus leaving the associate priest by himself, I agreed to do the 9 a.m. outside service one Sunday. This was because the associate had to do the 8 a.m. service which overlapped the 9 o'clock one. St. James' 9:00 a.m. service is only held in the summer and is very casual. Most parishioners arrive in shorts, or slacks, sandals or tennis shoes. It's also abbreviated with its own Rite 3 printed in a loose leaf note book for the priest to follow. A guitarist leads the music.

I was prepared certainly; nevertheless, after looking over the service and trying to figure it out, became apprehensive I might not do it the way they were all accustomed to having it done. So I started feeling nervous. About 3–4 minutes into it, I suddenly realized I had forgotten to light the altar candles. In my experience (other than when I'd been at Jackson) this is normally done by acolytes, so I hadn't paid much attention to this aspect of preparation.

For a moment, from the past, the Commission on Ministry, the disapproval, the ordination exams, the awful feeling I was a failure, the "Didn't they teach you anything in seminary?" comments all came crashing in on me. I wanted to leave, run away and never come back. Then, like the day I'd gone back to the Diocesan Convention in Florida and felt God's peace and presence near, suddenly, there in the courtyard, an invisible door opened. I didn't hear a voice, nor did I see or hear anything, but I <u>knew</u> God was there, and He was happy with me and smiling and could have cared less I'd forgotten to light those candles. He was reflecting the little homily I'd just given, coming back somehow through the little congregation before me, and God was saying "It's okay to be a klutz. I love klutzes, Marta!" That's certainly not what I'd preached about in my homily, but I had told them about the Seventy being sent out[73], how they had shared their faith, and how being faithful was what mattered. And how they'd told people what Jesus meant to them, that He was a forgiving God, a God with whom we could be intimate, who cared, and who raised people up. I'd told them about it intellectually, but right then and there, I *experienced* it, and it made so much sense. It was a moment I shall never forget.

I lighted the candles after the peace, during the offertory, before the communion liturgy began. And I think anyone not too observant would have probably assumed it's what I'd intended to do all along.

# END NOTES

## Part One

**1.** From the papers of Anne Newman Sutton: Of this story, she wrote: "The diary itself, written when a child, is more sketchy and factual than informing. The facts I have elaborated, the reactions written from memory. Yet there is no digression from truth. It is not difficult to understand why she walked alone. But the courage it took in those days of merciless criticism and silly fanaticism must have been stupendous. Yet she weathered it for half a century. Oddly enough, of her six children, father was the only one who shared her point of view. He walked alone too and found the going rough. Hence we, my father's family, are the only black sheep of a big Mormon 'tribe,' and although this does not spell the social ostracism it once did, yet there are times when we are keenly aware of discrimination. Let a 'gentile' try doing business in the smaller towns here in Utah, for instance, and he'll soon learn what boycott means."

**2.** Love is patient and kind; love is not jealous or boastful; it is not arrogant and rude. Love does not insist on its own way; it is not irritable or resentful; it does not rejoice at wrong, but rejoices in the right. Love bears all things, believes all things, hopes all things, endures all things. The New Oxford Annotated Bible Revised Standard Version

## Part Two

**3.** From *A Lifelong Love Affair—Memoirs of Lewis G . Weeks – Geologist* © Copyright 1978—Anne Sutton Weeks, assigned to Wisconsin University Foundation.

**4.** Rev. Rebecca McClain, National Stewardship Consultant 1990–94, from Diocese of Arizona. Quoted by permission.

**5.** 1 Corinthians 14:34

**6.** From an article by Frederick Burger, *Miami Herald,* September, 1977

**7.** James C. Fenhagen—*Mutual Ministry,* (Chapter 7, p. 105, Chapter 9, p. 129) 1977, Seabury Press, 815 Second Avenue, New York, N.Y. 10017

**8.** *Border Crossing* by Katie Funk Wiebe, Copyright © 1995 by Herald Press, Scottsdale, PA 15683. Used by permission.

**9.** Antarctica— "Reader's Digest Services Pty. Limited" (Inc. in NSW) GPO Box 4353, Sydney, NSW 2001 p. 2, 8, and 229) Quoted by permission.

**10.** February 9, 2001, NBC's Tom Brokaw reported on the nightly news about the remarkable story of Ernest Shackleton's heroic ventures in Antarctica and that it would soon be in IMAX movie theatres.

**11.** Australian Financial Times, Saturday, August 1, 1987

**12.** He brought to mind then, and for years after, the passage from Wordsworth's poem—London, 1802—*Thy soul was like a Star, and dwelt apart; Thou hadst a voice whose sound was like the sea; Pure as the naked heavens, majestic, free, so didst thou travel on life's common way, In cheerful godliness ...*

**13.** Exodus 3:5 (Then he said, "Do not come near; put off your shoes from your feet, for the place on which you are standing is holy ground." Joshua 5:15 ("the place where you stand is holy.")

**14.** Edward T. Holmes. Spirituality for Ministry, Harper and Rowe, p. 37. Quoted with permission.

**15.** Edward M. Hays, Secular Sanctity, N.Y. Paulist Press, 1980 p. 67

**Part Three**

**16.** The Episcopal Theological Seminary of the Southwest

**17.** Over the next five years, 450,000 people in the U.S. exploration and production industry lost their jobs.

**18.** According to Peter Schweizer's book, Victory, the trigger for the industry slide was a byproduct of a strategy devised early in the Reagan administration years to bring an end to the long Cold War with Communist U.S.S.R.. The key point of the strategy was to strangle the income of the number one revenue producer for the Soviet Union—oil exports—by lowering the price while upping the ante in the arms race, causing great expenditures. Meanwhile, the cash crunch would be exacerbated by increasing the material needs and expectations of the populous. (From an article by Larry Nation published in AAPG Explorer,© Jan. 1996 issue. Reprinted by permission of the AAPG whose permission is required for further use.

**19.** "He gave his people the lands of the nations and they took the fruit of others' toil."—Ps.105:44

**20.** From talks sponsored by the Department of Religious Studies of the University of Miami and the Florida Psychoanalytic Alliance, January 24, 1999.

**21.** Even though the House of Bishops in 1985 indicated it would not stand in the way of women's election and consecration to the episcopate, there were many who were upset with this. In the British flank of the Anglican Communion, one of the leading opponents to female clergy was the Rt. Rev. and Right Hon. Dr. Leonard Graham—Bishop of London—who in 1987 was the third ranking member in the Church of England's hierarchy. "The question of the ordination of women," he said "is a symptom of the larger problem of subjectiveness." He developed this by saying "one of the follies of subjectivism is to believe that if the standards we proclaim are violated with increasing and substantial frequency, then standards must be changed. The Bible and Creeds are no longer definitive for the church, which must modify its teaching to match contemporary practice. Too often church synods and conventions reflect the practices of secular bodies by equating the will of the majority with the true and the good and in so doing fail to operate under the judgment of God ... to substitute a woman for a man as priest is to do something quite fundamental to our relation to God.... .the polarity of the masculine and feminine is fundamental to the universe. It can no more be ignored than can positive and negative electrical charges." From the John Findley Green Foundation Lecture—The Tyranny of Subjectivism—given at Fulton, Mo. As reported in Insight (The Washington Times), October 19, 1987 issue.

**22.** On September 15, 1976 the House of Bishops had voted 95–61, with 2 abstentions, to amend the canons to provide that women as well as men were eligible for ordination as bishops, priests or deacons. The following day the House of Deputies also approved and the change took effect January 1, 1977. The House of Bishops also provided that each woman who had been ordained before 1977 could function as a priest after a "completion of the ritual acts performed" in Philadelphia or Washington.

**23.** Encouragement: The Key to Caring by Lawrence J. Crabb, Jr. and Dan B. Allender, Zondervan Publishing House, Grand Rapids, Michigan (1948) p. 60

**24.** Havelock Ellis—*The Dance of Life*

**25.** When referring to Christian paideia, we specifically refer to a system of education vis-à-vis the Bible coupled with the educational patterns of Hellenistic literature and philosophy. Christian paideia had as its objective the achieving of the wisdom of God, through the spiritual formation under the divine Pedagogue, the Logos, or the Word of God. Its final aim was true Gnosis, or Christian philosophy, whose end was the imitation of Christ.

**26.** A song based on a Gaelic melody and found in many church hymnals. It was popularized for the general public by Cat Stevens but the lyrics were copyrighted by Eleanor Farjeon.

**27.** Carolyn Tanner Irish (the Bishop of Utah) once wrote to me saying "As you may know, I now days receive Ember Day letters from seminarians, and every time I read one I jump right back into my own experiences at VTS. (Virginia. Theological Seminary). Images I recall of myself at that time were of being under water and also of being turned inside out."

**28.** D*ictionary of National Biography, p.1070*

**29.** This man had a doctorate in clinical psychology and told me the first week of school that after 39 years in the military, the most difficult thing at first for him in seminary was trying to decide what to wear each day. He said it was absolutely traumatic for him having to get up and make choices every morning. He said he always felt like a "fish out of water". Seminary presented us all with new experiences and problems.

**30.** One Episcopal Bishop who had had difficulty with alcohol once wrote to me: "As I have come to see it, almost everyone has problems, whether they acknowledge them or not, and I think those of us who were lucky enough to go to seminary and to engage in ministry develop a compassion for those who don't yet know what their problems are. (By 'problems' I of course mean the limitations of our finitude and also of our sinfulness.")

**31.** "Suppressed grief is like a time bomb. It goes underground and explodes later, causing much damage." In a column by Ann Landers.

**32.** A bar in the upper Florida Keys.

**33.** This is a theology which emphasizes event, becoming and relatedness as basic categories for its understanding rather than those of substance and being. Process theology maintains that what is real is essentially in process.

**Part Four**

**34.** Later, on December 4, 1996, Mr. Bond pleaded guilty in the Western Australian Supreme Court to two charges of failing to act honestly as a Director of Freehold Pty. Ltd. (A Weeks Petroleum Ltd. subsidiary) in entering into a $700 million facility arrangement with Bond Corp. and a further extension of that agreement.

**35.** "The church cannot be true or false. It can only be better or worse." Comment attributed to a University of Utah professor.

**36.** As recently as August 2, 2001, an executive of a major corporation spoke to the Economic Development Corporation of Utah and said: "Utah is a tough sell. If you have lived here all your life, you don't see this. But believe me, if you don't live here and you're looking in from the outside, otherwise educated, liberal open-minded people still look at the Utah environment and think that you guys are from Mars. I'm not kidding ... there's still a real perception that there's an undesirable lack of separation between church and state. Perception and reality are two different things. But if you are trying to attract CEOs, you have to attack that perception, because in today's world, that is not seen as appropriate." He went on to say "Your complex liquor laws are a bigger issue than you think ... The issue is one of personal freedom. In today's sophisticated global economy, whether I choose to drink a glass of alcohol or not, I don't want someone telling me when and how." (In the Business section of the *Salt Lake Tribune,* August 2, 2001.)

**37.** From the Latin meaning "And the Son," this is a dogmatic formula expressing the double procession of the Holy Ghost added by the Western Church to the Nicene-Constantinopolitan Creed immediately after the words "the Holy Ghost ... who proceedeth from the Father." It is no part of the original Creed.

**38.** *Women and the Episcopate in the Eastern Orthodox Tradition* by Rev. Canon William B. Green, Phil. D., Professor of Theology, Episcopal Theological Seminary, Austin, Texas.

**39.** The calendar, now in general use, introduced by Gregory X111 in 1582 to correct a slight error in the Julian calendar.

**40.** In July, 1997, President Boris Yeltsin rejected a bill that would place tight restrictions on religious groups in Russia, including the Mormons, evangelical Christians, Roman Catholics and Japan's Aum Shinri Kyo cult. But the Orthodox, under Patriarch Alexy 11, exerted a great deal of pressure saying this would threaten the structure of Russian society. They feared the law would be unable to restrict the activity of the sects and insisted the Russian Orthodox Church be given special recognition in its unique heritage in shaping Russian history and culture. They pledged "respect" for Islam, Buddhism, Judaism and other traditional religions, but asked that all other groups be expected to register with the government in order to own property or conduct public worship, and could not do so until they had been in the country for 15 years. With 80 million church followers (half of Russia's population) and the fact that the church helped get Yeltsin elected, getting along with the church was the politic thing for him to do. During his 7 years now as president, Putin's government has asserted greater state control over independent Russian media and business. It has also eliminated most political opposition in parliament and turned the country's governorships from elected to appointed jobs. The rules, contained in a law passed in April, 2006, have sparked outrage among human rights groups, churches operating in Russia and Western government, including the European Union. These rules would force churches and religious groups to report to the government on their services, sermons and sources of income. Religious leaders say the reporting requirements are onerous and a painful reminder of the religious suppression of the Soviet era. The Catholic Archbishop in Moscow—Thaddaeus Kondrusiewicz—says he thinks "it's wrong and even impossible to comply" with such a request. Victor Korolyov, who heads the division overseeing religious organization registration at the Federal Registration Service, says he would like to further discuss review of the rules as they apply to religious groups. He thinks the law will be difficult to enforce on nearly a million religious branches across Russia.

**41.** The Blessed Virgin Mary is important to the Russians. In a paper written by the Rev. Canon Dr. William B. Green for a chapter in a book relating to the eastern Orthodox view of women in the episcopate, Dr. Green writes: "Bishop Kallistos quotes with approval Fr. John Meyendorff who claims that 'the protestant rejection of the veneration of Mary and its various consequences (such as the really "male dominated" Protestant worship deprived of sentiment, poetry and intuitive mystery-perception)' is one of the 'psychological' reasons which explains the recent emergence of institutional feminism." (Used with permission.)
It's my personal feeling that feminism is a movement in our society trying to lead people out of a patriarchal system long endorsed by the church and that venerating Mary has only prolonged the change.

**42.** 1) *Helping and Hating the Homeless*—An essay by Peter Marin in *Harper's Magazine*
2) *Can We Be Good Without God?* By Glenn Tinder from *The Atlantic Monthly*
3) *Taking Action for Economic Justice* by James Perkinson. This was a theological assessment presented
at the July, 1988 General Convention in Detroit.

**43.** Whereas it was at that time the only program of its kind offering seminarians a structured experience in mission in the Episcopal Church outside the U.S.A., it was cancelled in 1999 due to no fewer than fifteen other such programs endorsed by various Episcopal seminaries ranging in sites from Appalachia and the Rio Grande area to Belize, Mexico, Uganda and the Holy Land. It was also believed that Latin America was no longer "in vogue" in the minds of many. Asia and events in Africa are now commanding people's attention. Years earlier, Bishop Ottley predicted that such a shift would occur.

**44.** This teaches that we should make an option for the poor, that we identify with the poor. It does not mean we become poor necessarily ourselves, but it does mean we have to understand where they are coming from and see things through their eyes. The long term goal of those who ascribe to liberation theology is to raise not only the consciousness of those in the Third World, but to help those in the more developed countries understand (from their view) how other theologies legitimize an unjust world order. It's to empower the people; it's to help them understand that they can improve their lives and not be so dependent. In most cases, these country's economies are geared to supplying primary commodities at low cost to the developed nations which are then used in the manufacture of expensive goods which are sold back to the poor countries. This results in an enormous chasm between the haves and the have-nots—the few who are wealthy, who control the land and the economy, and the many who are poor.

**45.** "I would like to tell you a lot more. But I want you to know that your presence simply as an American has been most valuable. Because here there is a tendency to think that a priest who dedicates himself to this kind of work with the poor is a communist. Now since you've been here, I've been absolved of that, because I am not one."

## Part Five

**46.** All except Dr. Green, our theology professor, who had an Iraqi student that played a "boom box" next door to him day and night. After 2–3 days of little sleep, Dr. Green finally gave up and moved out. Given the political situation at that time, he told us he had no desire to make waves with an Iraqi!

**47.** Tantum ergo sacramentum veneremus cernui
Et antiquum documentum novo cedat ritui.
Praestet fide supplementum sensuum defectui.
Genitori genitoque laus et jubilatio
Salus, honor, virtus quoque sit et benedictio
Procedeti ab utroque compar sit laudatio.

**48.** Author of *Principles of Christian Theology, In Search of Deity, The Concept of Peace and In Search of Humanity.*

**49.** Diocesan exams were somewhat different from the GOE's. The Diocese picked seven people who would examine me in seven subjects. And each examiner, I soon discovered, had his own style. As it turned out, my first examiner was a joy. The remaining asked fair questions, but everything was geared to their schedules. So, unfortunately, exams stretched over an entire summer. Instead of seven days in June which I had anticipated, it was late August before they were finished.

**50.** Affections are the "central dispositions of moral character that lead to particular ways of acting." *What Are They Saying About Scripture and Ethics?*—William C. Spohn

**51.** Wipe the slate, or erase the tablet.

**52.** Years later, I could resonate with what I heard Geralyn Wolfe, the Bishop of Rhode Island, say. As she put it: "I might willingly die for my faith, but I would never willingly die for the church!" I probably would never have appreciated her comment had I not been through the "process." I felt like getting up and cheering for her right in the middle of her talk!

**53.** A letter to me from Dr. Sugeno dated April 26, 2006 stated: "You certainly have permission to use my quotes. I continue to feel the same way about GOE's which continue to harass students and to impede the seminary efforts at theological education. It does appear that the GOE's are losing support in the church. The Diocese of Texas, I've been told, is about to discontinue their use."

**Part Six**

**54.** From the *Book of Common Prayer, p.*510—The Church Hymnal Corporation, NY and the Seabury Press, Kingsport Press, Kingsport, Tennessee, 1977.

**55.** Reminiscent of the Tail Hook scandal, the woman who had been abused in it said after doing time and measuring up to the professional standards imposed by the military, she'd expected to be treated the same among her peers. Like her, I'd done my time and had every right to be employed and treated like everyone else.

**56.** If only I could have known then that some years later, this same priest would be removed from his job and all priestly duties for far more serious behavior, it would have helped me through that humiliating day, but that revelation was still far off in the future.

**57.** *Peace is Every Step:* The Path of Mindfulness in Everyday Life by Thich Nhat Hanh—Bantam, 1992

**58.** Christian existentialism is a form of existentialism stressing subjective aspects of the human person considered as a creature of God, such a theory emphasizing: 1—the natural desire of the creature to seek his/her creator as in the philosophers and thinkers Augustine, Pascal, Nikolai, Berdyaev and Gabriel Marcel or 2—the distance between guilty man/woman and omnipotent God (as in Kierkegaard and the dialectical or crisis theology of Karl Barth and Emil Brunner.)—*Webster's New Third International Dictionary*

**59.** Synthesis—A Weekly Resource for Preaching and Worship in the Episcopal Church for May 24, 1992.

**60.** *Lesser Feasts and Fasts,* Third Edition (page 239) church Hymnal Corporation, 800 Second Avenue, New York, N.Y. 10017

**Part Seven**

**61.** The *Stanford Daily* is the student newspaper on campus.

**62.** Francois Rabelais was a 16th century French writer who for his contemporaries was an eminent physician and Humanist and for posterity is the author of the comic and satirical masterpieces *Pantagruel and Gargantua.* Many of his books were put on the Index of Forbidden Books.

**63.** This was the young student from that seminary murdered in Haynesville, Alabama August 20, 1965 during the turbulent times of the civil rights movement.

**64.** The Episcopal Church's national headquarters at 815 Second Avenue, New York, NY 10017.

**65.** California Divinity School of the Pacific, a western seminary of the Episcopal Church.

**66.** The summer catalogue, 2005, from CM Almy (which sells clergy clothing and other items) had 36 pictures of men in it and 21 of women. Early fall showed 37 for men and 22 for women. The spring and summer 2006 catalogues included 38 of men, 21 of women.

**67.** Cyrus had been king of Persia 559–520 B.C.. The later Biblical writers viewed God as leading Cyrus by the hand so that he could accomplish the task of liberating His people. Cyrus was a non-Israelite; nevertheless, he was considered "anointed."

Actually, petroleum in its various forms had been found long before the prophet Isaiah's time. Asphalt had been among the building materials in the oldest ruins of Ur in Mesopotamia dating to 3000 B.C. and "naptha" comes from an Akkadian word some 4,000 years old. Cuneiform tablets from excavations of ancient cities record contracts for the oil trade and complaints about shortages. The prices approved by King Hammurabi's trade commission about 1875 B.C. are officially reported. Bricks in the walls of Jericho and Babylon were cemented with bituminous mortar. Ancient literature of Greece and Rome contains many references to oil and gas. Heredotus, the gossipy historian of 450 B.C. complained about the evil smells of Persian oil, and the Byzantine emperor, Heraclitus, in 624 A.D. destroyed temples near Baku where fire worshippers had bowed down before burning gas wells since time immemorial. But the modern petroleum industry is traditionally viewed as beginning in 1859 A.D. with the oil well at Oil Creek near Titusville, Crawford County, in northwestern Pennsylvania. (From *The Trek of the Oil Finders: A History of Exploration for Petroleum* by Edgar Wesley Owen.) AAPG© copyright Reprinted by permission of the AAPG whose permission is required for further use.

**68.** *Screaming Hawk* by Patton Boyle—Station Hill Press

**69.** In this sense, born again refers to centering our hearts and lives on the person of Jesus Christ.

**70.** Psalm 16, and Psalm 18, part 2.

**71.** *The Book of Common Prayer*, page 355, Rite 2.

## Epilogue

**72.** Now Pro Player Stadium.

**73.** Luke 10

msw ... April, 2007

978-0-595-40501-5
0-595-40501-0

Printed in the United States
142778LV00002B/1/A